Eglise. Velines 24230

...ation

T Danie

...treet

Heath

N.S.W

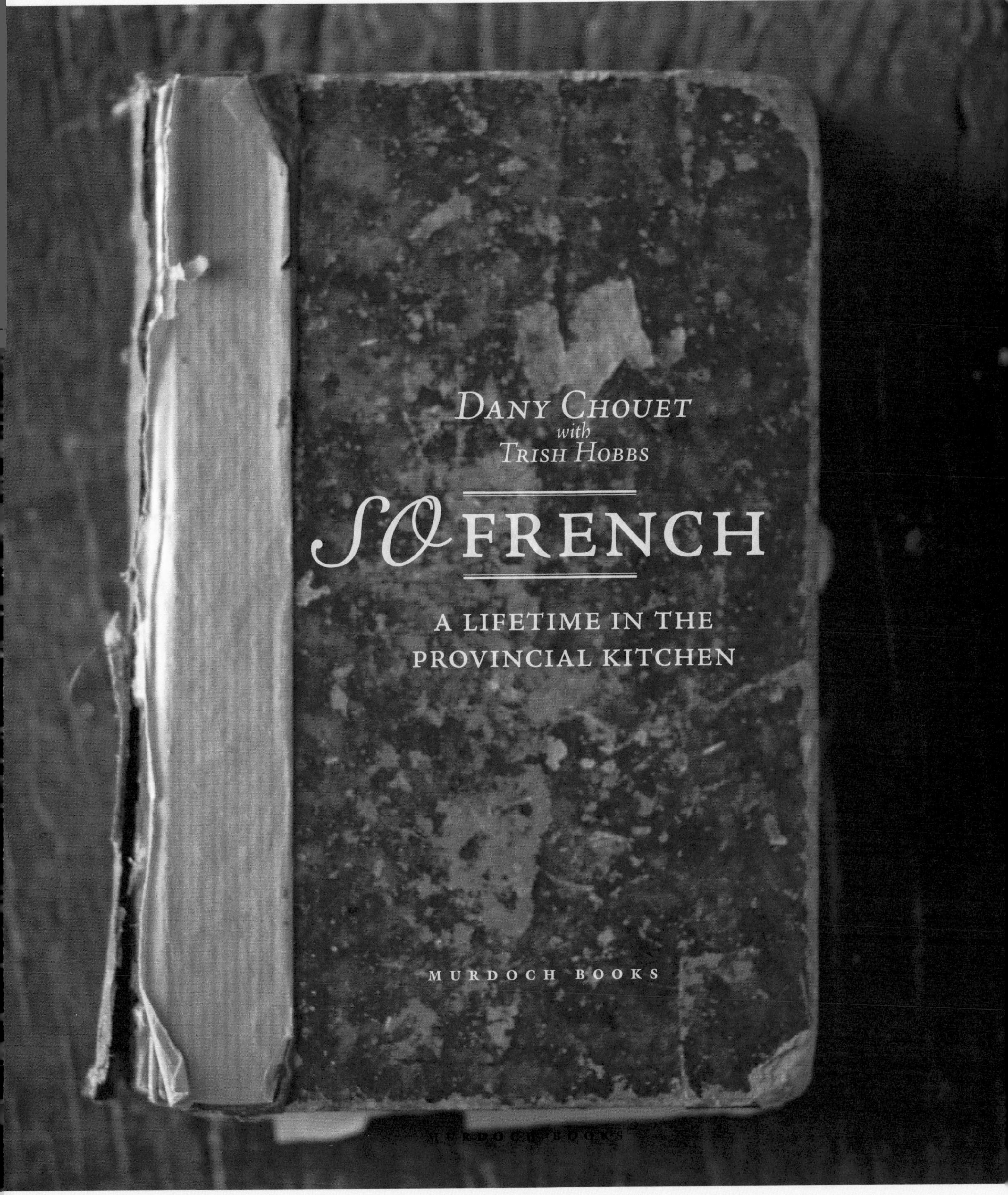

DANY CHOUET
with
TRISH HOBBS

SO FRENCH

A LIFETIME IN THE PROVINCIAL KITCHEN

MURDOCH BOOKS

This book is dedicated to the memory of the women who
taught me to cook: my mother, Madeleine Maurice-Chouet, and
my grandmothers, Rachel Maurice and Alice Chouet.

ACKNOWLEDGEMENTS

Foremost I want to thank Dana Facaros, who turned recorded conversations into written form, and then with
generosity, talent and humour guided and showed us the 'how' of book writing. Sincere thanks to Morgan
McBain who had the idea of seeking Dana's help, along with Barnaby Hobbs and Michelle Taylor who, all three,
encouraged and enthused from the beginning. Our dear friend Mary Moody introduced me to my agent
Lyn Tranter; and publisher Jane Lawson who loved and nurtured the idea from the start. Thanks to the
Murdoch team headed by Kay Scarlett, especially Carla Grossetti for her light touch with the editing.

My sister Monique Manners happily helped with memories of dates and family stories. Heartfelt thanks
to photographer Alan Benson for his understanding, creativity, patience and friendship; his love of
France and all things French shines through in his pictures. Bill Watts lent us props, made us laugh and
cheerfully helped cook during the photography. And finally, Trish, my 'personal stylist',
the only one capable of coaxing and cajoling me, who with enthusiasm, sense of humour and talent
has been there beside me for over thirty wonderful years.

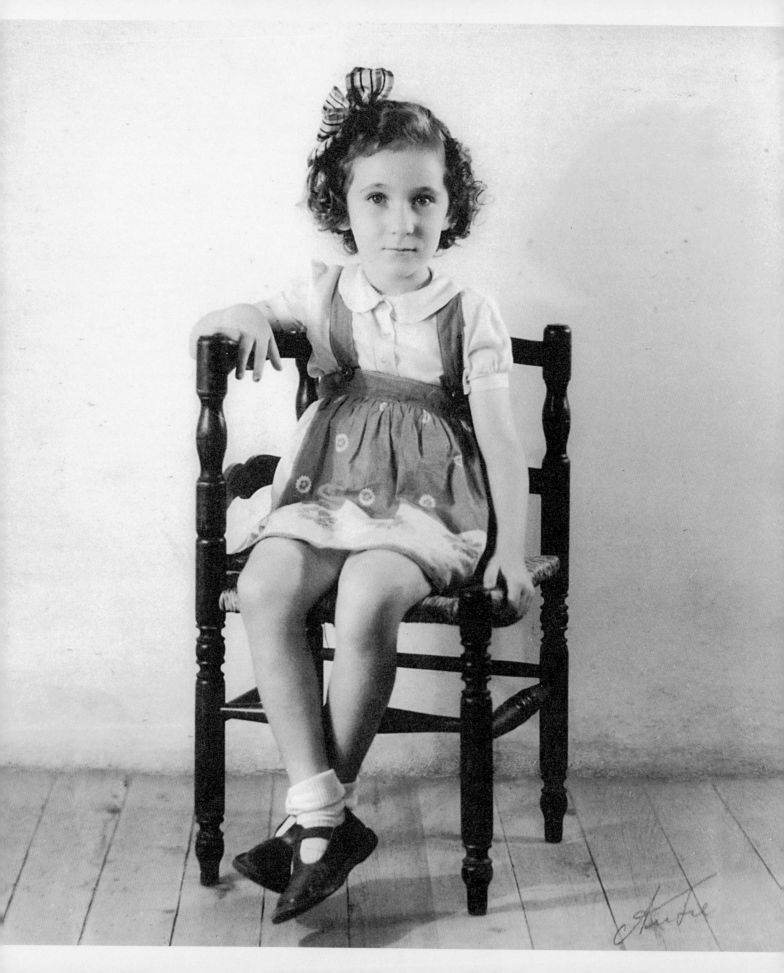

CHAPTER ONE

―――――――――

1942–1966

FRENCH BEGINNINGS

'This one will love to eat...'

DANY AT 4 YEARS OLD, THE BASSIN D'ARCACHON, 1946

MY MOTHER'S SISTER, MARIE-ANTOINETTE, AND I WERE SITTING ALL ALONE IN THE ENORMOUS DINING ROOM AT THE SPA AT LUZ-SAINT-SAUVEUR IN THE PYRENEES, AN HOUR BEFORE THE OTHER *CURISTES* (SPA CLIENTS) CAME IN FOR THEIR LUNCH. AT MY AUNT'S REQUEST, THE CHEF HAD PREPARED SOMETHING JUST FOR ME — A DELICATE DISH OF PAN-FRIED TROUT WHICH HAD BEEN CAUGHT IN A NEARBY MOUNTAIN STREAM. TATIE ANTOINETTE WAS GENTLE AND PATIENT, AND SAT NEXT TO ME, URGING ME TO EAT IN HER OWN, SWEET WAY: 'MANGE, DANY. MANGE, DANY.'

I WAS FOUR YEARS OLD AND SERIOUSLY UNDERWEIGHT; a little stick figure with hollow cheeks and matchsticks for limbs. I'd been refusing food for almost a year and nothing my parents did could persuade me to eat. They were at their wits' end, so when my aunt offered to take me along on her annual visit to the spa to try and fatten me up a bit they quickly agreed.

At home, my parents were always arguing. Although my father, Max, was a generous, good-hearted man, he lacked an education and had never learned to control his temper. My mother Madeleine knew just how to tease him and often provoked him into a full-blown rage. Sadly, this often happened just as the family sat down to eat: insults and shouts would be hurled across the table, followed by plates and saucers that shattered – *bang, boom, crash* – into one hundred pieces against the wall and the floor. When they weren't arguing, I hardly saw my parents. My Papa was always preoccupied with work and my Maman had neither the time nor the inclination for cuddles or caresses, reading stories or playing games. She would give me a few toys and then disappear. I had a brother, Michel, who was seven years older, but we had little in common and rarely spent time together. The only way I thought I could get any love and attention in my family was to starve myself.

There was, however, one thing I couldn't resist and that was the love and attention lavished on me by my kind, sweet Tatie Antoinette, who sat so patiently with me in the spa dining room that day, imploring me to eat. *'Mange, Dany. Mange, Dany.'* Finally, I gave in to her gentle pleas and ate properly for the first time in a very long time.

After finishing my meal, Tatie Antoinette took me back to our room for a *sieste* and went to enjoy her own lunch with the other *curistes*. The minute she was gone I leapt out of bed and bounced around the room, waiting, impatiently, for her to return. Although she was only away for about an hour, it seemed, at the time, to be an eternity; after lunch Tatie went and lay down on a chaise longue under a shady tree on a beautiful green lawn that sloped down to a stream. I know this because by standing on my tiptoes on a stool in the bathroom I could look down and spy on her. Along with the sound of her sweet voice coaxing me to eat, I can still recall that image of Tatie Antoinette relaxing in the dappled shade of the garden, listening to the gurgling stream and breathing in the fresh mountain air. She was, like the other guests, relieved that the war was finally over, that peace had come at last and that her funny little niece had decided to break her year-long fast.

Refusing to eat had been the perfect weapon to use against a family devoted to food. We lived in Sainte-Foy-la-Grande, a bustling market town on the Dordogne River just east of Bordeaux, on the border of the *départements* of the Gironde and Périgord. My father was the youngest of five sons, and had taken on his father's business as a *négociant en bestiaux* (a dealer in livestock). He rose at three o'clock most mornings to don the traditional dark-blue smock and overalls of a merchant, which protected his shirt and trousers from the filth. He would then lurch off in his rickety, old cattle truck to *les forails*, the livestock markets in the Limousin, Tulle, Brive and Cahors; sometimes he even went as far south as the Pyrenees. If Papa's truck didn't break down, he would return in time to sell the animals to local butchers in Ste-Foy's *marché*, a beautiful covered market located at the end of our street, on the edge of town.

My father's mother, Grandmère Alice, was famous for her cooking in Ste-Foy. In the late 1920s she ran her own *charcuterie* shop in the village, where she made sausages, pâtés, and meaty rillettes. It was there that she gave Maman her first lessons in commercial-scale cooking. Grandmère Alice's apricot tarts made from brioche dough were legendary and so large they couldn't fit into a conventional oven. Instead, she had to take them to the local *boulangerie*, where it was commonplace for customers to put dishes in the still-piping-hot ovens after the day's bread had been baked.

Another of her specialities was *boudin* (black pudding), some of which inevitably exploded while being poached. Grandmère would add vegetables to the *boudin* stock to make a delicious soup called *jimboura* that is unique to this pocket of France. Still, to this day, there is a *charcutier* in the Ste-Foy market that makes this dish in the winter months; whenever the blackboard sign outside the shop advertises '*Jimboura!*' the local elders queue up with their jars. Now, the villagers must pay for the soup, but back in my Grandmere's day, the neighbours came with their saucepans to collect their free portion.

But life in Ste-Foy wasn't always so sweet. Like my Papa, Grandpère Auguste was also notorious for his bad temper. In fact, on one occasion he was so angry he grabbed a huge basin of sausage meat that Grandmère Alice had made and threw the whole lot onto the street. Even though Maman got on well with Grandmère Alice, Grandpère Auguste was another matter: he was a difficult, angry, authoritarian figure whose word was law. He was the one person that Maman could not boss about.

In those days, the Ste-Foy tradition was for the youngest member of the family to live with their parents to care for them in their old age. In return for taking over his father's business and inheriting the family home this duty fell on my father's shoulders. Maman was always resentful that Papa neglected to inform her of this before they were married, as afterward, she was given no choice. Although Papa's four elder brothers had all left home, one of them who returned from time to time was my funny little Tonton Robert, a *pâtissier* on the *Pasteur*, a ship that sailed between Bordeaux and Indochine. When Tonton Robert returned from a voyage he would always bring treats for the family, such as coffee and porcelain tea sets.

MAMAN ADJUSTED WELL TO HER NEW LIFE WITH THE in-laws. In fact, she soon took her place as the driving force in the family. She was like a steamroller, endowed with tremendous confidence and energy and a practical, no-nonsense nature. Although she wasn't a thinker, Maman was enterprising and impulsive and, during the Second World War, became the glue that held the family together. She was young and attractive, and used to march around in a pair of knee-high red boots that she was particularly proud of. When Papa was away at the Front, Maman took charge of the house. Because Ste-Foy was in the unoccupied 'free zone' governed by the Vichy regime, many of my cousins and their wives came to live in the house. Maman looked after all of them, as well as the in-laws. During difficult times she could be extremely generous but, in return, it was understood everyone must do just as she said.

While Papa was away during the war, Maman even took over his business as a *négociant en bestiaux*. She had never even driven a car, let alone a truck, but she wasn't going to let a small detail like that stop her. Maman asked the *commis* (employee) for some basic instructions. She then pulled on her prized red boots for courage, climbed into the cab, turned the key and careened off down the road. Maman then drove the cattle truck out to the *forails*, where she dealt with the farmers, and bought lambs and pigs to sell to local butchers.

She was a natural, and proved adept at bartering. People would approach her and say: 'Oh, Madame Chouet, we would like a pig, but we don't have any money'. 'Oh, so you don't have any money? Well, then, what do you have? Linen sheets?' Maman would then promptly swap a pig for four linen sheets, which, as I recall, was the going rate.

She also swapped lambs and pigs for walnut oil which was extremely hard to get hold of in the Dordogne, as it had been requisitioned by the Germans. Maman would then stash the precious tins under the driver's seat. One day Maman was pulled over at a German checkpoint. If they had found the walnut oil, she would have been in big trouble! So she turned on the charm: she smiled and batted her eyelashes and pretended to adjust her belt while showing some leg over her tall, red boots. The Germans gazed on appreciatively and instead of inspecting the truck, they just walked around it, said she was a '*schöne Frau*' and let her go.

Even though we lived in the rich and fertile region of South-West France, there were still major food shortages during the war. To escape from hunger, many people survived by eating just one potato per day. But thanks to Maman's resourcefulness and our family

Morue en sauce

SALT COD AND POTATO RAGOÛT

SERVES 4

WHEN I WAS A CHILD LIVING WITH MY GRANDPARENTS, SALT COD WAS INEXPENSIVE. IT WAS EASIER
TO FIND THAN FRESH FISH AND HAD A VERY IMPORTANT PLACE IN OUR POPULAR REGIONAL CUISINE.
MY GRANDFATHER PARTICULARLY LOVED THIS RECIPE WHICH WE OFTEN ATE ON A FRIDAY.

1 kg (2 lb 4 oz) thick fillets of salt cod

75 g (2¾ oz/½ cup) plain (all-purpose) flour

80 ml (2½ fl oz/⅓ cup) olive oil

2 medium onions, finely sliced

8 medium waxy potatoes, peeled and cut into
1cm (½ inch) thick slices

4 large garlic cloves, sliced

1 bouquet garni (1 bay leaf,
5 parsley sprigs, 3 thyme sprigs)

2 tablespoons coarsely chopped flat-leaf
(Italian) parsley

You will need to start this recipe a day ahead of serving. The day before, cut each fish fillet into four pieces and place, skin-side up in a colander. Place the colander inside another container, and add enough cold water to cover. Make sure the fish is not in contact with the bottom of the dish where the dissolved salt from the fish is stagnating. During the first 24 hours, change the water at least 4 times. If the weather is very hot, place the container in the refrigerator.

After 24 hours, drain the fish, rinse under cold water and pat dry. Roll each piece of fish in flour. Heat 2 tablespoons of the olive oil in a cast-iron saucepan (cocotte) and fry the fish, in batches, for 1–2 minutes each side or until pale golden. Remove, set aside and keep warm.

Heat the remaining olive oil in the same pot, add the onion and sauté over low–medium heat. When the onion is transparent, add the potatoes and fry gently for 3–5 minutes, stirring gently to avoid breaking them. Pour in enough hot water to cover the fish pieces (about 1 litre/35 fl oz/4 cups), then add the garlic, bouquet garni and pepper to taste. Bring to a simmer and cook for 15 minutes, or until the potato is cooked but still firm. Place the fish pieces on top of the potato, half-cover with the lid and cook gently over low heat for 5–6 minutes or until the fish is tender and flakes easily with a fork. Serve sprinkled with the parsley.

connections, we were never that desperate, and every now and then we would slaughter a lamb on the sly. As a precautionary measure, Maman always shared the meat with our neighbours so they wouldn't report us to the Germans or the Resistance movement when they smelt it cooking. At the very least the meat would be confiscated, but my parents also risked arrest and imprisonment. Because there wasn't much refrigeration we had to eat the meat at every meal until it was finished. My bad-tempered Grandpère Auguste was in his eighties at the time and would wander the streets of Ste-Foy, complaining to everyone he met: '*Mon Dieu!* I'm getting sick of eating lamb every day!' It was very difficult to stop him; luckily everyone thought he was crazy, blathering about a luxury such as lamb that was impossible for the townsfolk to even imagine.

And so I was born in 1942. Apparently the doctor remarked about my little round tummy, 'This one will love to eat!'

In 1941 Papa was given leave to attend the funeral of his brother René, who had died of tuberculosis. While he was home for the funeral, the Nazis captured his regiment in the north of France. Because there was no longer a regiment for him to return to, he was stationed at an aviation camp outside of Bordeaux and allowed home every weekend. And so I was born in 1942. Apparently the doctor remarked about my little round tummy, 'This one will love to eat!'

Grandmère Alice was overjoyed. She had five sons and many grandsons and was absolutely besotted with me. Finally, a grand-daughter! Grandmère doted on me: she put me into her bed with her, gave me my bottle, changed me and dressed me. Maman hardly ever got the chance to touch or hold me. I was only two when Grandmère Alice died and I can barely remember her, but everyone said I inherited her character.

My parents initially wanted my Tonton Paul (one of Maman's brothers) to be my godfather, but he had been taken to Germany at the start of the war and forced to work as a farm labourer. Instead, they chose Marcel Ducandas, a man who lived across the lane. Marcel had worked as a purser with a big maritime company in Bordeaux called the Messageries Maritimes, but when war broke out he was stationed in Ste-Foy with all the company's paperwork, which he hid from the Germans. He and his wife Jeanne became friends with my parents and they asked him to be my godfather.

Tonton Paul, meanwhile, spent the entire war working as a farm labourer, in awful conditions and with never enough to eat. By the time he came back to Ste-Foy, his hair had turned grey; he was only twenty-eight. Even so, he still had a sparkle in his eye and remained one of my favourite family members.

After my doting Grandmère Alice died, I became quite a difficult child; very 'determined and wilful', or so they say. The truth is that above all, I missed Grandmere's attention. My brother, Michel, was at school and Maman didn't exactly leap in to fill

Grandmère's place. My year of refusing to eat was the only way I knew that I could get her love and attention.

I was five when my sister Monique was born in 1947. She was a pretty little thing with curly hair and blue eyes and I was overjoyed at her arrival. Finally I had someone smaller than me to boss around. Jealousy also came in to play and people were always saying: 'Dany, look at your sister. Why can't you be sweet like her?'

At the end of the war Papa didn't know what he was going to do to support the family. In 1944, his cattle truck had been requisitioned by the Resistance; one night he was simply told to drive it to the Bois de Monfaucon, a lonely forest north of Ste-Foy, and leave the keys in the ignition. He never saw his truck again. It was one of Papa's contributions to the Resistance. In later years, Maman would regale us with stories of her own deeds of bravery, but I was never able to separate fact from fantasy. It was certainly true, however, that at the end of the war she had managed to accumulate a large quantity of linen sheets and a major stash of cash in a suitcase under her bed. After selling the family home, my parents had enough money to buy a lovely 1930s villa on the edge of town. There was also enough money to pay for a new truck and trailer for Papa.

France changed dramatically after the war, but one change that directly affected us was the centralisation of livestock markets. There was no longer enough work for them

In those days, few people owned cars, so the baker, fishmonger, fruiterer and butcher drove around in their vans on appointed days of the week announcing their presence with a merry toot on the horn.

and so, my parents, then in their forties, decided to sell the villa, leave Ste-Foy and learn a new trade. My mother always said she would have loved to have owned a shoe shop or a *quincaillerie* (a hardware store) where nothing on the shelves was perishable. 'But oh no! Not us!' she often complained. 'We had to have a *boucherie-charcuterie*.' Learning to be a butcher was a natural progression for Papa because he knew a lot about meat: what to buy, what was good and what to kill when. What he didn't know was how to cut it up. Luckily, his friend Lucien, one of the best butchers and *charcutiers* in Ste-Foy, sent his son Michel to live with us for a year and provide on-the-job training.

My parents bought their first butcher's shop in Ambarès-et-Lagrave, a town about twenty kilometres north-east of Bordeaux. It was a huge shop attached to a large home with a courtyard across the lane that featured an abattoir and enormous kitchen where they prepared all the *charcuterie* – the terrines, sausages and *andouillettes*. My parents often worked through the night: they'd have to set an alarm to wake up and turn off the ovens, which were left on for hours. It was very hard work; we may as well have lived in a small factory. My parents hired a number of people to help out around the house including Paulette, employed full time to cook and wash, and Madame Hervoie, who was hired two days a week to manage a mountain of ironing and sewing. Paulette and I adored each other. She was somewhere between a big sister and a nanny and, unlike Maman, always had time to listen and reassure me.

In the mornings, Maman would go to the shop with young Michel and my brother (also Michel) to learn alongside my father how to cut and debone meat. Our two grey Citroën vans had to then be loaded up with masses of meat to *faire la tournée* – to do the rounds in the surrounding countryside. In those days, few people owned cars, so the baker, fishmonger, fruiterer and butcher drove around in their vans on appointed days of the week announcing their presence with a merry toot on the horn. I was in elementary school in Ambarès at the time but on Thursdays, when we did not go to school, I would get up at the crack of dawn to go on the *tournée* with Papa. I loved it! It was like a mobile shop. It had a curtain to protect the food from flies, a little refrigerator, a set of scales and a big wooden block where Papa cut up the meat to order. I was in charge of the cash drawer and giving out the change. Together, we zigzagged from village to village, hamlet to hamlet, and sometimes from house to house. A highlight of the *tournée* was our midmorning stop at a café to enjoy a second breakfast: a hot croissant or *pain au chocolat*. When the customers exclaimed: 'Oh, *celle-là, c'est bien la vôtre!*' (Oh, that one there, she's certainly yours!), Papa would blush and beam. Although he wasn't great at showing affection and never once said he loved me, I knew that he was proud of his little cashier. Every Monday afternoon, while Maman served customers in the shop, the animals would be slaughtered in the abattoir. There was always a steer, a couple of calves, two or three lambs and a pig. Papa paid a man who was somewhat of a slaughtering specialist to do all the killing for him. We called him 'Monsieur Croûte-Rouge' (Mr Red Crust) because of his rough red face. Monsieur Croûte-Rouge also had an alarming habit of drinking the warm blood from the *boeuf* he slaughtered to give himself strength.

Monique and I thought the abbatoir provided the best entertainment in the world! After school all the neighbourhood children would often sit on the wall by the abattoir and watch Monsieur Croûte-Rouge slit the throats of the animals. The animals would scream and squeal when they were taken, digging their hooves in and trying to resist their fate. Interestingly, we weren't disturbed by these blood-splattered slaughterhouse scenes; we regarded animals as being part of the food chain.

The communal back lane by the courtyard and abattoir was our playground. We played with Pepette, the daughter of the *ébeniste-matelassier* (cabinetmaker/mattress-stuffer), and Francis, the son of the *épicier* (grocer), who were both around the same age as Monique. Because I was the eldest, I was the boss. I made them play shop with me: I was always the *marchande* and they were the plebs; the customers. Francis would often get fed up and kick over the 'shop'. His parents sold sardines that came in big wooden boxes and we loved messing around in them. When we came in from playing, Maman would screech: 'Oh no, not again! You stink of sardines!'

I also liked to play the *coiffeuse* – much to the horror of the parents. I was particularly fond of cutting off Monique's blonde curls and scalping Francis. Playing 'the priest' was

Ris de veau au vin blanc

VEAL SWEETBREADS

SERVES 4

MY TATIE DENISE WHO LIVES IN THE CHARENTES NEAR COGNAC GAVE ME THIS RECIPE. SHE OFTEN USED TO COOK THIS DISH AS A SECOND OR EVEN THIRD ENTRÉE FOR OUR HUGE FAMILY BANQUETS. THESE FEASTS WOULD LAST AT LEAST FIVE HOURS AND ON SPECIAL OCCASIONS ENDED WITH A GLASS OF 1900 COGNAC.

750 g (1 lb/10 oz) veal sweetbreads
35 g (1¼ oz/¼ cup) plain (all-purpose) flour
1½ tablespoons duck fat (or oil)
10–12 French shallots, cut in half
200 ml (7 fl oz) dry white wine
1 small bouquet garni (1 bay leaf, 5 parsley sprigs, 3 thyme sprigs)
mushrooms, any type you like, added 5 minutes before the end of the cooking (optional)

Soak the sweetbreads in cold water with a pinch of salt for about three hours. Drain, wipe dry and remove membrane or fatty bits. Cut into portion size. Sprinkle a tea towel with the flour and roll the sweetbreads around in it to coat lightly. Heat the duck fat in a large frying pan, add the shallots and fry until golden, then add the sweetbreads and sauté gently for 5–10 minutes. Season with salt and freshly ground black pepper. Pour in the wine and reduce for 3–4 minutes, then add 200 ml (7 fl oz) water, and the bouquet garni. Watch it carefully, and after about 20 minutes, it should be a creamy consistency *mais pas écrasé* (not mashed).

another favourite: they had to sit in the sardine box while I married them. And there was strictly no kissing until I gave the word. Maman, who did excellent needlework and embroidery work often sighed and said: 'Dany, why don't you ever sit quietly and embroider?' Maman also liked to dress Monique and I in matching dresses and blazers and put silly ribbons in our hair. Every spring we would get new identical outfits to wear for our annual long weekend trip to Lourdes. I remember sitting in the back of the car, watching the countryside and villages roll past and looking at restaurants, thinking 'Oh, that one looks nice'. But outside of our annual trip to Lourdes, we rarely ate out. If we didn't eat at home, we ate at a relative's house.

We especially looked forward to Sunday lunch with Tonton Paul and Tatie Denise up in the Charentes, North-East of Bordeaux. Tatie Denise would prepare a wonderful *poule au pot soupe*, which was followed by a cold entrée and veal sweetbreads. The main course usually consisted of chicken from the soup, or roast beef with *cèpes* and then a platter of cheese and desserts. We would be totally stuffed at the end, which was when my uncle would bring out the family's cognac.

I often went to visit Tonton Paul and Tatie Denise on holidays. While there, I would help harvest the hay, or pick grapes for the cognac before tucking into the classic *vendanges* (grape harvest) lunch, which was an experience in itself. This great French tradition was the ultimate in over-indulgence: course after course of delicious food was served in quick succession with endless bottles of wine and cognac. I don't know how the workers went back to the vines after that, but they did.

FROM THE AGE OF SEVEN I PREFERRED TO MAKE MY OWN lunch on school days. That was because my parents never ate before 1.30 pm after they had closed the shop and unloaded all the meat from the *tournée*; if I waited to eat with them, I would be late back at school, which I hated. I would stand on a stool, pop a potato in a pot (there was always a pot of soup or stock on the stove) and then go into the shop and cut a piece of meat and cook it the way I liked it. Always fussy about what I ate, I was especially fond of a slice of *foie de veau* or beef steak, which was quick and easy to pan-fry. I was quite proud of my cooking expertise and I was never lonely in the kitchen: Madame Hervoie would chat to me from the sewing machine while I ate; and Paulette was always there to give me soup and vegetables from the substantial family lunches she prepared each day.

When it wasn't a school day, I still gathered with my parents and siblings, Paulette and all the boys from the butchery to share a meal. We sat in rush-seated chairs arranged around the long kitchen table covered with oilcloth. We each had our own linen napkin and the cutlery that was required for each course. For starters we'd have soup, a cold entrée or *charcuterie*. Next was a main course with vegetables, salad and fruit followed by a dessert such as *oeufs au lait*, or my favourite, *gâteau de semoule*. A big loaf of *pain de campagne* and bottles of red wine and water were always on hand. Because everyone had

TOP: THE FAMILY BUTCHERY, BORDEAUX, 1961

BOTTOM: CLOCKWISE FROM LEFT — TATIE GERMAINE, PAPA, GRANDMÈRE RACHEL AND MAMAN

PREPARING CÈPES, SEPTEMBER, 1969

been up working hard since dawn, lunch was the most substantial meal of the day. Papa always put water in his wine, as did the others. He used to buy big *barriques* of wine from *viticulteurs* he trusted in nearby Saint-Loubès or Ambarès; it was good-quality wine, but the men still had to work in the afternoon, so they dared not over-indulge. Like most French children, I added about one tablespoon of red wine to my water, to give it colour. The *'vins fins'* were reserved for Sunday lunches and special occasions.

On Sundays, lunch was truly a major production. Paulette would stay overnight, sleeping in my big double bed, so she could help with the late-night and early-morning preparations. The dining room was like a shrine: it was kept shut and polished and smelt of beeswax. The table extended to seat sixteen; it was set with exquisite, embroidered linen, tablecloths and napkins before being laden with our best china, glassware and

After coffee, all the women would converge in the kitchen to wash up a mountain of dirty china, silver and glassware and to chat and gossip away from the men. The men, meanwhile, continued to get louder and more red-faced, as they compared cognacs, smoked cigars and ranted about politics. I much preferred to be in the kitchen with the women, listening to their secrets.

silver. Delicious little morsels were served with the aperitif before the serious eating began. The lunch inevitably started with a soup such as *consommé au vermicelle fin*. Big platters of oysters with *crepinéttes* or platters of mixed seafood or cold hors d'oeuvres then preceded a fish course, such as sole with *moules*, and the main *plat* (beef or game or poultry) with *haricots verts*. This extravagant feast would finish with cheeses and desserts brought by our guests. I loved those desserts! Our guests competed with each other to buy the most elegant little *gateaux* or beautifully decorated constructions from the top local patisseries. The best Bordeaux wines were then served with the lunch amid much chatter from a table of guests who all considered themselves to be expert connoisseurs. It wasn't terribly interesting for the children: we sat through the interminable lunch, wiggling in our chairs, waiting for the dessert. Apart from lively discussions about wine, there was also a certain amount of not-so-good-natured banter between Maman and her brother-in-law, Jacques, which often finished with her flouncing out of the dining room. Calm was not a word to describe the atmosphere *chez nous*.

After coffee, all the women would converge in the kitchen to wash up a mountain of dirty china, silver and glassware and to chat and gossip away from the men. The men, meanwhile, continued to get louder and more red-faced, as they compared cognacs, smoked cigars and ranted about politics. I much preferred to be in the kitchen with the women, listening to their secrets. After lunch, it was time for the entertainment – where everyone was expected to perform. Maman, Tatie Antoinette and Tonton Paul all loved to sing and they all competed for compliments. I remember standing, reluctantly on the table, reciting a poem or performing a duet with Monique. Grandmère Rachel (Maman's mother) and Tatie Denise would join in the chorus while Grandpère Armand (Maman's father), played the clarinet. My cousin Jacqueline, Tatie Antoinette's only child, was nine years older than me and accompanied all the singers on the piano. I hated performing and much preferred those Sundays when I went to watch the rugby with Papa.

When Monique started school my parents sent her to a Catholic school closer to home as they thought she was too sweet and gentle for the rigours of public education. I offered to cook Monique's lunch, too, but she would shake her head and squeak: '*Non, non, j'attends Maman!*'

Every summer I looked forward to joining my godparents at the seaside, at their summer home in La Teste, on the Bassin d'Arcachon. My godfather Marcel was back at sea with the Messageries Maritimes, but his wife Jeanne and her mother would invite me for a month-long holiday. Although I found Jeanne quite odd, I adored her mother, who was gentle and good-natured. Jeanne's mother kept oyster beds. She got up at five o'clock every morning to go out on the water in her *pinasse*, the traditional wooden boat of the Bassin, to tend to her oysters. I often went with her as she plucked oysters from the sea and we would have a *casse-croute* right there on the boat, slurping down the freshest, tastiest oysters imaginable.

Then, in the summer when I was eight, I asked Maman: 'So when am I going to La Teste?'

'You aren't,' she said.

This was very sudden. 'But why not?' I asked. 'I always go!'

'No, not this year. You weren't invited.'

'But why not?'

'Oh I don't know,' she said, with a shrug. 'Sometimes it's like that, you know. *C'est comme ça.*'

I was furious! So I went to the shop and got myself a postcard, and I asked Maman for a stamp. 'I'm going to write to Jeanne,' I announced.

'All right,' she said, and gave me an envelope for the card. I only had one word for Jeanne: '*MERDE!*' which I wrote in big letters across the card. I put the card in the envelope, wrote down the address, stuck on the stamp and posted it in the box across the street. Maman was busy at the time and so a few hours later, when she thought of it, asked: 'So what did you write to Jeanne, then?'

'I wrote "*MERDE*",' I said.

Maman threw up her hands and rushed to the post office but was too late; the letter had been sent. I never knew why my oyster-eating summer holidays came to such an abrupt end. Maman angrily said, as she often did, that it was because I was '*un chameau*' (a difficult beast) and that no one would ever love me. Thankfully, she was proved wrong. At school I did so well that my favourite teacher, Madame Dubreuilh, recommended I

Daube de bœuf

BRAISED BEEF IN RED WINE

SERVES 6

BEEF BRAISED IN RED WINE IS ONE OF MY PARENTS' MOST SUCCESSFUL DISHES. IT WAS SOLD IN THEIR BUTCHERY IN BORDEAUX, READY TO TAKE HOME AND HEAT UP. MAMAN'S ORIGINAL RECIPE IS FOR VAST AMOUNTS OF BEEF; THIS IS A MORE MANAGEABLE AMOUNT FOR SIX AND CAN BE DOUBLED FOR TWELVE.

Bring a saucepan of water to the boil, add the pork skin and blanch for 8 minutes. Drain and rinse the pork skin under cold running water then cut into 2 cm (¾ inch) squares and set aside.

Heat the duck fat in a large frying pan over medium heat and cook the beef (you will have to do this in batches to avoid 'stewing') until browned, season with salt and pepper to taste. Remove and set aside. Add the onions to the same pan and sauté for 5–7 minutes or until softened. Set aside.

Preheat the oven to 150°C (300°F/Gas 2). In a large heavy-based, ovenproof casserole dish, place the meat and vegetables in two layers starting with half the pork skin, beef, carrots, onions, lardons, garlic and French shallots. Repeat. Add the bouquet garni and sprinkle with the spices, hot wine and cognac. Pour over the stock, it should be level with the meat and vegetables but not fully submerge them. Bring to the boil. Meanwhile, combine enough flour and water in a bowl to make a thick gluey paste, then smear the paste around the rim of the dish and press on the lid to completely seal.

Place the casserole dish on the bottom shelf of the oven and cook for around 3½ hours. Lift the lid carefully to check the meat – it should be tender. Let it stand a little, then skim any fat from the surface and remove and discard the bouquet garni. Serve with boiled potatoes or fresh tagliatelle tossed in olive oil.

200 g (7 oz) pork skin, with no fat

60 g (2¼ oz/¼ cup) duck fat

3 kg (6 lb 12 oz) shin of beef on the bone, sliced into 4–5 cm slices

4 onions, diced

4 carrots, sliced

250 g (9 oz) smoked speck (or bacon), cut into lardons (2 cm x 1 cm pieces)

4 garlic cloves, sliced

6 French shallots

1 bouquet garni (1 bay leaf, 2 cloves)

¼ teaspoon four spices (quatres epices)

750 ml (26 fl oz/3 cups) red wine, heated

100 ml (3½ fl oz) cognac (or brandy), heated

500 ml (17 fl oz/2 cups) veal stock

plain (all-purpose) flour, for paste

be sent to the Lycée Mondenard in Bordeaux, an excellent girls' school where I would board during the week. I was only ten at the time and it was a big shock to the system: for a start, the school dinners were revolting! I hated boarding and was completely demoralised. I didn't know anyone and was shoved at the back of the class, where the teachers forgot all about me. My grades suffered, and on Sunday nights I would become physically ill at the prospect of having to go back to Bordeaux, so ill that I couldn't get out of bed. Dr Massena, our family physician, came to see me, and eventually told my parents: 'You really have to take Dany out of Lycée Mondenard. She's never going to do well there, and if she stays there, she's going to lose a year of school.'

My parents took me out of Lycée Mondenard in the middle of the school year. There wasn't a *lycée* (secondary school) in Ambarès, so they asked Grandmère Rachel and Grandpère Armand, who lived in Port Sainte-Foy, if I could live with them so I could attend the *lycée* in Ste-Foy, which was only a short bike ride over the bridge. It was a big decision for my grandparents: Grandpère Armand, then in his sixties, was a retired *chef de gare* (stationmaster); Grandmère had always been a housewife; and their youngest son, Jeannot, who was only three years older than me, was still at home. Even though they survived on Grandpère's pension, they very graciously took me in. Jeannot left home soon after to do an apprenticeship at my parents' butcher shop and I was left alone with them in their little house on the edge of a vineyard, overlooking the Dordogne River.

I LIVED WITH MY GRANDPARENTS FOR FOUR MARVELLOUS

years. My grandparents were wonderful, patient, kind and peaceful people who rarely argued. It was quite a change from my family home, which was complete chaos and carnage: as well as being noisy day and night there were people coming and going, to and fro, all the time; lots of shouting; and animals squealing and being butchered and cooked in big pots of *charcuterie*. Although I did have to repeat the *sixième* class, my marks soon shot up again once I was removed from my misery in the school in Bordeaux. I had few distractions to my studies in Port Ste-Foy: Grandmère Rachel washed all my clothes; meals were always ready on the table for me and I never had to cook for myself.

Every second week, my parents and Monique came to visit and always brought meat and money to help pay for my food. But we could never convince Monique to stay even one night with me – she always wanted to be with Maman. Grandmère and Grandpère would sometimes tell me: '*Mais avec toi, c'est différent!*' (We love all our grandchildren just the same 'but with you, it's different'). With them I was never difficult; we shared a close bond because I was happy!

Grandpère Armand grew much of what we ate – all the fruit, potatoes, leeks, lettuce, onions and vegetables. Grandpère had a *potager* near the house and a little *charmille* under the vines where he liked to sit and watch people pass by. He also had ten rows of vines up towards the *château*, where he cultivated vegetables and fruit trees between the rows. Every day Grandpère Armand would pedal over to the garden on his bicycle to take care of his crops. He was a happy, jolly man who had an eye for the ladies. As well as tending to his garden, he busied himself by having a flirtation in the vines with the *bonne* (maid) from the *château*. Grandmère suspected as much and would often ask me to ride my bike over to investigate: 'Dany, can you ride over and see if there are two bicycles in the ditch under the vines?' I knew why Grandmère wanted me to do this and although I often found the two abandoned bicycles, I always informed her there was just the one. This little white lie kept everyone in the household happy!

Grandmère's style of cooking was both simple and excellent. Her mother, Marcelline, worked as cook in a château in the Charentes and was renowned for her refined dishes. She in turn taught Tatie Antoinette and Maman everything she knew. Although Maman was a very good cook, Tatie Antoinette's food was exquisite. Before every meal there was always, always *la soupe* made from a pot of stock that Grandmère kept simmering away on the woodstove. Besides the main house kitchen, Grandmère had an *arrière cuisine* – a larder or coolroom – where she had a fireplace for cooking her conserves using everything from tomatoes to green beans.

Grandmère had a wonderful way of making pastry, too: after rolling out the pastry she would use her thumb to spread little dollops of soft butter in even rows on the surface before folding it over and rolling it out again, then adding more dollops of butter and repeating the exercise. The result was her delicious version of flaky pastry, which she used to make wonderful fruit tarts. I can still conjure up the heavenly aroma of hot pastry, butter, sugar and apricots plucked fresh from the orchard.

Grandpère, on the other hand, was a great hunter. He went out at dusk with his Brittany spaniel Youki and often returned with a fair number of thrushes. If he came back from the *chasse* with a certain smile on his face Grandmère would know straightaway: '*Ah, tu as une bécasse!*' she would exclaim. She would then reach around behind his back into his hunting pouch to produce a woodcock. Even then woodcocks were rare and a great delicacy and cooking them was always quite a ceremony. Grandmère would first hang the bird in the *arrière cuisine's garde-manger* (a screened, wooden frame box). After being suspended from the ceiling for a few days, the bird would then be plucked and roasted together with its partly decomposed intestines, which had been flavoured with a little cognac. When the roasted bird was cut open all those tiny bits – the intestines and liver and so on – would be melded together beautifully. Grandmère would then spread the intestines on top of a tray of croutons to make a *tartine*, which was served under the gamey meat. Ooh, la-la, was it good! Woodcocks only eat insects and wild berries, which may be why their guts tasted so delicious.

On Fridays we ate sardines (which were cheap) or *morue* (salt cod) or fish caught fresh by Grandpère from the Dordogne. Grandpère had his own boat and would catch eels and little river fish called *gardons*. Grandmère would then clean the fish and fry them very quickly in the pan. They always tasted fresh and delicious.

Though Grandpère Armand was a jolly old soul he wasn't a big drinker. Despite this, one of his greatest pleasures was getting his visitors tipsy. Whenever anyone stopped by, even for a chat, he would get out a bottle of Sauternes or sweet Monbazillac.

Terrine de foie de porc

MAMAN'S PORK AND LIVER TERRINE

MAKES ENOUGH FOR TWO 1.5 LITRE (52 FL OZ/6 CUP) TERRINES

WHEN I FIRST LEFT HOME TO LIVE IN PARIS, MAMAN WOULD MAKE LOTS OF WONDERFUL TERRINE MIX AND PUT IT IN SMALL TINS WHICH SHE WOULD TAKE TO THE MAN IN THE BICYCLE SHOP IN VÉLINES TO BE CRIMPED SHUT. SHE WOULD THEN COOK THEM FOR THREE HOURS TO STERILISE THEM SO THEY WERE EASY FOR ME TO TRANSPORT AND KEEP. YOU'LL NEED TO START THIS RECIPE AT LEAST 24 HOURS IN ADVANCE BEFORE YOU WISH TO SERVE IT. IF YOU HAVE A MEAT GRINDER, IT IS PREFERABLE THAT YOU DO YOUR OWN MINCING. IF YOU DON'T HAVE A MEAT GRINDER AT HAND, ASK YOUR BUTCHER TO MINCE THE MEAT FOR YOU.

In a frying pan, place the duck fat, shallots and cook over medium heat until golden. Set aside to cool.

Line the terrine moulds neatly with the slices of pork back fat, bottom sides and ends trying not to overlap.

Combine the pork meat and liver with the shallots and remaining ingredients and mix with your hands for a long time, until it becomes sticky and a bit elastic. Put the mix into the terrine moulds, folding back the fat and covering the top as well. Place a bay leaf in the centre of each and firmly seal the terrine with either a lid or aluminium foil.

Preheat the oven to 200ºC (400ºF/Gas 6). Place a thin cloth at the bottom of a heavy roasting pan, place the terrines on top and add boiling water until it reaches half way up the sides of the terrines. Cook in this bain marie for 20 minutes, then lower the heat to 180ºC (350ºF/Gas 4) and continue to cook for 1–1½ hours. Check regularly and add more water if needed. After an hour, pierce with a wooden skewer, when the juices run clear, the terrines are cooked.

Remove the lids or the aluminium foil and place on a rack to cool. When the terrines are cool but not set, cover with plastic wrap, place a heavy weight on top and refrigerate. Leave them to set for a couple of days before serving. They will keep well sealed in the refrigerator for up to one week.

NOTE: The saltiness of this dish will assist in preservation and will mellow with age.

½ tablespoon duck fat

150 g (5½ oz) French shallots, finely sliced

800 g (1 lb 12 oz) pork back fat, finely sliced

1.6 kg (3 lb 8 oz) pork, minced (800 g/1 lb 12 oz fatty belly, and 800 g/1 lb 12 oz pork neck)

600 g (1 lb 5 oz) pork liver, minced

4 garlic cloves, crushed

2 eggs

40 g (1½ oz) fine salt

8 g (¼ oz) freshly ground black pepper

¼ teaspoon freshly grated nutmeg

30 ml (1 fl oz) cognac (or brandy)

2 bay leaves

He would then proceed to keep filling their glasses while only pouring a drop in his own. Grandmère would either serve what biscuits she had on hand or whip up a cake called a *tôt fait* ('quickly made'). The guests would be served a slice of cake with glasses of Sauternes until – much to Grandpère's amusement – the conversation became animated.

I was living with my grandparents in Port Ste-Foy when I celebrated my *Communion Solennelle* at age twelve. In France, a *Communion Solennelle* always called for a huge family lunch in a restaurant. I was never really religious and – as usual – I was joking around as Tatie Antoinette helped me into my long, white dress. Tatie Antoinette, who was a devout Catholic, admonished me for my behaviour: 'You know, Dany, you really should be in a contemplative mood on the day of your *Communion Solennelle*. It's a very important moment in your life. You should reflect on your holy state and have pious thoughts.' Alas, in spite of all my trips to Lourdes, I was a complete failure when it came to practising pious thoughts.

After the church service we went to the restaurant. I still have the printed menu, dated 11 Juillet, 1954, where I am pictured replete with veil and pure white lilies. That angelic image was merely a short-lived illusion. At the restaurant I was seated next to Grandpère Armand who played his little trick on me – he poured too much wine in my glass and made me tipsy. When the *communiants* returned to church to make our solemn procession up the aisle I tripped over the hem of my dress and fell flat on my face.

Although religion didn't capture my attention, the art of photography certainly did. Not long after my Communion, I managed to save up enough pocket money to buy a Brownie Flash, which became my pride and joy. Monique was my favourite subject: I used to torment my sister whenever we were together, following her around and taking her picture and making her pose for me. She often ended up in tears, which provided me with what I thought were perfectly candid, artistic portraits.

My favourite subject at school was drawing. I tried so hard to impress my art teacher and – like many of the girls – I had a huge crush on her. I did, however, suspect that my crush was different to what the other girls were feeling, so I decided to go and visit Paulette. Even though Paulette was now married with little children of her own, we had remained friends and she was the only person to whom I could confess my secret. When I broached the subject of my sexuality Paulette laughed and hugged me and told me not to worry, that my feelings towards members of the same sex were normal and would pass and that I would grow up and meet a nice boy and marry. In my heart, I didn't believe this was just a passing phase; I continued to apply myself in art class, believing that my talent would attract the attention of my art teacher, who remained totally impervious.

When I was fourteen, my Tatie Germaine (who was formerly married to Papa's late brother René) and her new husband Emile invited me to Paris for a week. By the end of my stay, I was completely besotted with the capital and vowed to return and live there some day. I thought Paris was the most beautiful place I'd ever seen and that week-long visit inspired me to get out and explore the world. I told Grandpère how I wanted to visit Tahiti. 'Oh *pah*,' he replied. 'You don't have to go anywhere. This is the most beautiful country in the world right here!'

Around the time of my third year in Port Ste-Foy, my parents sold their business in Ambarès and bought a corner shop in Bordeaux on Boulevard Brandenburg, out by the Grand Pont over the Garonne. The shop sold meat and groceries and fruit and vegetables. It had a cellar to store groceries and a courtyard, but no garden. It would be much less hard work for them. Though there would be no more killing animals and no more *tournées*, Papa still got up very early each day to pick up the fruit and vegetables and meat from Bordeaux's wholesale market. At the back of the shop was a dining room and kitchen that measured two by one and a half metres – so small that only one person could stand in it at a time. There was a shower and sink off the kitchen and – upstairs – the smallest flat in the world. Although Maman and Papa had a large bedroom, Monique and I had to share a double bed in a room the size of a cupboard. They hired Thérèse, a young married woman with children, to be our housekeeper. I got along really well with Thérèse – she used to tell me all sorts of gossip about Maman – and if there was ever an argument she always took my side.

During the school holidays I worked in the new shop – slicing the cheese and terrines, weighing the vegetables and serving the customers. I loved everything about the job and one day announced to Maman that I wanted to leave school and work in the shop. 'Well, all right, then,' Maman said at once. 'Let's go in tomorrow morning to the *lycée* to tell the *directrice* and see what she says.' So my parents got all dressed up – '*sur leurs trente-et-un*' – as we say in French, and off we drove to Ste-Foy. The *directrice* received us in her office, where she lectured me about how much I would regret leaving school, what a waste it was to give up my studies and how I would one day thank my parents for forcing me to stay on. Reluctantly, I agreed to stay, but I made my parents promise that after I finished the *brevet* at Ste-Foy (the exam at the end of *troisième*) I could go to the *lycée* in Bordeaux to finish my studies for the *baccalauréat*. I was ready for the big city – especially if I didn't have to board and eat those awful school dinners!

The Lycée de Jeunes Filles was in the centre of Bordeaux on Rue de Cheverus and one of the teachers lived near my parents. We had fabulous teachers at the Lycée and I made some great friends, especially Anne-Marie and Marie-France. We were always together. I chose to major in philosophy and I loved to carry on about problems that couldn't be solved. Maman never understood what I was studying. One of the books we had to read was Camus' *Le Mythe de Sisyphe*, where in the very first sentence he asks if the realisation of the absurdity of life requires suicide. Maman found the book – she was always nosy and ferreting about in my room – and when she read that sentence threw the book straight into the stove. For days I searched about, saying, 'I can't believe this! Where is my Camus?' Finally she confessed: 'I burned it!' She was afraid I might kill myself! Maman continued to look through my books and burn those she thought would lead me astray.

NEITHER OF MY PARENTS HAD ANY INCLINATION OR interest towards books – although, admittedly, nor did they have much time to read.

Lapin rôti farci

ROAST FARM RABBIT

SERVES 4–6

MY GRANDMOTHER AND MY MOTHER BOTH BRED THEIR OWN ORGANICALLY FED RABBITS. THEY HAD THAT
HAZELNUT-FLAVOURED WHITE FLESH STILL FOUND TODAY IN RABBITS IN COUNTRY FRANCE.
A *LAPIN FARÇI* WAS ALWAYS COOKED FOR SPECIAL OCCASIONS, OR WHEN I CAME HOME FROM PARIS.

1½ tablespoons duck fat, warmed (this can be
   substituted with grapeseed oil if unavailable)

2 large French shallots, thinly sliced

1–1.5 kg (2 lb 4 oz–3 lb 5 oz) rabbit with belly
   flaps, liver and kidneys intact (if there are
   no livers, substitute with 2 chicken livers)

40 g (1½ oz) Bayonne ham (or prosciutto) ½ fat,
   ½ lean, not too dry, skin removed and finely diced

1 large garlic clove, crushed

¼ cup coarsely chopped flat-leaf (Italian) parsley

2 savory sprigs, coarsely chopped (if unavailable
   can be substituted for thyme)

1 small egg

1 piece of crustless bread (about 20 g/¾ oz),
   soaked in 125 ml (4 fl oz/½ cup) milk and
   squeezed out to the size of 2 walnuts

12–16 smoked speck, thinly sliced

Preheat the oven to 210ºC (415ºF/Gas 6–7).

Heat ½ tablespoon of the duck fat in a small frying pan over medium-heat. Add the shallots and fry without colouring for 2–3 minutes or until just starting to soften. Allow to cool completely.

Remove the liver and kidneys from inside the rabbit, remove the nerves but reserve the fat and set aside. Place the ham in a food processor and process until minced. Add the liver and kidneys and process again for 1 minute, scraping down the inside of the bowl. Add the shallots, garlic, parsley, savory, egg, and salt and freshly ground black pepper to taste along with the soaked bread. Blend the ingredients well.

Spoon the stuffing into the rabbit belly, fold over the flaps and then, using a trussing needle and kitchen string, sew the flaps together to enclose the stuffing. Season the rabbit on the exterior with salt and pepper but take care not to use too much salt. Wrap the rabbit with the slices of smoked speck, quite close to each other, and secure with string. Place the rabbit in a roasting pan and drizzle with the remaining duck fat.

Roast for 20 minutes, and then turn over and roast for a further 20 minutes. Insert a skewer into the thickest part of the thigh, when the juices run clear, it is done. Depending on the size of the rabbit, it may need another 5 or 10 minutes, but not much more. Transfer the rabbit to a plate and keep warm.

Place the roasting pan over medium heat and deglaze with 250 ml (9 fl oz/ 1 cup) water, bring to the boil and cook for 5–10 minutes or until it has reduced by half and the sauce has thickened slightly.

To serve, cut and remove all the string from the rabbit, pile all the speck in the middle of a serving platter, using a sharp knife remove the 4 legs and chop the saddle into thick slices, keeping the stuffing with each slice. Arrange the slices around the platter and spoon over the hot sauce.

After lunch Papa would pore over the *Sud-Ouest*, Bordeaux's daily newspaper, for a few minutes before he fell asleep in his chair. And Maman had little patience if I tried to discuss some of the issues we were studying in *philo*. 'Oh, that's enough of that!' she'd cut me off, not wanting to know, and would add her equivalent of 'get lost', which was: 'Why don't you go out and buy us a camembert?' Often, while I was trying to study, Maman would burst through the door to my room and say: 'Your father and I are too busy to make supper. Can you make it, Dany?' Though I hated having to put aside my books, I loved that Papa enjoyed my cooking because I always used cream (which is never used in traditional south-west dishes). He was always requesting my special *gratin aux macaronis* with cream and cheese.

My parents sold the shop on Boulevard Brandenburg while I was at the *lycée* and bought a smaller *boucherie-charcuterie* on Avenue d'Eysines on the outskirts of Bordeaux. No more *épicerie* and vegetables – Papa wanted to once again concentrate on his beloved meat. Thankfully, the flat was larger, with its own front door, so you didn't have to access it via the shop. There was also a little garden near the kitchen. Maman did a lot more cooking when we moved to the new shop: she made strongly flavoured tripe dishes and *daubes*. I could always smell them as soon as I got off the bus from the *lycée*. Back then there were no plastic containers or aluminium *barquettes* so she bought hundreds of small Duralex glass bowls that she filled with individually portioned stews, which the customers would take home and heat in a saucepan.

Maman also made a delicious *poitrine de veau farcie* (stuffed breast of veal), which she sold like a terrine. After stuffing the breast, she wrapped the whole thing in a big piece of gauze to keep it in a long sausage shape while it cooked. Once it had cooled, she would remove the gauze.

I took my *baccalaureat* in 1961 and scored well in philosophy, which compensated for my lousy marks in maths and physics. I wanted to go to the Beaux Arts to study drawing and photography but my parents said: 'No, it's time to go to work.' My father thought that a '*bac*' meant a job; he didn't understand that first you got the *bac* and then you learned something useful. In the early 1960s there was a shortage of teachers in France, so anyone with a *bac* could immediately start teaching in the elementary schools; you'd start in class for five days a week and on the Thursday take classes in teacher training. Maman thought this was great: 'You can apply to get a job in Bordeaux as a teacher!' I didn't want to be a teacher, but Maman insisted: 'Look, Dany, teaching is a great job. You get a good retirement and pension.' As if a nineteen-year-old could care less! But Maman had it in her mind that I had to be either a teacher or a pharmacist, because they made good money. I didn't want to know about it. Instead I took a few classes at the Beaux Arts in Bordeaux while Maman continued yammering like a broken record: 'Apply to be a teacher! We can't afford to have you around studying and not working.'

Finally, I came up with a cunning plan – one that would satisfy Maman and indulge my own secret passion to go and live in Paris. I applied to be a teacher but chose only one *département*: the Seine, the *département* of Paris. I received an offer in the post, but because I was nineteen and considered to be a minor, my parents had to sign an authorisation

TOP: DANY, AT HOME — FREE AT LAST IN PARIS

BOTTOM: VISITING THE FAMOUS ACTOR MICHEL SIMON

form to let me go. They refused: 'Oh, no. You can't go to Paris. There must be teaching positions for you here in the Gironde!' I shook my head and looked morose. 'Oh, no, no. *Pas de places dans la Gironde*. You wanted me to be a teacher but the only places available are in Paris.' Reluctantly, they agreed – on the condition that I stayed with my cousin Max – who had lived with us during the war – and his wife Colette. They lived in Saint-Leu-la-Forêt, *en banlieue*. It was hardly what I had in mind but I planned to change that arrangement once I was settled.

The job the education ministry gave me was in an *école maternelle* for disadvantaged children, run by the *mairie* (local council) in Saint-Denis, the poorest part of Paris. The school was located just behind the very first Gothic Cathedral, the Basilique de St Denis, dedicated to the patron saint of Paris. It was the burial place for most French kings – none of which saved it from being in the middle of a slum! I was in charge of a class of three-year-old urchins; even in the middle of winter they would come to school in thin, raggedy shorts with their little stick legs bright red from the cold. I've never been very maternal, but I did feel very sorry for the little souls. For most of them the hot lunch provided by the school was the only nourishing meal they ate all day. My job was to keep them amused with songs, games, stories and craft. At the end of each day I caught the train back to Saint-Leu-la-Forêt, which is not where I wanted to be. I wanted to be in the heart of the action – in the centre of Paris. As soon as I had saved enough money from my wage to afford the fees, I applied to a private art school, the Atelier Met de Penninghen in Rue du Dragon. The *école maternelle* finished at 4 pm, so I'd hop on a train and attend classes where I trained to be an art teacher.

That was when living in Paris became a lot of fun. I soon made some great friends at art school, including Francine, of Brive, who was hilarious. Like me Francine was a teacher as well as an art student and earned extra money as a guide on the tour buses in Paris. Not long after we met, Francine and I decided to rent a flat together in the centre of Paris by the Gare de l'Est. I was so happy to leave my life with Max and Colette behind: they fought and screamed almost as much as my parents. Although my new flat with Francine was grotty and vile it had one redeeming feature: a great big bathtub, where Francine would often end up sleeping at night, preferring it to the wretched, smelly old sofa bed. '*Oooh, c'est très confortable!*' she'd laugh. But Francine was rarely home – she spent most of the night out gallivanting in her yellow Deux Chevaux, which she called the '*corps jaune*' (yellow body). I soon bought a car, too – a little Renault sports car – as this was back in the days when you could still get a parking spot in Paris.

When classes at the Atelier finished at 10 pm, many of the art students spilled out into the city streets. It was a great time to be young in Paris. Everyone was excited about the music scene and New Wave cinema, Godard and Truffaut. Like many girls, I wore my hair short like Jean Seberg in *A Bout de Souffle*. One of our favourite haunts was the little triangular Le Petit Sauvignon on a corner near the Atelier. It was a shop/café known as a *vins et charbons* for its main products: coal and wine, owned (like nearly all the *vins et charbons* in Paris) by a couple who had arrived in Paris early in the twentieth century from the Auvergne. Dressed in their matching blue aprons, Monsieur and Madame would stand behind the old zinc bar along with their daughter (who runs it to this day). Here we would down gallons of rosé, accompanied by goat's cheese, terrines, ham from the Auvergne and thick slices of country bread. Another favourite meeting spot was the Café des Sports on Rue du Four. The night I remember most vividly was that of 22 November 1963, when someone burst through the door and shouted that John F. Kennedy had been assassinated. All we could do was sit in stunned silence.

The little café-theatres along Rue de la Montagne Sainte-Geneviève were also a major part of the scene for art students. We'd all squash together in smoky little rooms to listen to celebrated French singers and actors such as Jacques Brel, Anne Sylvestre and (Marcel) Mouloudji, who – for just a few *sous* – would sing and play for the students. It was thrilling to hear all that beautiful poetry and music performed live for the first time.

As a result of these late-night jaunts, I often turned up at Saint-Denis feeling less

When classes at the Atelier finished at 10 pm, many of the art students spilled out into the city streets. It was a great time to be young in Paris. Everyone was excited about the music scene and New Wave cinema, Godard and Truffaut.

than fresh. I always looked forward to when my little pupils took their *sieste* after lunch so that I could catch a few winks, too. After the year at the *école maternelle* at Saint-Denis, I used my family connections to get a less strenuous job as a *surveillant* or *pion* (monitor) in a *lycée* in Montgeron and, later, in Sarcelles, another Paris suburb. Being a *pion* was like being a police sergeant; because we weren't much older than the students we had to look authoritarian. We had a strict dress code which consisted of conservative jackets and skirts in the hope they would take us more seriously. Outside of work, however, I was a typical 1960s art school bohemian. We all smoked like fiends and I even puffed on a pipe – I loved the taste of it and it even made me a little bit high.

As twenty-year-olds do, we laughed at everyone and spent a lot of time poking fun at the directors of the *lycée* and our teachers at the Atelier. It pains me to confess that we would also pile into Francine's famous 'corps jaune' and drive past the best restaurants in Paris tooting our horns, laughing and mocking the bourgeois clients.

It was at the *lycée* in Sarcelles that I met my first girlfriend, Françoise, who was a maths teacher. Françoise was quite beautiful and wore her hair in a fashionable bouffante. Her father was a great intellectual and scholar and had taught her to love the arts and music and she seemed to know everything. One night, after attending a concert on the Pont des Arts with a group of teachers from the *lycée*, one of my male colleagues kissed me. That was when the penny dropped: I knew the person I wanted to be kissing was Françoise. With much trepidation I approached her and declared my feelings. To my

Gâteau de semoule

CARAMELISED SEMOLINA CAKE

SERVES 6-8

THIS MOIST DESSERT IS VERY 'HOMEY'. I LOVED HELPING COOK THIS RECIPE WHEN I WAS A CHILD. IT CAN BE COOKED EITHER IN A SAVARIN MOULD OR IN INDIVIDUAL RAMEKINS. IT IS BEST WHEN PREPARED A DAY IN ADVANCE.

Preheat the oven to 160°C (315°F/Gas 2–3).

Combine 80 g (3 oz) of the sugar and 2 tablespoons water in a small saucepan over medium heat, bring to the boil and cook for 5–10 minutes until the caramel is light golden in colour. Working quickly, pour the caramel into a 1 litre (35 fl oz/4 cup) savarin mould or divide between six 125 ml (4 fl oz/¹⁄₂ cup) ramekins, rotating to coat base of mould with caramel. Set aside.

In an ovenproof saucepan, combine the milk, butter, remaining sugar, vanilla bean and seeds, lemon and orange zest and a pinch of salt and bring to the boil. Sprinkle the semolina into the pan and stir well. Cook in the oven for 20 minutes.

Remove the saucepan and increase the oven temperature to 180°C (350°F/Gas 4). Remove vanilla bean and spoon mixture into a bowl, add egg yolks and cream and beat well to combine.

Using an electric mixer, beat the egg whites until stiff, then fold into the semolina mixture. Spoon the mixture into the savarin mould or ramekins, then place in a roasting pan with enough water to come halfway up the sides of the mould. Bake for 15 minutes or until the cake springs back when pressed. Allow to cool. It is best to leave the cake in the mould for a few hours or overnight in the refrigerator so the caramel has more time to be absorbed. The caramel will make a sauce for the cake when turned out. Serve with seasonal poached fruit or berries if desired.

140 g (5 oz) caster (superfine) sugar
500 ml (17 fl oz/2 cups) milk
50 g (1¾ oz) unsalted butter
½ vanilla bean, split and seeds scraped
finely grated zest of ½ lemon
finely grated zest of ½ orange
pinch of salt
125 g (4½ oz/1 cup) fine wheat semolina
3 eggs, separated
40 ml (1¼ fl oz) cream

great surprise and delight she told me she had been waiting for such a declaration. Françoise and I soon found a nice flat together, this time near the Gare du Nord. But even though we were living in the heady days of the sixties – when love and freedom and women's liberation were in the air – it was wise to keep the fact that we were gay to ourselves. To the rest of the world, we were simply flatmates.

Alongside my new-found love for Françoise and passion for art, my obsession for food remained. On Sunday mornings at five o'clock, I would often drive south of Paris to the huge market at Issy-les-Moulineaux to earn a bit of cash helping my Tonton Jeannot. Though Maman's brother had trained to be a butcher with my parents in Ambarès he had since moved into poultry, taking over the family business that had belonged to his wife's parents. It was a major enterprise, selling ducks, chickens, eggs and game in the markets. A highlight of these Sunday excursions was the lunch that Jeannot's mother-in-law would have waiting for us at 3 pm after we came back from the market and unloaded everything. She used to cook wonderfully rich foods using butter and cream as well as pastries and terrines, foie gras and game dishes all accompanied by superb wines. Prior to these family feasts I had only ever drunk Bordeaux wines, but Jeannot introduced me to red Burgundies such as Pommard and white wines from the Loire Valley. They were delicious!

Like his father Grandpère Armand, Jeannot was also a great hunter. He and some friends shared a *grande chasse* and had a big hunting lodge in the forest of Sologne, between Paris and the Loire Valley. I often accompanied them – not to shoot guns, but to shoot pictures. It was a tradition for these wonderful *chasse* lunches to last all afternoon and feature endless courses of game served with rich sauces and perfectly matched wines. Those were the good old days, when calories and cholesterol didn't enter the equation.

Meanwhile, back near Bordeaux, my parents had sold their shop and moved once again. Before I left for Paris, my parents had invited an elderly couple to live with them. The wife was a cousin of Papa's and she and her husband – both in their late eighties – had become too old and frail to live on their own in their home in Vélines, a village outside Sainte-Foy. Papa's cousin died six months after moving in with my parents; her husband survived for another few years, living to the ripe old age of ninety-two.

In exchange for taking care of them, the couple willed my parents their home in Vélines: it was a big, beautiful nineteenth century house in the centre of the village with a terrace and front garden and two hectares of land that boasted lovely views of the countryside. It was a dream come true for Maman and Papa who had worked so very hard all their lives – often in cramped conditions. Finally, they could take it easy. Papa still did a bit of business buying and selling lambs and Maman kept chickens, ducks and rabbits and tended a big vegetable garden.

After selling my old Renault Floride I bought a newer Citroën Diane so I could drive down to visit them during the holidays. Monique was still living at home. Unlike me, Monique wasn't champing at the bit and was happy to stay near my parents. After getting her *brevet* in the Catholic school system, she went on to a secreterial school in Bordeaux.

One Easter holiday, Monique and I were both supposed to stay with Grandpère Armand and Grandmère Rachel. I had a two-week break from teaching but wanted to spend the first week with my friends in Paris, so Monique arrived on her own. Grandpère Armand died suddenly that night. Monique told me that when she had arrived that morning at the station in Sainte-Foy, Grandpère's face had fallen to see that she was alone. '*Mais Dany n'est pas là,*' he had said sadly. We never saw each other again. Years later, it is something I still regret.

———

AFTER LOSING GRANDPÈRE, GRANDMÈRE RACHEL MOVED

into my parents' spacious new home in Vélines. Grandmère Rachel was as lovely as ever and the perfect caricature of a little French granny: she twisted her long white hair into a bun on top of her head and wore black stockings and an apron every day. Papa was very fond of Grandmère Rachel and always took her side during family squabbles. I can still picture her sitting quietly in the kitchen, shelling peas, or helping Maman to prepare vegetables from the garden. She was always gentle, smiling and quiet.

On the few occasions I had invited Françoise along to visit my family in Vélines, Maman had been so rude to her that we had been forced to leave early. Although Françoise and I slept in separate bedrooms, Maman was always making loaded comments about what she suspected was my dark, depraved Parisian existence. Of course, the person she blamed for leading me astray was beautiful Françoise, who often left the house in tears.

Although I loved my visits to Vélines for the holidays, I had to accept that I must make the journey minus Françoise if I wanted to avoid causing Maman any stress. I would then return to Paris with an assortment of wonderful terrines that had been sealed tight in little tins using a machine at the local bicycle shop. I would scarcely set foot in my Paris flat when the phone would start to ring: 'Allo, Dany? What have you got to eat?' Everyone knew I always returned laden with goodies from the Dordogne.

Back in Paris I had started to veer away from drawing and develop my long-held passion for photography. After four years in the department of education, I said to myself, 'Well, Dany, you can't remain a *pion* forever. It's time to start earning some real money!' And so began my search for work as a photographer. I very quickly landed a job in a commercial laboratory at the Arc de Triomphe and advanced quickly, working on some major advertisements and publicity campaigns. Our group of friends, Françoise and I spent our spare time excitedly planning the films we would make and rushing from our day jobs to the cinematheque to watch the same films again and again. We even gate-crashed the opening of Jean Renoir's Pigalle cinema. We got close enough to talk to him and after giving me the once-over, he remarked that I could become a great character actress. But oh no, I did not want to be an actress, I wanted to direct!

My parents were not at all pleased that I was working in a film laboratory; when I visited Vélines, Maman would introduce me as 'My daughter, Dany, who *could* be a teacher.' Maman was always much happier with Monique, who, after finishing school had worked as a secretary in Bergerac and Port Ste-Foy, never far from home. The fact is that Maman knew little of photography and was never sure of what I did in Paris. She would often try to entice me back, saying brightly:'We will buy a photographic shop in Ste-Foy, where you could have a studio and take wedding pictures.''No, no!' I'd groan,'That's the last thing I want to do!' Not I, who dreamed of making films worthy of Jean Renoir and mixing with Picasso and Claude Sautet! Maman could never say,'I love you' or,'I miss you', but she certainly tried to lure me back. Even when I moved to Australia she would write,'Come back and I'll buy you a sports car.'

Working in a film laboratory meant I was positioned on the periphery of all the upheavals in Paris in May 1968 (when the largest general strike in French history stopped the country's economy). Back in Vélines, Maman read about the riots and bread shortages in the capital and decided I would soon starve to death. She made a beeline to the local *boulangerie*, bought an enormous *pain de campagne*, wrapped it in linen and stitched the entire parcel together. She then addressed it in her beautiful, flowing script and posted it to me in Paris, thus ensuring I averted certain starvation.

It was mid-1968 when I moved to another film laboratory where I was given more responsibilities and occasionally sent to company headquarters in London. My Dutch boss often asked me to work until 4 am – so I made some really good overtime money. He would then take me to the glamorous Champs Elysées for something to eat because it was the only place in Paris that was still open. For a girl from Sainte-Foy-la-Grande – these were very exciting times. As well as having a fulfilling job that I loved, I was dining out in hip cafés and visiting art galleries, movies and theatres with my friends and living in beautiful Paris. Although I felt I couldn't ask for a better life, there were a few dark clouds on the horizon. Flirtations outside home made Françoise jealous and my personal life was becoming complicated. I thought everything would be resolved if I buried myself in work so I put off making difficult decisions and concentrated on having fun.

Terrine de foie de volaille 60
Cucumber salad   .50
Garlic brains   .55
Mexican fish salad   .60
Quiche lorraine   .80

                        1.20
Oysters
                        1.50

Steak < maitre d'hôtel
        au poivre   2.00
Filet de boeuf "strogonoff" 1.80
Rôti de porc à l'orange 1.50

Lamb steak "prov
Sauté de veau m
Cheese
Chocolate
Cherry
Galade

CHAPTER TWO

1966–1972

UPSTAIRS DOWN UNDER

'There are no leeks in Australia…'

THE FAMILY HOME IN VÉLINES, DORDOGNE, FRANCE

MY MOTHER WAS FOND OF FINDING THE DRAMA IN EVERYDAY LIFE. WITH TYPICAL FRENCH FLAIR, SHE ONCE SAID: 'THAT DAY I WALKED ACROSS THE SQUARE IN VÉLINES WAS THE DAY I SENT MY TWO DAUGHTERS TO AUSTRALIA ... TO THE OTHER SIDE OF THE WORLD.'

IT WAS SPRING 1966 AND I HAD ONCE AGAIN DRIVEN down from Paris to visit my family in Vélines for the duration of the spring holidays. Since arriving in the village, I had been trying to convince my sister Monique to move away from the family and start a new life in Paris. Of course, our parents were deadset against the idea of me nudging Monique out of the nest. They ignored our protests and promises of good behaviour and said: '*Non*! It's out of the question. Dany leads a depraved life in Paris.' And that was that. End of discussion. *Merde*! But even without me egging her on, Monique had already begun to cast her gaze further afield: she was nineteen and wanted to go to England. She was in love with the English language – it was one of her passions – and if Paris was not an option then perhaps she could persuade our parents to let her go to the United Kingdom. Monique's reasoning was simple: even though London was further away, at least it wasn't like Paris – a city seething with depraved perverts!

On one particularly fateful afternoon during my stay, when the back-and-forth negotiations with my parents had stalled, Monique and I retreated to the front doorway of the family home where we stood with our arms crossed, feeling restless and fidgety. As usual, there wasn't much happening in the village on that sleepy spring day and so we chatted idly, dreaming of action and adventure in far-off lands. In the distance, a dog was barking. Nearby, little blue butterflies flitted and flirted in circles. The lace curtains in the neighbourhood windows shifted in the breeze. Walking back from the *boulangerie*, with their daily *pain* tucked under their arms, was a slow procession of elderly folk. Across from us, in the main square of the village, loomed the church; the tolling of its bells marking the hours of our lives drifting away.

Suddenly, the routine sameness of the day was disturbed by the revving of a Range Rover that was trailing a caravan and pulling into the *place*. Back then, in rural France, people could camp just about anywhere – even in the village square. But this Range Rover had British plates, which in those days was very rare. Monique and I wandered down to the front gate and watched as an older man and a much younger woman set up camp and prepared to spend the night. This promised to be quite an event! 'Maman!' we called towards the house. 'Come look! There are *des Anglais* in the square!'

'*Ah bon?*' she exclaimed, rushing to look. She then turned to Monique: '*Vas-y-toi!* Off you go! Go and talk to them. You speak English.' We looked at each other, both horrified by her pushy impetuousness; one just didn't go and talk to strangers. Whatever would they think? Although the English are renowned for their good manners we both knew Monique's English was not up to the task of having an actual conversation. Still, Maman remained as determined as ever, and, when it became clear we weren't about to budge she opened the gate and strode straight across the square to the caravan!

'Maman, what do you think you're doing?' we called out, cringing with embarrassment. 'Don't worry about it!' she shouted back, before disappearing inside the caravan, where she stayed for more than an hour. Given that she couldn't speak a word of English beyond 'Hello', Monique and I were baffled by Maman's behaviour and wondered what the hell she was up to. We stood nervously, hopping from one foot to the next, until she finally emerged. She appeared triumphant: strutting across the square with her shoulders back and her head held high. It was a walk that announced to the world that she had just done business. 'So there. It's all arranged!' Maman said as she marched towards us. 'What? What's arranged?' We were crazy with curiosity.

'*Ils sont charmants*! They are charming. Now off you go and talk to them Monique because in three months' time you will be going to live with them in England to take care of their baby.'

'What baby?'

'There's a little baby boy in there and you will be his *au pair* for one month.'

The young mother, Mercedes, was Spanish and was the third wife of the older man who, though English, had been trained as a French teacher and understood everything Maman had said. The couple were on their way to Spain when they decided to settle in Vélines for the night. That chance meeting with Maman actually proved very fortuitous for Monique: the modest English gent just happened to be George Perry-Smith, the so-called 'Father of modern British cooking' and owner of The Hole in the Wall, a legendary restaurant in Bath. Known for his great sense of humour and adventure, George was hardly the type to say 'No' to a pushy French mother in the middle of nowhere.

And so Monique's wish was granted and, in January 1967, off she went to England to take care of Andrew Perry-Smith. Monique loved living abroad so much that George invited her to stay for another twelve months to wait on tables at The Hole in the Wall. It was a wonderful opportunity for Monique to practise her English language skills. George was a self-taught chef and a huge fan of Elizabeth David, the pre-eminent British cookery writer of the mid-twentieth century. Both Elizabeth David and George Perry-Smith have been credited with introducing postwar Britain to the pleasures of good food and were great believers in using the finest ingredients available and treating them with respect. As well as offering lengthy menus with lots of choices per course, George had an innovative approach to staffing. Those employed at The Hole in the Wall were encouraged to try their hand at different stations: waiters would help prep; chefs would

Cervelles en persillade

GARLIC LAMB'S BRAINS

SERVES 4

THIS IS MY MOTHER'S RECIPE FOR GARLIC BRAINS — SOMETHING SHE USED TO COOK FOR US WHEN WE WERE CHILDREN. MY MEMORIES ARE OF DELICIOUS WARM AND CREAMY FOOD AND THE SMELL OF FRESH GARLIC STIRRING THE APPETITE, HOW COULD ANYONE NOT WANT TO EAT THEM? FOR MY BUSY MOTHER IT WAS A DISH THAT WAS QUICK AND EASY TO PREPARE AND FULL OF NOURISHMENT. IT TOOK A CERTAIN AMOUNT OF PERSUASION TO CONVINCE AUSTRALIANS OF THE DELIGHTS OF OFFAL, BUT IT EVENTUALLY BECAME A SIGNATURE DISH AT UPSTAIRS, MY FIRST RESTAURANT.

Soak the brains in cold water with 1 tablespoon of the vinegar for an hour or until they are white with no traces of blood. Change the water and vinegar at least once and then drain. Peel membranes from the brains if necessary.

Place the brains in a saucepan, cover with cold water, add parsley sprigs, onion, thyme and bay leaf. Bring to the boil, reduce the heat to very low and simmer for 5–7 minutes or until just cooked through. Remove from the heat and let the brains cool down in their court bouillon. When cold, cut the brains into large chunks and set aside.

In a non-stick frying pan over a low flame, melt the butter with a little olive oil, add the garlic and fry without colouring, then add the brains, stirring very gently for 3–5 minutes until lightly golden. Add the lemon juice and chopped parsley, then season with salt and freshly ground black pepper and serve immediately on warm plates with lemon wedges and some fresh, crusty bread.

6 lamb's brains

2 tablespoons white vinegar

2–3 parsley sprigs

1 small onion, thinly sliced

1 thyme sprig

1 fresh bay leaf

50 g (1¾ oz) unsalted butter

olive oil

4 large garlic cloves, finely chopped

juice of 1 lemon, plus extra lemon wedges to serve

⅓ cup chopped flat-leaf (Italian) parsley

wait tables; the dishwasher would make the soup. This meant the kitchen brigade worked in sync with the wait staff as they understood what it was like to work the floor; and the wait staff all had intimate knowledge of the dishes featured on the menu because they had helped create them.

As well as offering lengthy menus with lots of choices per course, George Perry-Smith had an innovative approach to staffing. Those employed at The Hole in the Wall were encouraged to try their hand at different stations: waiters would help prep; chefs would wait tables; the dishwasher would make the soup.

One of the chefs who came to work at The Hole in the Wall restaurant was Michael Manners, a recent graduate from the École Hôtelière de Lausanne, Switzerland. Just months after meeting, Michael and Monique fell in love and in February 1969 were married during a real French village wedding in Vélines. Maman was in her element: she organised everything and everyone and loved being the mother of the bride – a role she had begun to suspect she would never enjoy with me. Maman kept asking me what I would be wearing to Monique's wedding but I insisted it would be a surprise. As indeed it was. Determined not to be forced into wearing a frock, I waited until moments before the ceremony to reveal my outfit of pants and a jacket that I'd had tailor-made in Paris. Maman was not impressed, but it was too late for her to do anything about it.

As the unofficial wedding photographer, I had the perfect excuse to ignore the fifty-year-old 'cavalier' Papa had provided to accompany me to the wedding. I certainly did not want to dance with him; I was more interested in Monique's bridesmaid Francine. Despite my misgivings about my dinner date, everything ran smoothly until Monique announced that she and her new husband were going to Australia. What? I hadn't even registered that Michael was an Australian – he spoke English, after all. I had to consult an atlas to even locate Australia, a country I knew next to nothing about. After dropping this bombshell, Monique and Michael departed for their honeymoon – travelling around Greece in a VW van before selling it and leaving for Sydney. Using his old connections, Michael soon found work as a chef while Monique got a secretarial job in the city.

It wasn't long before letters began to arrive from Monique, describing how wonderful and different it was in Australia and how much I would like it. Although I remained unconvinced of this, my personal life in Paris had become incredibly complicated and the thought of escaping my crisis of overlapping love affairs seemed to be quite an attractive option. I loved my country and didn't want to live anywhere else but I also felt a change of scenery might do me good. To my surprise, staff at the Australian Embassy in Paris told me that I could actually travel free to Australia on the condition that I stayed in the country for two years. Labour shortages in Australia were acute after the Second World War and the country had welcomed many refugees from Greece, Italy and Yugoslavia to employ on the huge public works projects that were then underway. Most of these workers were men. What Australia needed was women to redress the imbalance of the sexes; it needed women for these men to marry. A free ticket was hard to refuse and, besides, if I didn't like it, I would only have to refund the price of the ticket. Needless to say, I neglected to inform the embassy staff that I was gay.

AND SO IT WAS THAT TWO YEARS AFTER MAMAN MADE

Monique walk across the *place* in Vélines that I also left France bound for Australia. Although Maman did have a love of the 'dramatic', it's also true that her actions on that sleepy spring day did prove to be a defining moment in all our lives.

Because of the Six Day War between Israel and the armies of the neighbouring states of Egypt, Jordan and Syria, the Suez Canal was closed, which meant the journey by sea would take six weeks or more. I opted, instead, for a charter flight out of London where I was joined by a very international group of passengers destined for Down Under. We arrived at dawn on 19 December 1969 after flying in over Sydney and its harbour: the view was absolutely magnificent, one of the most beautiful cityscapes I had ever seen. A few minutes later, the plane landed at the 'airport' – which was nothing more than a wooden shed with a tin roof. It was 6 am, I hardly spoke any English, and I sincerely hoped Monique and Michael would be waiting in that shed. Of course, they were, and they drove me to their home in Paddington. Apart from the stunning aerial view, my first impressions of the city were that it seemed so foreign and lacklustre; Monique assured me that the rows of tiny, cramped terrace houses were becoming fashionable but it was not at all like my beautiful Paris. Where were the cafes and terraces teeming with people? The city looked empty and soul-less.

Although I was keen to get a job straight away, Monique said I should relax and wait until the holiday period was over. Relaxing, at their house, was certainly easy to do. It was completely unlike Paris, where it's possible to have lifelong friends that have never once visited your home. At Michael and Monique's house, people drifted in and out all day and night – chatting, laughing and drinking. Compared to Paris, Sydney seemed so incredibly casual: people even wore shorts in the street!

Michael worked as a chef in a restaurant called Patrick's, on Jersey Road, only a short walk away from their house. In typical Aussie fashion, he would kick off his shoes the second he was home and, to my horror, often go barefoot to the pub at the end of the street. I only went to the pub once: it was full of men all drinking large quantities of beer and I couldn't decipher a word they said. But the girls – much to my delight – were all beautiful. They were tall, leggy and tanned and all so friendly and seemingly interested in the French girl who had just stepped off a plane from Paris. Sydney was beginning to look promising. Sandy Pearce, an old friend of Michael's, and his French-Vietnamese

Poivrons à la Monaco

MONACO-STYLE RED CAPSICUM SALAD

SERVES 4, AS AN ENTRÉE

MY MOTHER SENT ME THIS RECIPE: PERFECT FOR A HOT SUMMER NIGHT, AS PART OF A BUFFET OF HORS D'OEUVRES, OR TO ACCOMPANY COLD CHICKEN AND A GREEN SALAD FOR LUNCH UNDER A SHADY VINE WITH A GLASS OF ROSÉ. IT CAN BE MADE AHEAD OF TIME AND KEPT IN AN AIRTIGHT CONTAINER IN THE REFRIGERATOR.

40 g (1½ oz) sultanas (golden raisins)
60 ml (2 fl oz/¼ cup) olive oil
100 g (3½ oz) baby spring onions
(scallions), trimmed
200 g (7 oz) fresh tomato concassé (see recipe page 230) or tinned whole tomatoes, drained and chopped
1 small garlic clove, finely chopped
1 bouquet garni (6 parsley sprigs, 1 thyme sprig, ½ bay leaf)
1 pinch saffron threads
1 pinch cayenne pepper
100 ml (3½ fl oz) dry white wine
1 teaspoon brown sugar
2 large red capsicums (peppers), thinly sliced
20 g (¾ oz) black olives

Soak the sultanas in warm water for 20 minutes. Then drain and set aside.

Place a tablespoon of the olive oil in a heavy-based saucepan and gently sauté the spring onions over medium heat until starting to colour. Then add the tomatoes, garlic, bouquet garni, saffron, cayenne pepper, wine, sugar and salt and freshly ground black pepper to taste and cook for about 15 minutes.

In a frying pan, over medium heat, quickly sauté the capsicum in the remaining olive oil without browning, then add them to the sauce. Add the sultanas and olives to the sauce and cook for another 15 minutes, or until the capsicum is tender but not collapsed. Place into a salad bowl and serve cold. It can be kept in the refrigerator for 2 or 3 days.

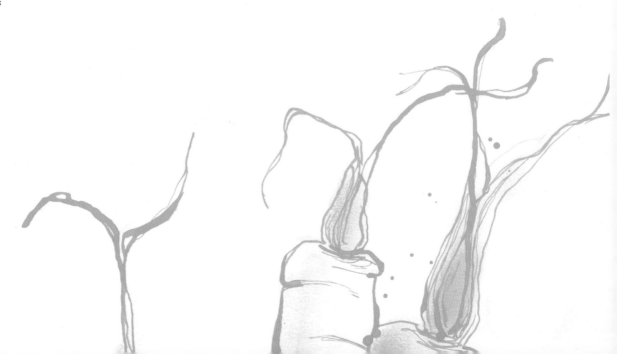

DANY AND FRIENDS, CRUISING ON THE GOOD SHIP *ORCADES*, 1970

wife, Colette, visited our house all the time. When Monique and Michael had first arrived in Australia, they had stayed with Sandy and Colette while house-hunting. Because we could all speak French, we became inseparable.

But I was not one to sit around being idle. Even though it was December – the month Monique said Australians aimed to do as little work as possible – I was constantly reading the 'Help Wanted' ads and keen to start earning some money. I applied for the first job that jumped out at me – for a photographer to work on a cruise ship that travelled to Tonga, Fiji and Auckland. I even donned a proper girlie dress for the interview; it was blue with '*petits pois*' (polka dots). I got the job. It was only later when I met the other photographers working aboard the *Orcades* that I realised the woman who interviewed me only employed gay women for the job. We were hired to take happy snaps and then develop the pictures to sell to the tourists. Each night, the three of us converged to our own table in the dining room. One evening, while we were eating, one of the photographers, a rather butch German girl, whispered: 'Eh, Dany, those two girls at the next table are giving us the eye. Why don't you turn around and look?'

I was shocked! That wasn't how we did things in Paris. I suddenly felt very shy. 'Oh no, I can't do that! I can't turn around and look at her!' Although I felt timid at the time, I wasn't too shy to meet with Carol in the darkroom later that night.

The job on the cruise ships wasn't fulltime and so I continued to see Carol for a few months back in Sydney. One of the places Carol took me to was the Fork 'n' View in the Blue Mountains. Run by a French-Australian named Sophie, the restaurant was housed in an old ice-cream parlour and boasted extraordinary views of the mountains. Although Sophie was a good cook, the Fork 'n' View was much more than a restaurant; dining there was a major event. Sophie was one of those people who had done many things in her life: as well as claiming she had been shipwrecked in Darwin, stories of her singing Edith Piaf songs in Sydney restaurants often did the rounds. While the service at her restaurant was slow – she only had one helper – Sophie's regulars would come prepared; they staggered into the restaurant with bottles of wine and drank prodigious amounts of it while they waited. Sophie didn't care – she would come out from the kitchen to have a chat and a glass of wine with the customers she knew, while the others thought, 'Ooh, la-la! Aren't you supposed to be in the kitchen cooking my dinner?' So slow was the service that there was even enough time for people to play *pétanque* between courses. The idea was to go to the Fork 'n' View to spend the whole day, eating and drinking and letting time drift by.

When I wasn't working on cruise ships, I loved to do the cooking at home, which made Monique so happy she kept telling me to stop looking for a job and stay home and cook for her and Michael. It was fun. I began to get a feel for what was fresh and seasonal in Sydney and discovered a huge variety of wonderful fresh seafood and exotic tropical fruits that I had never seen nor heard of.

It was around this time that my career path took a few unexpected twists and turns. One day, when the dishwasher at Patrick's restaurant didn't show up, Michael called and asked if I could take his place. On another occasion, he needed help peeling vegetables. A few days after that, he was desperate for someone to help make desserts. Because our

Langue de veau, sauce piquante

VEAL TONGUE IN PIQUANTE SAUCE

SERVES 4 AS A MAIN COURSE

THIS IS FRENCH BOURGEOIS FOOD OF THE SORT SERVED IN FAMILIES WHERE SPENDING TIME AND EFFORT ON EVERYDAY MEALS WAS CONSIDERED QUITE NORMAL. WHEN OUR PARENTS HAD A BUTCHERY AND CHARCUTERIE NOTHING WAS EVER WASTED AND FOOD FADS WERE NOT TOLERATED. WE WERE EXPECTED TO EAT AND ENJOY A WIDE VARIETY OF FOODS AND SO GREW UP WITH AN APPRECIATION FOR ALL PARTS OF THE ANIMALS. I COULD NOT UNDERSTAND WHEN PEOPLE SAID THEY WOULD NOT EAT WONDERFUL THINGS SUCH AS VEAL TONGUE.

Soak the tongue for 2 hours in cold water to drain the blood. Remove tongue and place in a large saucepan full of cold water, making sure it is fully submerged. Bring to the boil over medium heat, then lower the heat and keep skimming the froth coming to the surface until it stops. Add the vegetables, herbs and spices all at once and let simmer for 1½ to 2 hours, or until a skewer easily pierces the thickest part of the tongue. Leave to cool in the stock.

When cool enough to handle, remove and peel off the hard skin covering the tongue, and also remove as well any small bones or gristle at the back. Strain the stock and set aside.

TO MAKE THE SAUCE PIQUANTE: In a heavy-based saucepan, fry the onion gently in a little olive oil over medium heat until golden, deglaze with the vinegar and let it reduce totally. Add the tomatoes, bring to the boil, add 250 ml (9 fl oz/1 cup) reserved tongue stock and the garlic, and cook slowly for 15 minutes. Season with salt and freshly ground black pepper.

At this stage you can purée the sauce, or leave it chunky. I like it chunky. Slice the tongue into 1.5 cm (⅝ inch) thick slices, and reheat gently in the sauce, for about 5 minutes. Just before serving add the cornichons and capers and serve sprinkled with the parsley leaves.

2 fresh veal tongues (1.25kg/2 lb 12 oz)

1 onion, studded with 4 cloves

2 large carrots, thickly sliced

2 large celery stalks, thickly sliced

1 large bouquet garni (1 bay leaf, 3 thyme sprigs, 20 parsley sprigs)

¼ teaspoon quatres épices (four-spice mix)

1 tablespoon rock salt

½ tablespoon black peppercorns

1½ tablespoons olive oil

SAUCE PIQUANTE

1 onion, finely diced

olive oil, for cooking

100 ml (3½ fl oz) sherry or red wine vinegar

400 g (14 oz) fresh tomato concassé (see recipe page 230) or tinned whole tomatoes (900 g tomatoes, blanched, peeled and seeded = 400 g fresh concassé)

1 garlic clove, chopped

8 cornichons (baby gherkins), very thinly sliced

1 heaped tablespoon baby capers (optional)

2 tablespoons flat-leaf (Italian) parsley leaves

house was situated so close to the restaurant, it was easy for me to pop down to Patrick's, as required. As I became more comfortable in the kitchen, I began producing my own signature fruit tarts, making my own pastry and filling the kitchen with a lovely aroma. Tony, one of the owners, was a great gourmand and loved my creations. 'You're a great cook,' he said more than once. 'You really should open a restaurant!'

'Oh no, no, no,' I said. 'That's not what I've trained for. I don't want to be a cook!' And it was certainly true. I had never considered cooking as a job – it was just something that I grew up doing. In my family, cooking was as natural as breathing – Maman, my grandmothers and my aunts were all wonderful cooks but a career as a chef wasn't something French women from that era would ever consider. There were just a small handful of women we called 'les mères', who ran simple restaurants and did the basics. And besides, I considered myself to be a photographer, not a cook.

Yet perhaps Tony's words did sink in. A few months later, Colette, Monique and I were sitting around the house when I suggested that we all go out to a *bistrot*.

'No, we can't,' Monique said glumly.

'But why not?'

'Because, Dany, there aren't any *bistrots*. There's nothing like that here. Nothing.'

'Well, if there aren't any, we should open one,' I said, tongue-in-cheek.

Remember, this was the seventies, and restaurants in Sydney were often staid, formal and dark. Many were run by people from Europe who wanted to start a new life in Australia; opening a restaurant was the one thing they all felt they could do. They also believed stylish dining meant descending into a dark cellar. There would be the ubiquitous red tablecloths and candles, Chianti bottles and plastic grapes festooned from the ceiling. There were a few French restaurants that offered garlic prawns, garlic prawns and more garlic prawns. The garlic prawns were served in a little metal dish on a wooden board and sprinkled with odd-tasting flecks of preserved garlic that swam in searing-hot oil that you ate at your own peril. Alternatively, you could order a dish such as veal stroganoff that was *flambéed* at your table using equipment that dominated half the dining room. There were Italian restaurants, too, most of which were pretty dismal. They were all dark panels and low lighting and often featured violinists on Saturday nights.

It's safe to say that Sydney was ready for something different. The city was young, dynamic, energetic and full of promise. The sixties had changed everything. The American artist Christo had come to Sydney's Little Bay to make the world's largest sculpture, *Wrapped Coast*; film director Tim Burstall was reviving Australian cinema; the Sydney Opera House was nearly finished; and 1972 welcomed a new Labor government into power. More and more Australians were going on grand tours of Europe, living and working a year in London before travelling to countries on the Mediterranean, where they sat with their feet in the sand, eating sardines fresh from the sea. When these travellers came back to Australia to resume their regular lives, they yearned to find something similar at home.

MONIQUE AND I STARTED TO DISCUSS THE POSSIBILITY

of opening a French café. We thought it might be fun and we talked about it off and on, but never too seriously. Michael, however, thought our ideas had merit and one day declared that it was a long-held dream of his to open a restaurant and we should all do it together. Like his mentor George Perry-Smith, Michael was a devotee of Elizabeth David and wanted to own a restaurant that served real food made from fresh, quality ingredients. Michael's interest and enthusiasm meant our somewhat whimsical ideas might just become a reality.

After this conversation, our dear friend Colette came over, bursting with excitement. 'I've found a *bistrot!*' she announced. 'It's called Le Continental, over in Palmer Street. There's a French woman there called Madeleine and she cooks French food but she doesn't have a telephone.'

I had nothing planned for the afternoon, so I said: 'Oh, okay – I'll go around and have a look and book us a table.' Le Continental, as it turned out, was located above a seedy-looking Maltese club in a grotty neighbourhood that had its fair share of prostitutes. Luckily, it was broad daylight so I felt safe enough to clamber up the stairs to Le Continental, which was where I found Madeleine, shuffling about the little kitchen. '*Ah, c'est vous*, Madeleine,' I said. '*Vous voilà!*'

'*Oui oui, c'est moi,*' she said.

'Can I book a table for this evening?'

'Of course,' she said. But then she looked at me closely. 'How long have you been here?'

'A couple of months.'

'And what are you going to do?'

'I don't know! Maybe I'll start a restaurant,' I said, jokingly, another one of my famous throwaway lines!

'Well, this one is for sale,' she replied seriously. 'I want to sell this restaurant.'

'Oh, really?' I exclaimed. 'How much?'

'Three thousand dollars.'

After talking to Madeleine I drove straight to Patrick's restaurant to see Michael. 'Michael! Guess what? I found a restaurant for sale!' Immediately, he began firing questions at me. When I told him it was in Palmer Street, he hesitated: 'Hmmm. Well, it's not in a very good area, but I suppose that doesn't really matter. How much does she want for it?' Although I hadn't been in Australia long enough to understand the real value of the currency, Michael assured me that three thousand dollars was not a great deal: 'Oh that's nothing! My mother's got that. She'll lend it to us.' Later that evening Monique, Colette and I dined at Le Continental. I hate to say it, but the food was seriously bad and what has stuck in my mind was the pâté covered in cold, rotten ratatouille that had been taken in and out of the fridge once too often. It was absolutely disgusting!

Despite this, we returned the next day with Michael in tow and, together, the three of us bought Le Continental's lease. Two months later, we had the keys in our hands and ten

Clafoutis aux cerises

CHERRY CLAFOUTIS

SERVES 6

THIS IS A SIMPLE FAMILY DESSERT TO MAKE WHEN JUICY RIPE BLACK CHERRIES ARE IN SEASON. THIS ORIGINAL RECIPE — WHICH APPEALS TO CHILDREN AND ADULTS ALIKE — WAS GIVEN TO ME BY MY TATIE ANTOINETTE, MY MOTHER'S SISTER, WHO HAD A REPUTATION IN THE FAMILY FOR ELEGANT AND REFINED COOKING.

500 g (1 lb 2 oz) pitted very ripe black cherries

1 tablespoon kirsch (or cognac)

40 g (1½ oz) unsalted butter

3 eggs

55 g (2 oz/¼ cup) caster (superfine) sugar

35 g (1¼ oz/⅓ cup) ground almonds

200 ml (7 fl oz) thick cream, plus extra to serve

¼ teaspoon natural vanilla extract

¼ teaspoon natural almond extract

finely grated zest of 1 lemon

Preheat the oven to 200ºC (400ºF/Gas 6).

Place the cherries in a mixing bowl with the kirsch, let them marinate, tossing from time to time, for about 15 minutes or until the juices are released. With some of the butter, grease a 25 cm (10 inch) pie or flan dish and set aside in a cool place.

In a bowl, whisk together the eggs and sugar, add the ground almonds, cream, extracts and lemon zest and mix well. Strain the cherries and add their juice to the cream mixture. Spread the cherries in the dish, pour over the cream mixture and dot the remaining butter over the surface. Bake on the middle shelf of the oven for 25–30 minutes or until set and golden brown. Serve lukewarm or cold with the extra cream.

TOP: MICHAEL MANNERS AT THE PASS.

BOTTOM: DANY CHOUET AT THE STOVE, UPSTAIRS RESTAURANT

days after that, in May 1970, we opened Upstairs. Those were ten very difficult days: we removed piles of mouse and cockroach debris; scrubbed the filthy commercial gas cooker until it sparkled; painted over a 1960s mural of Italian peasants and tidied the tiny galley kitchen from top to bottom. Michael then set up a blackboard to write down the day's menu, which added an authentic French touch. The three of us shared a lot of excitement over printing up the business cards, which Michael distributed to everyone he knew. There was to be no signage, no phone and no bookings; the restaurant would simply be called Upstairs and it would be first-come, first-served for those in the know. Without Michael, Monique and I would never have been able to fulfil such a grand vision. Michael had the training, technique, organisational skills and confidence to manage everything from the fit-out to the food. The menu featured five or six entrées followed by a choice of about seven main courses.

What was I thinking? In a moment of wild panic, I wrote to Maman: 'Help, help, help! Please send recipes!' Apart from the dishes I always made at home, what did I know? I didn't even own a cookbook. I asked Maman to send *La Cuisine du Monde Entier* and *La Vraie Cuisine Française* and I also subscribed to *Cuisine et Vins de France*. Maman also sent a little book, *Le Guide Marabout de la Pâtisserie et des Desserts*. Armed with my new books and magazines – which were filled with reliable recipes – I felt confident to launch into my new career. But it was also my memories of France that I carried into the Upstairs kitchen. I remembered the aromas in my grandmother's kitchen and, through these recollections, recreated the glorious tastes of my childhood.

THE DAY UPSTAIRS OPENED THERE WERE FOUR OF US

– Michael, Monique, myself and a French girl, Mimi, who Colette had picked up hitchhiking. Finding Mimi was another happy coincidence: there weren't that many French people in Australia and it's not every day that you would find one wandering down a road. Colette had befriended Mimi and suggested to us it would be great to have a French waitress on the team, too. Michael and I were in the kitchen; while Monique and Mimi waited tables. At the time, I was twenty-eight, Michael, twenty-six, Monique, twenty-three, and Mimi, twenty-one. In those days it was usually only older people who owned restaurants, so the fact we were all in our twenties meant we seemed *très chic* to our customers. The food we cooked was also very authentic – no fusion – so Upstairs was seen as 'a little bit of France' tucked away in Darlinghurst.

Of course, we never dreamed that Upstairs would be such an instant sensation. We were in the right place at the right time and word spread like wildfire across Sydney. There were queues forming by the middle of the first week, when we suddenly went from zero to about three sittings, serving about 150 people per night. As well as being *the* place to go for young people, the local French community hurried to check us out. In our first week of operation, we took more than one thousand dollars.

191 PALMER STREET, SYDNEY

LUNCH—NOON TO 2 p.m., TUESD,

DINNER—FROM 6 p.m. TO 10 p.m.,

up
stairs

-FRIDAY

JESDAY-SUNDAY

It wasn't long before Mimi and I became an 'item' and started living together in a wonderful old Potts Point flat with harbour views. Upstairs had glowing write-ups in the newspapers and magazines and it was proving to be a real crowd-pleaser. But although this was an exciting time, it was also a lot of hard work. From the moment we opened the Upstairs doors at 6 pm a great wave of customers would rush in. When I heard them coming up the stairs, I would quickly rush to the toilet, knowing that it may be my last chance to go that evening. Within ten minutes we'd have sixty-five orders to deal with. This first wave of customers would leave at about 8 pm to go to the cinema or a show and we would ready ourselves for another steady stream. The third sitting at 9.30 pm attracted fewer people and a more bohemian crowd; everyone was talking about *La Nouvelle Vague* (French New Wave) cinema and after feasting on a Jean-Luc Godard film it seemed only natural to then dine in a French bistro until late at night.

Our customers were also attracted to Upstairs to see the nightly show performed by André, our dishwasher–waiter. Spanish-born André was raised in France and – apart

I remembered the aromas in my grandmother's kitchen and, through these recollections, re-created the glorious tastes of my childhood.

from exclaiming, 'Ooooh, daaaaaaaahling' whenever he sashayed past a male customer – his English was appalling. Towards the end of the third sitting André would tie his apron on his head and start camping it up in his very own ad-lib drag show. He was very funny – we never knew what he'd get up to next.

Upstairs was BYO – and the average customer brought a half-gallon flagon of wine. The queue would start on the rickety wooden steps and snake out onto the street. We would hand glasses out the kitchen window so they could enjoy a drink while they waited. Having crowds lining the stairs near their club was new for the Maltese community, too. They sat in the club all night wearing their flat caps, playing cards, smoking and drinking. I thought they were rather scary looking, but somehow they were fond of us 'mad kids' as they called us back then. The parking police would come around and mark the side of our car tyres with chalk. Fifteen minutes later, they'd be back to issue tickets if the cars were still there. When they saw parking police coming, our neighbours would whistle a warning and we'd hurtle down the stairs to move our cars.

OF COURSE, UPSTAIRS WAS MUCH MORE THAN JUST A novelty act. It was not just our youthful exuberance or the fixed menu for $1.75 that packed in the crowds. It was, above all, about the food, which was authentic French cuisine that was good value and prepared from scratch using fresh ingredients. The secret to our success was that we applied the principles of home cooking to our restaurant – which, although rewarding, resulted in a lot of extra work. We only had four small home fridges to use for cold storage and everything we made sold out every day. The galley kitchen was so tiny and cramped we had to squish past the fridges just to get into the kitchen, which was so narrow that our bottoms touched when we cooked.

To cope with the large number of customers that spilled through our doors, Michael and I had to do much of our preparation in advance. Michael managed most of the main courses and he was forever stirring large pots of *Poulet sauté Marengo*, *sauté de veau* and *boeuf Bourguignon*. I ate so much *boeuf Bourguignon* during this time that I have struggled to eat it ever since. Michael also pre-prepared steaks (using sauces such as *maître d'hôtel* and *chalonnaise*) as there simply wasn't the space or time available to cook everything *à la minute*. Mushrooms in red wine were also on the menu and served as an entrée. Every now and again I would create a main course, too, such as *tripes Charentaises*, a dish Maman made and sold in the *boucherie*. When I was about sixteen and going to the *lycée* I detested the smell of tripe cooking. I would bring a friend home to have a chat about Simone de Beauvoir and the air would be thick with its pungent smell. It made me feel so ashamed. I used to say to Maman: 'Please close the door to my room when you make that stuff!' But there I was cooking it myself!

For the most part, however, I was in charge of the entrées. I made *salade Mexicaine* and *escabeche* (raw marinated fish), *tarte aux aubergines*, *moules de Grandmère* and *moules marinières*, and *poivrons à la Monaco* (sweet, red peppers cooked with tomatoes, sultanas and black olives). Back then, many of these dishes were quite daring for the average Australian palate, but their strong flavours also made them well suited to a hot summer night in Sydney.

Classics such as quiche Lorraine also tempted many tastebuds. While working at Upstairs, I made enough quiche Lorraine to repave the roads between Sydney and the Blue Mountains. Because we had to cook in such large quantities, I could never make individual tarts; instead I had to bake the quiche in a large, square pan and then divide it into slices, as they did in my school *cantines*. I also made lots of terrines – *terrine de foies de volaille*, *pâté de campagne* – which were easy to serve as the orders piled in. As with the *tripes Charentaises*, a real home-made terrine was something many Sydneysiders had never tasted before. Maman was always thinking of new ways to make money for the *boucherie* and terrines ticked all the right boxes: they sold well, were thrifty to make and luxurious to eat.

As the daughter of a butcher, I had absorbed the recipe for this versatile staple almost by osmosis. But replicating the taste of many of my favourite French dishes wasn't always easy. One day, I asked our vegetable supplier for some leeks as I wanted to make a *pot au feu*. 'No, Dany, forget it,' Michael said. 'There are no leeks in Australia!' I found this very difficult to believe and so I kept asking around until finally someone told me I had to drive to Leichhardt, Sydney's 'Little Italy' where there were some excellent greengrocers. Feeling triumphant, I purchased some leeks, which I proudly proffered to Michael. As

Tarte soufflée aux abricots

APRICOT SOUFFLÉ TART

SERVES 6–8

THIS TART IS INSPIRED BY A RECIPE I GOT FROM A FRIEND IN PARIS DURING THE SEVENTIES.

Preheat the oven to 200ºC (400ºF/Gas 6).

Roll out the pastry to 3 mm (1/8 inch) thick and line a 27 cm (10 3/4 inch) tart tin. Refrigerate while preparing the soufflé mixture.

In a saucepan bring the milk and vanilla to the boil over medium heat.

Using an electric mixer, whisk egg yolks and sugar until white and foamy, add the cornflour and keep mixing. Pour the boiling milk on to the egg mixture and continue whisking. Rinse out the saucepan and pour egg mixture into it. Cook over low heat, whisking constantly for 3–5 minutes, or until the mixture thickens and is cooked. Remove from the heat, discard the vanilla bean, scraping out the seeds. Allow to cool.

In another bowl (or using an electric mixer) beat the egg whites until firm peaks form and fold into the lukewarm mixture.

Remove the pastry case from the refrigerator and fill with the soufflé base mixture. Gently place the apricots on top of the mixture, skin side down and bake for 30–40 minutes, watching the colour – the cream areas should be light brown and puff up. Remove from the oven to a wire rack, glaze the fruit with warmed apricot jam and dust with copious amounts of icing sugar, if desired. Serve alone or with whipped cream.

300 g (10 1/2 oz) pâte sucrée (sweet short crust pastry)
(see recipe page 329)
500 ml (17 fl oz/2 cups) milk
1/2 vanilla bean, split, or 1/4 teaspoon natural
vanilla extract
5 eggs, separated
100 g (3 1/2 oz) caster (superfine) sugar
50 g (1 3/4 oz) cornflour (cornstarch)
12–15 large ripe fresh apricots
(about 1 kg/2 lb 4 oz), halved, stones removed
2–3 tablespoons apricot jam, warmed
icing (confectioners') sugar, for dusting (optional)

well as being happy to prove Michael wrong, I was glad I had got to know Leichhardt: while weaving around this colourful suburb I discovered some great delicatessens selling a wonderful selection of quality olive oils and smallgoods that were unavailable anywhere else in the city.

I'VE ALWAYS COOKED WHAT I LIKE TO EAT AND IN

France the animal's innards are regarded as tasty and nutritious. In Sydney in the seventies, however, nobody ate offal and therefore nobody bought it, which meant it was amazing *rapport qualité prix* (value for money). It never failed to amaze me that calves' livers – a luxury in France – were so cheap in Australia. Why didn't Australians like liver? I later found out that offal had been the cheapest food during the Depression and so had acquired the reputation of being 'food for the poor'. I suspect it may have been badly cooked as well. Convincing my customers to eat my *cervelles à l'ail* was quite a coup.

It was while walking slowly down Oxford Street one day that I spotted lamb's brains in a butcher's shop. They came in boxes of six and each brain cost only nine cents. What a bargain! Growing up in France, I ate lamb's brains all the time and loved the soft, creamy texture and taste. When I went back to the restaurant I said, 'Hey Michael, I found cheap brains. I could make garlic brains as an entrée – they're delicious.' 'Well, you can try,' said Michael, 'but I doubt you'll convince Sydneysiders to eat brains.' Initially, of course, he was right; no one wanted them. 'Oh no, no,' they'd say. 'We don't eat brains. We don't eat stuff like that!' Despite the negative reaction towards this revered French delicacy, I remained convinced I could convert my customers if only they would just try the dish. And so I would wind my way around the restaurant, encouraging my customers to branch out: 'Listen, just try these. If you don't like them I will give you something else.' Before long, we were going through up to sixteen boxes of lamb's brains per day. It was fun cooking for people who were so open and ready to try something new.

So, what did we do after we had finished the third and final sitting and all our customers had gone home? We cooked some more, of course! Because there was only one stove and minimal storage space, we would make the terrines and desserts for the next day, staying up until the early hours of the next morning. It was a crazy lifestyle. But for a year or so it was fun. After that, we all recognised that despite the fact we were all young, we were also rundown. We knew we had to give up something to survive – either smoking or drinking – so we gave up the cigarettes and stuck to the red wine.

Nevertheless, the cycle of exhaustion and stress that came from cooking for queues of people each day was beginning to take its toll. Now, in tune with the feet going 'boom, boom, boom' up the stairs, my head began to go 'boom, boom, boom' too. I started to feel hemmed in and hated the proximity of it all: the bum-against-bum grind in the cramped galley kitchen. As the tensions mounted, Michael and I began to disagree. We had both come to cooking from very different backgrounds; he was professionally trained and devoted to Elizabeth David who meant nothing to me (my English wasn't good enough

for me to even bother opening her books); and I was someone used to cooking only what I wanted to eat. I was getting bored. Always interested in initiating new ideas, I became obsessive about reading my French cookbooks and discovered all kinds of interesting main courses I thought we should try. I hated restaurants that served the same dishes over and over again. In fact, I was somewhat notorious for creating dishes that everyone loved only to take them off the menu when I became bored of preparing them.
The French expression '*Se prendre au jeu*' means that one starts off just playing a game

The French expression 'Se prendre au jeu' means that one starts off just playing a game until one becomes so involved it is no longer a game. That is what happened to me. I now knew I could cook, but I wanted to do it better.

until one becomes so involved it is no longer a game. That is what happened to me. I now knew I could cook, but I wanted to do it better. I wanted to cook more refined dishes, spend more time creating recipes and focus more on quality, than quantity. I began to dream of having my own restaurant, but I didn't think I could do it without Monique and Michael.

At the same time I also felt tired and wanted to return to France. What else could I do? I was nearing the end of my two years in Australia and although I missed Paris, I would be swallowed up working in a restaurant in a city of that size. It seemed to me that my surprise career as a chef was coming to an end and I felt enormous regret that I would never have the chance to show the world what I was capable of in the kitchen.

It was inevitable that Michael and I would have a falling out. Here were two couples – Monique and Michael; Mimi and I – working gruelling hours with almost no time off. We were physically and emotionally on top of each other and a storm was brewing. Resentments and petty problems had been simmering away for some time.

One day, while working in the kitchen and talking about wanting to move on, another *concours de circonstances* changed my life when the dishwasher suddenly piped up: 'I know where there's a café for sale.'

'Oh?' I responded. 'How do you know about it?'

'Well, it's mine,' he said. 'I have a café where my partner and I do yoga and sell sandwiches. It doesn't work so we've decided to sell it.'

I knew it was time to move on. I didn't want to stay where I was, doing what I was doing. It was decision time. Should I go back to France and pick up the pieces of my old life or stay in Australia and forge ahead with something new? It was my partner, Mimi, who encouraged me. 'Don't worry! We can do it together.' 'Okay,' I said. 'Why not?'

GOING IT ALONE

The famous Restaurant X

THE FIRST BUSINESS CARD FOR AU CHABROL, DANY'S FIRST SOLELY

OWNED RESTAURANT

THE IDEA OF OPENING ONE'S OWN RESTAURANT SOUNDS QUITE ROMANTIC.
THE REALITY IS THAT IT'S MORE LIKE A FEAT OF ENDURANCE. LONG BEFORE
THROWING OPEN THE DOORS AND WELCOMING NEW CUSTOMERS MIMI AND I FACED
THE TASK OF CONVERTING THE EXISTING YOGA-STUDIO-CUM-SANDWICH-CAFÉ INTO
A PROPER RESTAURANT SPACE. ALTHOUGH THE KITCHEN CAME WITH AN EXCELLENT
SIX-DOOR FRIDGE, WE NEEDED TO PURCHASE PRETTY MUCH EVERYTHING ELSE —
FROM POTS AND PANS TO PANTRY STAPLES. THE LIST SEEMED ENORMOUS.

AS WELL AS FORKING OUT FOR THE LEASE, WE ALSO HAD
to buy a new stove, fans, tiles, plates, glassware and cutlery. It was an expensive exercise
and the truth is I didn't hold out much hope of getting a loan from my Kings Cross bank
manager. Why would he give me any money? I had only been in the country for eighteen
months, didn't speak the language very well, had no credit references and had never run
a business. To my surprise, he just smiled and said: 'I see you need some money. Let me
loan you some. The only bad thing that can happen is that it won't work!' What a lovely
man! He had been a customer at Upstairs and his appetite for my rustic French fare had
given him faith that I would succeed. When he later dined at the new restaurant he had
helped fund, he patted his stomach and declared: 'I'm so happy I lent you that money!'

Once we had bought the lease, Mimi and I got to work. Although it was located on
Victoria Street, just a few streets away from Upstairs, our new neighbourhood wasn't
nearly as grotty. In fact, with St Vincent's Hospital and St Margaret's Maternity Hospital
in the immediate vicinity and a dozen doctors' surgeries dotting the streets in between,
we were well placed to cater to hordes of hungry medical staff.

A hairdressing salon was located next to the café and the owner – a nosy woman
with a blue-rinse hairdo – came over to see what Mimi and I were up to. 'What? You're
going to start a restaurant?' she scoffed. 'Oh, forget it! You'll never make it work. Not
here. No way. And it's going to be French? Ha, ha, what a joke! Who eats French food
anyway?' 'Don't worry,' I told her. 'You'll see!' As soon as the project began to take shape,
I was filled with confidence. I knew from my experience at Upstairs that people liked my
cooking and I felt sure it would succeed.

The name of the restaurant was Au Chabrol in reference to the expression 'faire
chabrol'. The term referred to an old peasant custom in the Périgord, in South-West

France, which was said to be a tonic; it involved tipping about half a glass of red wine into the last spoonfuls of bouillon in the bottom of a soup plate and slurping it down all at once. It was not a refined or delicate custom, but one that was very French: as a child I had witnessed my grandfathers and uncles and father all relish this ritual around the kitchen table. And so, on opening night, I insisted all the guests *fassent chabrol*, too. This led to a lot of laughter as those participating in the fun were left with a lot of pink liquid trickling down their chins.

My vision was to make Au Chabrol a bit more upmarket than Upstairs, so instead of Pyrex tumblers, I bought sturdy glasses with little stems. I felt quite pleased with myself – not only did they look chic, but unlike long-stemmed glasses they were *très pratique* because they didn't tip over as easily. That feeling of self-satisfaction diminished somewhat when I was told they were, in fact, beer glasses! Well, *tant pis*! I used them anyway. Although I searched high and low for *toile cirée* (oilcloth) it just didn't exist in Sydney in 1972, so I had to settle for beige vinyl car upholstery. Although the vinyl was stiff and unwieldy, it was cheap and easy to clean. I didn't have the time or money to do anything about the yellow-and-black-flocked wallpaper, but it didn't seem as important as the cuisine. I would make my style statement in the kitchen.

AU CHABROL CATERED TO A MAXIMUM OF THIRTY-SIX

customers. I wanted people to relax and enjoy the food and not feel pressured to make way for the next round of diners. This freed me up to create more cuisine *à la minute*, instead of relying on big pots of pre-prepared dishes that only had to be reheated and served. Of course, there were still some stews on the menu because, with Mimi out front, I was the only one in the kitchen. There was no phone in the restaurant but we erected a sign above the door and printed some business cards, too. Au Chabrol was open Monday to Friday, for dinner only. My experience at Upstairs had shown that Saturday night diners usually went out to get drunk, have fun and eat steak, steak and more steak. I didn't want to be cooking steak after steak; I wanted to be challenged. No kidneys, no liver, no tongue also meant no fun!

On Au Chabrol's official opening night – in May 1972 – we only did nine covers, which suited me fine; I certainly didn't want a repeat performance of what happened at Upstairs, when we were assaulted from the start. Instead, I wanted to build custom slowly, to give me time to gain confidence in the kitchen. While working at Upstairs I had come to know food critic Leo Schofield, who wrote a very influential column in the *Australian*. When Leo came into Au Chabrol not long after it had opened, I implored him not to write anything about the restaurant because I did not want to be overwhelmed with customers. There I was, an absolute nobody, begging a famous food critic not to write a review. It made Leo laugh. 'Okay Dany,' he agreed. 'But suppose I write something and don't mention the name of the restaurant or where it's located? Would that be all right?' I thought about it. 'Well if you must write something, then sure,

LA MAZILLE

la
bonne
cuisine
du
Périgord

Restau

"YOU'VE SCREWED up enough good restaurants, Schofield," cried my copywriting colleague. "I almost think there'd be some profit in manufacturing false facades for places like Upstairs so that when the ravening hordes approach they whip down a blind painted like a theatrical backdrop and the eatery suddenly becomes a light engineering works or a debt collection agency. Thanks to you, you can't get into Upstairs, you can't get into —."

I cut him off in mid sentence by telling him about a **sensational** new restaurant I'd discovered. Just ambled in after the movies to be greeted by groans from at least six of the customers. "It's a goner," cried one. "Eat, drink and be merry for tomorrow we queue," cried another. Even the owner begged me not to tell anyone about it because, like Mary Magdalene says, they just couldn't cope.

So I told my copywriting colleague that if he could guess it in 10, I'd spill the beans.

"Is it in the city?"

"No."

"Then is it close to the city."

"Very."

"What sort of food? French?"

"Right."

"Good French?"

"Nothing short of sensational French. The night the guests groaned, I had Jambon Persillee that would bend your mind, to say nothing of your hachoir. Closely followed by Canard au Citron. Now duck with orange is duck with orange but duck with lemon is an altogether different taste territory. Woweee!

"The little lady had crab soup that tasted like it was air expressed from Toulon. And, because her tastes are as delicate as her looks, followed up with another entree, the old Cervelles with garlic.

"Then fo
tart. Thinks
be those sq
mandarin s
Ya boo su
Fine pa
luscious cre
on top real
each one
and arrang
looked like

28 Mai 72

The taste? Amazing. Does that answer your question?"

"Have you eaten there more than once?"

"Yep. Went there the next night. Even better. Had La Mouclade de Grand-Mere."

"This doesn't count as one of the 10 questions, but what's that?"

"That's just what I said to the waitress. Well, it was like a mussel stew. The soup plate was filled with a greyish liquid which looked like glue and tasted like Isolde's love potion. On top were scads of mussels crumbed and grilled. And if I might just bore you with a few more details . . . that night the duck was cooked with turnip and it's a real toss-up whether it was just marginally more sensational than with the lemon. And the Tripes Charentais! And the Leatherjacket Meuniere! And the bill — $11.70 for three. But I'm boring you. Go on."

"Is it licensed?"

"No."

"Has it been open long?"

"No"

"Is it hard to get in?"

"Not at the moment."

"Is the atmosphere pleasant?"

"Exceptionally so."

"No complaints at all?"

"Only that because the staff is small the service is a little slow. But everything is well worth waiting for. I'd wait a decade for the duck if necessary. And that's your last question."

"Are we up to 10 already?"

"Yes. And you've missed out. I can't tell you where it is because I gave my oath to the patronne. But you're bound to hear about it. Some Melbourne-based food writer will leap on it in six weeks time and call it "trendy." One last clue. I doesn't look a bit like a light engineering works."

RESTAURANT X. Unlicensed. Open 6-11. Closed Sunday. No phone. No reservations. Within a mile of the Sydney GPO. Good luck!

1 mandarin
etcha they'll
tinned Jap
caterers use.
They're not.
scrummy-
atisserie and
darin pieces,
gly dezested
each slice
Oldenburg.

Tourain Périgourdin

GARLIC AND ONION SOUP

SERVES 4–6

THIS SOUP IS EATEN ALL OVER THE SOUTH-WEST AND PARTICULARLY IN PÉRIGORD. IT IS TRADITIONALLY MADE WITH WATER AND POURED INTO THE *SOUPIÈRE* OVER A VERY LARGE THIN SLICE OF COUNTRY BREAD. IN THE OLD DAYS THIS SAME SOUP — TO WHICH WAS ADDED LOTS AND LOTS OF PEPPER — USED TO BE PRESENTED IN A CHAMBER POT TO NEWLYWEDS IN BED ON THEIR WEDDING NIGHT. THEY BOTH HAD TO DRINK IT OUT OF THE POT IN FRONT OF GIGGLING FRIENDS — THAT IS WHY THE NEWLYWEDS LIKED TO KEEP SECRET THE PLACE WHERE THEY SLEPT. THIS IS MY VERSION OF THE *TOURAIN*.

Heat the duck fat in a saucepan, add the onions and cook over medium heat until lightly browned, then add the flour and brown slightly. Gradually pour in the chicken stock, add the garlic, and stir constantly. Cook gently for 30 minutes.

Put this through a mouli using the largest holes and put back on the heat. Drop the egg whites into the soup. When they have set, lift them out with a strainer. Allow the egg whites to cool then dice and set aside.

Just before serving, heat the soup, whisk the egg yolks with vinegar and a ladleful of soup, then whisk this back into the soup on a very low heat – do not boil. Serve with the diced egg white.

1 tablespoon duck fat

3 large onions, finely sliced

1 tablespoon plain (all-purpose) flour

2 litres (70 fl oz/8 cups) chicken stock

3 large garlic cloves, finely sliced

3 eggs, separated

2 tablespoons sherry (or red-wine) vinegar

2 handfuls vermicelli or angel's hair pasta, to serve (optional)

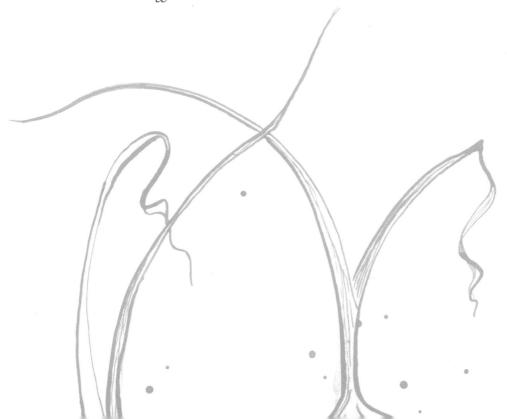

do it like that!' The resulting review of 'Restaurant X' was very favourable and attracted a lot of attention. Even four years after Leo's review was published, customers would come into Au Chabrol for the first time and say, 'A-ha! We have finally found the famous Restaurant X', as if they had solved a great riddle.

Offal also became a firm favourite: my famous lamb's brains developed quite a following; and new dishes such as pig's trotters in red wine and veal kidneys in pastry considered Au Chabrol classics.

To ready myself for the position of head chef, I spent a lot of time reading and studying recipes, teaching myself classic French dishes and sauces and then tweaking them to suit my own taste. I experimented a lot and if I thought a dish tasted delicious, I'd put it on the menu. My expansive collection of regional and country French cook books provided much inspiration and La Mazille's *La Bonne Cuisine du Périgord* was my bible. Here were recipes for dishes I had grown up with – all the traditional *plats* cooked by family members – each with its own little '*truc*' or personal twist. It was like having a reference book for my memories. As an *autodidacte* without any formal training, I was fearless when it came to trying new and interesting recipes.

The menu at Au Chabrol often featured duck: *canard au citron*, which had a fresh, zesty taste; and duck with turnip or apples, too. I made the sauce from scratch each service, frying bones and vegetables together, reducing the liquid and straining the sauce. This was how it was done in French homes. I had no idea that professional kitchens used a vat of veal stock for everything or, even worse, relied on big tins of 'boosters' (commercial taste enhancers). I made roast pork served with *chouée* (cabbage stew), a play on my surname, Chouet. I also made a lot of seafood dishes: *soupe de poisson*, which was very complicated to prepare; *mouclade*; Russian blinis with smoked salmon and caviar; a hot trout paté and flathead *beurre blanc*. Flathead is not available in France, but it's a fish that I adore; it has a sweet, delicate flesh that is simply delicious when poached. For dessert, there would be *Paris Brest*; *Flaugnarde aux pruneaux*; and seasonal fresh fruit tarts. I was constantly testing the recipes as I wanted to perfect the pastry and filling and make the finest desserts possible.

Rumsteak was another popular choice with my customers. When treated right, I believe rump to be the juiciest cut of beef. I would buy an entire rump and hang it in the coolroom until it was nearly black. This was the method I learned from my family and it resulted in the meat becoming so tender you could cut it with a butter knife. Many of my customers came solely for that steak; up until eating at Au Chabrol, most of them had only eaten very fresh meat, which is quite tough. If I ran out of rump steak, I'd say, 'Sorry. Sold out', as I would never contemplate replacing it with meat that hadn't been hung.

Offal also became a firm favourite: my famous lamb's brains developed quite a following; and new dishes such as pig's trotters in red wine and veal kidneys in pastry considered Au Chabrol classics. I also served a few decent Australian cheeses alongside a range of French ones, which were now finally being imported.

When Au Chabrol first opened, I changed the entire menu every week. This meant devising five entrées, five main courses, and about four desserts every seven days. It wasn't long before I realised this was an insane approach: as well as taking a lot of time, energy, organisation and planning to achieve, it meant I wound up wasting ingredients, which I never liked to do. I didn't want to be bored, but I soon learned there were limits!

It was around this time that the Australian wine industry began to take off. Even though Au Chabrol was, like Upstairs, a BYO restaurant, our customers started to wise up about wine; they began bringing top drops to dinner – in proper bottles with corks – rather than lugging half-gallon flagons along to every occasion.

Although there was no phone at the restaurant, I did accept bookings by way of notes slipped under the door. Long before I knew her, my partner Patricia Hobbs had heard about Au Chabrol through some friends in Paddington who described it as the 'new place run by the breakaway sister from Upstairs'. Trish dutifully put a note under the front door booking a table for 8 pm, before venturing out for drinks with friends and losing all track of time. When Trish arrived, twenty minutes late, she was greeted by a 'very angry French woman' who came storming out of the kitchen like a tornado in all its fury. 'Just who do you think you are coming here twenty minutes late? It's not fair to the other customers! If you're going to book you be here on time!' After being duly reprimanded, Trish and her friends never dared arrive late again. But it wasn't until years later, when we started Cleopatra restaurant and guesthouse together, that she fully understood my rage.

Au Chabrol now averaged two sittings per night and about sixty-five covers. Some customers filed in early before going off to a film while others would show up after 9 pm. Monday nights were my favourite as the restaurant was never busy – we did about forty covers on a Monday night – and the crowd we attracted was, without exception, an interesting bunch of regulars who loved good food and great wine. It was liberating to be under less pressure in the kitchen and a real pleasure to cook for them. My list of regulars included: a gregarious group of girlfriends who came in every Wednesday; a diverse mix of doctors and hospital staff; and a group of actors, directors and musicians who came in after concerts. The club-like atmosphere made Au Chabrol conducive to meeting people and some of my customers became my closest friends.

So what was my secret? Well, part of it was my lack of training. Michael Manners taught me that to survive in the restaurant world you had to charge a minimum of three times the price of the ingredients of each dish to cover expenses: the staff, utility costs, rent and your own wage. But what I failed to understand were the food-costing formulas that chefs are taught in culinary school: how to calculate everything to the nearest cent. Most of my accounting skills were intuitive: if I had *rumsteak* on the menu then I'd have economical dishes, too, such as pig's trotters and garfish. The fact that I inherited my family's frugal gene also helped keep our finances under control. I cooked what I

Mouclade

MUSSELS GRATIN

SERVES 4

THIS IS A RECIPE FROM MY MOTHER'S FAMILY WHO ARE ALL NATIVES OF THE CHARENTES.
THE MEASUREMENT OF INGREDIENTS CANNOT BE VERY PRECISE — IT IS DIFFICULT TO SAY EXACTLY THE AMOUNT
OF MUSSEL JUICE — IT DEPENDS ON THE SIZE OF THE MUSSELS AND THE SALTINESS OF THEIR LIQUID.

1.25 kg (2 lb 12 oz) mussels

2 large French shallots, diced

250 ml (9 fl oz/1 cup) dry white wine

40 g (1½ oz) unsalted butter, plus
    extra for grilling

40 g (1½ oz) plain (all-purpose) flour

2 garlic cloves

½ teaspoon curry powder

1 egg yolk

50 ml (1¾ fl oz) cream

juice of ½ lemon

20 g (¾ oz/¼ cup) fine fresh breadcrumbs

Scrub the mussels thoroughly under running water and pull out the hairy beards. Do not soak them or you will lose their precious liquid. Once clean, place them in a bowl and set aside.

In a deep stainless steel or enamel saucepan combine the shallots and wine and gently bring to the boil over medium heat. Cook for 3–4 minutes only. Add the mussels, cover and shake them around. Continue to cook for 5 minutes, then discard any mussels that have not opened.

With a slotted spoon remove the mussels to a bowl, and strain the remaining juices through a fine strainer into a tall container so the 'mud' sinks to the bottom. Remove and discard the empty half of each mussel shell, and arrange the mussels on one large or four individual gratin dishes. Set the dish(es) aside and keep warm.

Melt the butter in a saucepan over low heat, add the flour, stirring until sandy in texture. Gradually stir in the mussel juice, being careful not to add the sediment from the bottom of the container. Whisk until smooth, add the garlic and curry powder and cook gently for about 5 minutes or until it thickens. Check seasoning and thickness – if too salty or too thick, add some water. In a bowl whisk together the egg yolk and cream with a few drops of lemon juice and a few grinds of black pepper. Whisk this mixture into the sauce.

Preheat the grill to high. Pour the sauce around and over the mussels, sprinkle with a thin layer of breadcrumbs, dot with the extra butter, and gratiné under the grill for 3–5 minutes or until golden. Serve immediately in their dish(es).

liked and never once accounted for what would sell well. I trusted my own taste and convictions: if I liked a dish I was confident others would, too. And they did. In 1972, as well as opening a restaurant, I put down a deposit on a house in Five Dock and bought a new Renault 12. *Mon Dieu*! Reflecting on my good fortune, I knew I would never have achieved all this within a twelve-month time frame if I had been in France!

Before too long, Mimi and I definitely needed more help and so hired Yvette, who had been recommended through Sophie, of Fork 'n' View fame. Yvette was looking for a second job and was happy to help with everything from washing-up to preparing vegetables. Yvette was so efficient and organised that we felt her talent was wasted in the kitchen; we wanted her out front with Mimi. After a bit of gentle persuasion, Yvette agreed and soon excelled in the busy task of waiting tables, too. Through Yvette we met Maryse, who then became my kitchenhand. It was an extraordinary coincidence that both these girls actually hailed from Bergerac, a town just twenty-five kilometres from Vélines. Now, here we were together in Sydney, on the other side of the world.

ANOTHER DOSE OF FRANCE ARRIVED WHEN MAMAN came to visit Australia. She stayed at Monique's in Paddington but would wander over to Au Chabrol and look for things to do. Even in retirement, she was never one to sit still. 'Give me a job,' she'd demand.

One afternoon Maman showed up to find me filled with despair: one of my assistants hadn't showed up; the waitress couldn't make it and there was no sign of the dishwasher, either. Although I had done a bit of prep work and finished one pile of dishes, the place was a shambles. 'Listen, Maman,' I told her. 'I'm going to close. I can't cope with so many people missing. I just can't do it by myself.'

'I'll help,' she said, as confident as always. '*Il faut ouvrir*, Dany. Look at all that food there! We don't want it to go to waste.' To Maman, *gaspillage* was a dirty word and there was no use arguing the point with her. True to form, she was amazing! After she'd served all the entrées she got a bit enthusiastic and started grilling the *biftecks* as soon as the orders came in. I was constantly coaxing her: '*Doucement*, Maman. Let them eat their entrée first.' During this time, Leo Schofield happened to write a review of Au Chabrol and he thought it was very amusing indeed to see Maman bossing me about in my own kitchen. But by far the biggest nightmare in my kitchen was finding someone to do the washing-up! I hired people from all walks of life. They were mostly young, but they would only stay on a few days or, at most, a week, before they'd disappear and leave Yvette, Mimi and I to rotate the task among ourselves. There were some dishwashers who would vanish without bothering to pick up their wages! I tried everything to keep them — from being sympathetic to offering them cake and wine after service. Finally, I decided to put an ad in the paper. Though quite a few people applied for the position, none of them were right for the job. I didn't even bother trying them out. Then, one day, Mimi came in and said: 'There's an old man at the door who wants the washing-up job.'

'No, no,' I said impatiently. 'I don't want an old man. Tell him to go away.'

So Mimi went away. A minute later, she was back. 'He's insisting. He says he "really, really wants the job". And he's French. He looks like he could do well. He says at least give him a trial run.'

'Oh, all right then! Send him in.'

Armand and I had a chat. He was from Nancy and he must have been in his late thirties or early forties, which seemed old to us at the time. He said he had fought in the Indochina War and had done odd jobs ever since. I asked him when he could start, and he said: 'Well, I could start right now and show you what I can do.'

So Armand went to the sink and he did a good job. He came back every night for a week and was very punctual, polite, clean and tidy. I said to him. 'Eh, Armand. What do you think? Do you want to stay?'

He looked me in the eye and said: 'Dany, I will be with you forever. I will be with you until I die.'

We couldn't believe our luck! Yvette and Mimi got down on their knees and thanked the gods they would never again have to do the washing-up. And it was true: Armand was an angel. On Saturdays, when I tended to my flower garden, did the accounts and experimented in the kitchen, he would come to my house and, as we say in France, 'bricoler'. He'd tinker about doing little odd jobs – from painting to planting. He helped me create a small herb and vegetable garden and also built a coop to contain our chickens. I was shocked to see so few vegetable gardens in Sydney. In true thrifty French fashion, I wondered why on earth you would have a useless expanse of lawn when you could be producing eggs and fresh herbs each day?

If I had nothing to 'bricoler' on my Sundays, which were usually spent at home planning menus and ordering my produce for the week, Armand would go to the restaurant and clean the kitchen from top to bottom. The health inspectors used to bring their trainees to Au Chabrol to show them what a clean restaurant should look like. I couldn't give Armand enough cake and wine! He was a gem.

Another person who really helped me at Au Chabrol was Jacques, or Mémère ('Granny') as we called him. Mémère was a mad queen who worked as the pastry chef at St Vincent's Hospital. He was considered the black sheep of his very well-to-do family in France and so was banished to Australia. By the time I met him, he was in his late fifties, was very large and struggled to move about. Mémère, who had snow-white skin and a big, bald head, was also extremely intelligent and refined. In his prime, Mémère had worked in the city's top restaurants and, for years, was the Fairfax family's personal chef. He really knew his stuff. Mémère started his shift at the hospital at 5 am. At about 2 pm, he'd pass by Au Chabrol with his nose twitching in the air. He would come into the kitchen, sit on a stool and have a chat and a coffee while I worked. He was a wealth of information and shared many recipes and offered great advice. I learned a lot from Mémère; he would ask me my method of doing things before explaining his in exact detail. As well as being generous with his knowledge, Mémère was never insulted if I didn't adhere to his advice. New ideas have always thrilled me and Maman inspired a medieval phase at Au Chabrol

Flathead avec sauce hollandaise

FLATHEAD WITH HOLLANDAISE

SERVES 4

THE FIRST TIME IN MY LIFE I MADE HOLLANDAISE SAUCE I SERVED IT WITH A WHOLE, POACHED FLATHEAD
ON THE PLATE COMPLETE WITH ITS HEAD. WHEN I PRESENTED IT TO MY CUSTOMERS AT AU CHABROL
RESTAURANT THEY SCREAMED: 'TAKE IT AWAY, IT'S LOOKING AT ME!'

4 whole plate-sized flatheads, cleaned, scaled
    and heads removed (if you prefer) – ask
    your fishmonger to do this

COURT BOUILLON
2 litres (70 fl oz/8 cups) water
200 ml (7 fl oz) dry white wine
1 large onion, finely sliced
1 celery stalk, finely sliced
50 g (1¾ oz) mushrooms, finely sliced
1 bouquet garni, (parsley sprigs, coriander roots,
    thyme sprigs, ½ bay leaf)
1 teaspoon salt
1 teaspoon whole white peppercorns

HOLLANDAISE SAUCE
30 ml (1 fl oz/1½ tablespoons) white wine vinegar
30 g (1 oz) French shallots, finely chopped
½ teaspoon whole white peppercorns, crushed
2 tablespoons water
2 egg yolks
150 g (5½ oz) unsalted butter, diced and brought
    to room temperature
1 teaspoon chopped chervil
juice of ½ lemon

TO MAKE THE COURT BOUILLON: Place all the ingredients in a large saucepan, bring to the boil, then reduce to a simmer for 20 minutes. Remove from the heat and allow to cool. You can either strain the court bouillon into a deep flameproof baking dish large enough to fit the fish, or leave the vegetables in, for flavour, but that makes it more difficult to handle when serving. Set aside on top of stove.

TO MAKE THE HOLLANDAISE SAUCE: Place the vinegar, shallots, peppercorns and water in a small saucepan and bring to the boil. Reduce to 1–1½ tablespoons, then strain, pressing out all the juices into a medium-sized mixing bowl. Add the egg yolks, whisk together and place the bowl above a saucepan of gently simmering water. Whisk energetically and constantly until the mixture swells, becoming white and frothy. Add a few drops of water to keep it light. When the mixture holds the mark of the whisk, it is time to incorporate the butter. Add the butter a few cubes at a time, whisking gently after each addition to incorporate. Add the chervil and a few drops of lemon juice at the end. Cover with a lid and set aside in a warm corner.

Bring the court bouillon to the boil, lay the flatheads carefully in the baking dish and turn the temperature to a low simmer. Cover the baking dish with aluminium foil and cook the fish for 12–15 minutes depending on the size. Lift each fish on to serving plates, and spoon some hollandaise sauce over each one.

NOTE: The left-over court bouillon can be strained to make a fish soup, using the reserved fish heads.

Tripes Charentaises

TRIPE WITH LEEK, WHITE WINE, COGNAC AND PARSLEY

SERVES 4–6

THIS IS AN ADAPTATION OF THE RECIPE MY MOTHER USED TO COOK IN HER BORDEAUX SHOP AND SELL
IN LITTLE PYREX DISHES, READY TO REHEAT. AS A TEENAGER, I WAS ASHAMED OF THE SMELL,
PENETRATING THE WHOLE FLAT, AND MY BEDROOM. MAMAN USED VEAL TRIPE AND CALF'S FEET;
IN AUSTRALIA I HAD TO USE BEEF TRIPE AND PIG'S TROTTERS.

1 kg (2 lb 4 oz) beef tripe, cleaned but not
    bleached if possible

dash of white vinegar, for soaking

2 large pig's trotters

1 onion, skin on, studded with 2 cloves

1 bouquet garni (2 thyme sprigs, 1 bay leaf,
    6 parsley sprigs, celery stalk)

2 large leeks, separate the green and white

500 ml (17 fl oz/2 cups) dry white wine

1½ tablespoon duck fat or olive oil

3 large French shallots, thinly sliced

1 tablespoon plain (all-purpose) flour

3 large garlic cloves, chopped

30 ml (1 fl oz) cognac (or brandy)

½ cup finely chopped flat-leaf (Italian) parsley

Soak the tripe and trotters together in cold water with a dash of white vinegar for about 1½ hours. Clean the trotters thoroughly and rinse in a few changes of water. Cut the tripe into 3 cm (1¼ inch) pieces.

Place the tripe and trotters in a saucepan with the onion, bouquet garni and the green part of the leeks tied in a bundle with string. Pour over the wine and enough water to cover. The tripe will melt and produce liquid. Season with salt and pepper. Bring to the boil, then reduce the heat to low, cover and cook gently over low heat for at least 3 hours or until the tripe is very tender. Test with the point of a knife. Set aside to cool.

With a slotted spoon remove any fat from the top of the cold stock, then strain into a large container. Remove the tripe and trotters, debone and dice the meat from the trotters, and set aside. Discard the onion, bouquet garni and bundle of leek greens.

Rinse out the saucepan, return to a low heat and add the duck fat, shallots and the white part of the leeks. Sauté gently without colouring. Stir in the flour to make a roux, then add about 375–500 ml (13–17 fl oz/1½–2 cups) of the reserved stock a little at a time, do not use it all if there seems to be too much, as the mix must not be too liquid.

Add the diced pig's trotter and tripe and garlic and cook gently for about 30 minutes. My mother's written instructions say 'the sauce is delicious when it starts to be sticky'. Taste and adjust the seasoning if necessary. Five minutes before serving, add the cognac and chopped parsley.

Serve very hot accompanied with boiled potatoes and toasted, rustic-style bread rubbed with garlic.

TOP, FROM LEFT: ZABU, ARMAND, MIMI AND MARYSE WEARING T-SHIRTS EMBLAZONED
WITH THEIR FRENCH HOMETOWNS, IN THE AU CHABROL KITCHEN, 1974
BOTTOM: FAMILY LUNCH AT TATIE ANTOINETTE'S, LA REOLE, 1975

when she sent me Céline Vence and Robert Courtine's *Les Grands Maîtres de la Cuisine Française*. Robert Courtine was one of my heroes — as well as writing a food column for *Le Monde* in the 1960s and 1970s, he edited *Larousse Gastronomique* and was a regular contributor to *Cuisine et Vins de France*. *Les Grands Maîtres* covered five centuries of French cooking and included recipes dating back to the 1200s — supposedly adjusted to suit the modern cook. I tried my hand at a few archaic delights including *artichauts à*

There is a scene in the film entitled 'Lunch at Au Chabrol' where the French 'mafia' were co-opted as extras.

la galérienne, from 1740, which, though labour-intensive, tasted great. But my attempts to replicate past recipes didn't always succeed. One such dish was called *galimafrée*, a name that I adored; it means 'having a good time, eating a lot and being *joyeux*'. It was a dish from the fourteenth century, from Guillaume Tirel's time. Tirel, who was known as Taillevent, was a cook known for penning the first French book dedicated to cuisine. The recipe called for left-over lamb to be cooked with onions. It was a bit like a French shepherd's pie but the result was nowhere near as exciting as its name. It was not at all '*trés joyeux*'.

Another one of my misguided innovations involved the use of blackfish, which looked like dark bream. The fish was so cheap that I thought I was onto something. Sadly, no one ordered it. Weeks later I learned why: blackfish was used as bait by local fishermen.

———

AU CHABROL HAD BECOME *THE* HOT PLACE TO GO AND was now receiving rave reviews that revealed its name and address. In 1974 I was invited to a cocktail party in honour of Paul Bocuse and Michel Guérard, who were visiting Australia for the first time. I was desperate to meet them — *nouvelle cuisine* was shaking up the world of French gastronomy and these two were the stars of the movement. The problem was the party took place during service time at the restaurant. I needed someone to replace me and so asked Mémère for a favour: 'Hey Mémère, I was wondering if you could do the service here while I go to a cocktail party? I promise I'll only be away for one hour.' '*Mais oui*, Dany! Of course I can do it.' Mémère arrived in the afternoon so I could brief him. I was feeling very nervous; this would be the first time I had ever left the restaurant during service. The plan was for Maryse to help with entrées, leaving Mémère free to concentrate on the main courses. Armand was also there to lend a hand.

The party was at a *très chic* house in Darling Point. I was standing there chatting in French with Paul Bocuse and Michel Guérard when one of them said: 'Look at the time! We have to go into the city; there's a formal function being held in our honour.'

Canard au citron

DUCK WITH LEMON SAUCE

SERVES 4

DUCK À L'ORANGE WAS STORMING SYDNEY, SO I THOUGHT DUCK AU CITRON WOULD BE DIFFERENT, PARTICULARLY WITH ITS OWN SAUCE MADE FROM SCRATCH, 'SANS DEMI-GLACE'.

Preheat the oven to 220ºC (425ºF/Gas 7). Season the duck inside and out with salt and pepper and finely grate the zest of 1 lemon over the breasts and the legs. Peel the white pith from the lemon, cut it into quarters and place inside the duck. Place the duck in a roasting pan on the middle shelf of the oven and roast for 50 minutes to 1 hour, keep checking the duck, basting with the pan juices and turning it to ensure it cooks evenly. Peel the rind from the remaining lemons and cut into julienne, then juice the lemons and set aside.

To prepare the sauce, heat the oil in a frying pan, add the speck and allow to brown before adding the carrot and onion. When the vegetables are slightly caramelised, sprinkle over the flour and cook for 2–3 minutes, mixing well. Gradually stir in the stock, add the bouquet garni and let it simmer.

Combine the sugar and vinegar in a small saucepan and stir over low–medium heat until the sugar dissolves. Bring to the boil and cook for 5–10 minutes or until light golden in colour (blond caramel). Remove from heat and add the reserved lemon juice along with 2 tablespoons of the sauce, being careful as it may splatter. Simmer until the caramel is dissolved, then add to the rest of sauce, return to a simmer and cook for 30 minutes or until the sauce is reduced and lightly coats the back of a spoon.

Meanwhile, place the julienned lemon zest in a saucepan of cold water, bring to the boil and cook for 5 minutes, then strain. Repeat and set aside.

Strain the sauce through a sieve pressing down firmly to get all the juices from the vegetables and the bouquet garni, then strain again through a fine strainer back into a clean saucepan. When the duck is cooked, remove it from the roasting pan and place breast side down on a warm plate so juices can absorb back into the breast. Set aside and keep warm.

Remove the fat from the roasting pan, and deglaze with a spoonful of the sauce over high heat. Add this to the sauce, then add the julienned lemon zest. Check the seasoning and stir in the orange liqueur.

Serve the duck with the sauce and lemon zest spooned over.

1.5–1.7 kg (3 lb 5 oz–3 lb 12 oz) duck
3 lemons
1 tablespoon grapeseed or sunflower oil
60 g (2¼ oz) speck, finely diced
1 carrot, finely diced
1 onion, finely diced
2 teaspoons plain (all-purpose) flour
500 ml (17 fl oz/2 cups) duck stock
    (or chicken stock)
1 small bouquet garni (1 bay leaf, 10 sprigs
    parsley and thyme)
2 tablespoons caster (superfine) sugar
2 tablespoons white wine vinegar
2 tablespoons orange liqueur (such as
    Grand Marnier or Cointreau)

I offered to give them a lift. 'I have to get back to my restaurant and it's in that direction. Let me take you.'

They happily agreed, but asked if I could drive them past my restaurant so they could have a quick look.

'Yes, of course,' I said, thinking it would give me a chance to see how Mémère was getting on and let him know I'd be back within minutes. Mémère was tired and old and I'd been fretting about leaving him. I parked the car outside Au Chabrol and said to my two famous passengers: 'I'll be back in two minutes. I just have to go to the kitchen to make sure everything is okay.' I presumed they just wanted to look at the restaurant from the outside. It was 8.30 pm, smack-bang in the middle of service; there were plates clattering, pots boiling and staff rushing to and fro. I asked Mémère: 'How are you doing?' 'Dany, everything's fine! Don't worry,' he said. And it was true; he had everything under control. I promised to be back in ten minutes to take over and so raced back through the dining room before the customers noticed I was dressed for a party and not in the kitchen, where I belonged. To my astonishment, I found Mimi standing there arguing with Paul Bocuse and Michel Guérard, who had plonked themselves down at a table! She was trying her best to get rid of them because they hadn't made a booking. Of course, she hadn't the slightest idea who they were and I stood there feeling stunned. I didn't know what to do! Standing at the door were some of my regular customers waiting for a table occupied by two of the greatest chefs France had ever produced. They were perusing the menu and pondering what they might like to order. Mimi wasn't having any of it. 'No, no, no,' she insisted. 'You can't order, you can't stay. You didn't book a table!'

'But we did!' they said.

'*Mais non*! What did you say your names were?'

'Romanov,' said Michel Guérard. 'And Vladovsky. Are you sure our names aren't in your book?' I quickly tried to remedy the situation: 'Mimi, don't you recognise who they are? It's Michel Guérard and Paul Bocuse you are talking to!'

'Oh my God!' Mimi cried, slapping her hand over her mouth in horror. 'Oh. Sorry, sorry, sorry!' Although the pair thought this was hilarious, I still had to insist they vacate the table. 'Come on. Get up and come with me to your dinner because you really are taking up someone else's table!' That's when Michel Guérard gave me the greatest compliment of my life: 'It's too bad. We would rather stay and eat here. This place reminds me of the Pot Au Feu, my very first restaurant in Paris.'

Michel Guérard and Paul Bocuse weren't the only famous people that Mimi or the rest of us failed to recognise. While ensconced in our little French enclave we were often oblivious to what was happening outside the walls of Au Chabrol. It was our regular customers who would take the waitresses aside and whisper: 'Oh, my God. Don't you know who's sitting over there?' One night we had Don Dunstan, the then premier of South Australia, queuing at the door together with future prime minister Bob Hawke and some government ministers. We played host to Labor Party heavyweights alongside artists, musicians and actors … but no one received any preferential treatment! There were plenty of well-known restaurateurs who frequented Au Chabrol, too, but they never

We played host to Labor Party heavyweights alongside artists, musicians and actors … but no one received any preferential treatment! There were plenty of well-known restaurateurs who frequented Au Chabrol, too, but they never introduced themselves. Maybe I was too scary?

introduced themselves. Maybe I was too scary? Don Dunstan, however, did introduce himself; he was warm and funny and full of enthusiasm. One of his grand plans was to import Au Chabrol to Adelaide and help us set up in South Australia. 'Adelaide! Where's that? It's even more remote than Sydney.' You could say we truly lived in our own little francophone world. Nothing mattered to us outside that kitchen and dining room. The only time we wound down was late at night when we'd have a few laughs with friends and drink copious amounts of red wine; current affairs and politics weren't on the menu.

Running Au Chabrol was an all-consuming task and enjoying some of life's little luxuries – such as watching a show or going to a concert – was never an option. Although I never took time off, I was energised with the excitement that comes from success. The more I succeeded, the harder I worked. My dishes became more elaborate, more adventurous, more interesting. Maman got very excited, too; the magazines and recipes streamed forth in a torrent of Gallic gastronomic dreams from Vélines to Sydney, including many recipes written by my grandmother in her beautiful, flowing script. The décor at Au Chabrol improved, too. I finally painted over the yellow-and-black-flocked wallpaper and bought beautiful red tablecloths to replace the vinyl covers.

———

TO BE REALLY SUCCESSFUL, HOWEVER, I NEEDED A licence to serve alcohol, which – in the 1970s – meant adhering to a stringent set of requirements. For starters, you needed to have at least fifty-two seats and separate toilets for men and women. I had only one toilet, located at the end of the alley and you had to ask the waitress for the key. I began to dream of buying the hairdressing salon and annexing it to the restaurant.

Somehow, I never followed through with this grand plan. I was simply exhausted. By late 1975, Mimi had lost interest in everything – including me – and wanted to return to France to start a family and be closer to her parents. I became very depressed. The love affair was over.

It was Michael and Monique who came to the rescue. They had sold Upstairs a couple of years before and travelled to France and England. They were now back

Gratin de poires aux noix chocolatées

PEAR, CHOCOLATE AND WALNUT GRATIN

SERVES 4

A HOT DESSERT FOR WINTER WITH SEASONAL PEARS, WALNUTS AND
CHOCOLATE, BROWNED UNDER THE GRILL WITH A SABAYON SAUCE.

Combine the sugar and 600 ml (21 fl oz) of water in a medium saucepan, bring to the boil, stirring to dissolve the sugar. Add the pears and cook gently, turning them if necessary, for 10–12 minutes – test with a wooden skewer, they should be tender, but not falling apart. Remove to a colander to drain.

TO MAKE THE CHOCOLATE WALNUT SAUCE: Combine the sugar and water in a medium saucepan. Bring to the boil and cook over medium heat until light golden (blond caramel). Remove from the heat and pour in the cream, whisk well then add the honey, cocoa, chocolate, 50 ml of the pear cooking syrup and walnuts. Return to the heat and cook, stirring with a wooden spoon, for about 3 minutes or until the sauce thickens. Set aside to cool in the saucepan.

TO MAKE THE GRATIN SAUCE: In an electric mixer (or in a bowl, by hand), whisk the egg yolks with the sugar until white and frothy. In a separate bowl, whisk the cream until soft peaks form, fold through the egg yolk mixture and then fold through the pear brandy. Set aside.

Preheat the grill. Slice the poached pear halves and set aside. Spread the chocolate walnut sauce over the bases of four 250 ml (9 fl oz/1 cup) capacity gratin dishes (or flat soup plates), arrange the pear slices on top, and cover with the gratin sauce. Place the dishes under the grill for about 2–3 minutes, rotating them once so they cook evenly. When golden brown, remove and serve immediately (being careful as the dishes will be hot).

200 g (7 oz) caster (superfine) sugar
4 pears, peeled, cored and halved

CHOCOLATE AND WALNUT SAUCE
50 g (1¾ oz) caster (superfine) sugar
45 ml (1½ fl oz) water
125 ml (4 fl oz/½ cup) cream
1 tablespoon honey
1 tablespoon unsweetened cocoa powder
50 g (1¾ oz) dark chocolate, grated
180 g (6½ oz / 1½ cups) walnuts, roughly chopped

GRATIN SAUCE
4 egg yolks
50 g (1¾ oz) caster (superfine) sugar
100 ml (3½ fl oz) cream, for whipping
1 tablespoon pear brandy

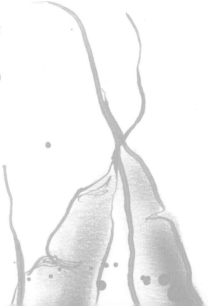

in Sydney and looking for a place to buy in the country. Michael and I had an understanding: we could cook together; I could employ him; or he could employ me. He was also capable of looking after my business. The restaurant was less than a kilometre from their house in Paddington. Michael said: 'Dany, take a few months off. Go to France and have a big rest. You need it. Monique and I will keep the doors open at Au Chabrol. I'll do your menu and your food, exactly the way you want it.' I was relieved to go and just as relieved to return a few months later to find the staff happy and the customers full of compliments. Michael and Monique had another surprise up their sleeves: 'While you were gone we found that place in the country we've been looking for.'

'That's great news,' I said, pleased for them.

'There's only one problem – we need you to come with us!'

'But I can't! I already have a restaurant.'

'Sell it!' they urged.

Au Chabrol was my baby; I had built it up from scratch. But when I looked in the mirror, I saw a tired, thin, pale woman staring back at me. Little by little, I came around to the idea that it might indeed be time to move on again.

Within a few days of placing an ad in the newspaper, a French-Swiss chef named Paul Elser contacted me wanting to buy Au Chabrol. Paul was a kind-hearted, sympathetic man. He could see I was still upset over the sale. 'Listen, Dany,' he said soothingly. 'Come back as many times as you like. Bring your friends once a week. I want you to feel like it's still your place.' It was very kind of him and I did pop in every now and then. I used to drink gin and tonics, and he always had the ingredients on hand. Whenever I showed up, a glass would appear at my table. Though Paul had a very different approach to cooking – he used a lot of cream and cheese – he, too, achieved great success at Au Chabrol.

In October 1976, at a farewell dinner for the staff and all our friends, Armand, my angel, became very distressed. 'Dany, you know I wanted to stay with you always but Michael has asked me to go to their new place in the Mountains. What will I do?' 'What do you mean, Armand?' I asked. 'You will be with me always because I'm going with Michael and Monique, too!'

Flaugnarde aux pruneaux

PÉRIGOURDIN PRUNE FLAN

SERVES 6—8

I DECIDED TO GIVE THIS FLAN MIXTURE A CASE TO MAKE IT MORE ELEGANT TO SERVE. IN FRANCE LIVING AMONG FIELDS OF PRUNES *D'AGEN* I OFTEN COOK THIS DESSERT, PARTICULARLY FOR MY UNCLE WHEN HE VISITS. IN SYDNEY IN THE SEVENTIES IT WAS AN AUTHENTIC TASTE OF MY COUNTRY — THE PÉRIGORD.

500 g (1 lb 2 oz) large prunes, stones removed

1 tablespoon armagnac (or brandy)

300 g pâte sucrée (sweet short crust pastry)
 (see recipe page 329)

2 eggs

1 yolk

2 tablespoons caster (superfine) sugar

2 tablespoons cornflour (cornstarch), sifted

1 teaspoon orange flower water

½ teaspoon natural vanilla extract

300 ml (10½ fl oz) cream

If the prunes are a little dry, cover in mild, hot tea and soak for about 1 hour, or until soft. Drain well and combine in a bowl with the Armagnac, set aside to marinate.

Roll out the pastry to 3 mm (⅛ inch) thick, or until large enough to fit the base and sides of a buttered, 27 cm (10¾ inch) loose-based tart tin. Line the tin with pastry and trim away the excess. Make sure there are no holes or cracks in the pastry. Place in the refrigerator for 30–40 minutes or until the pastry is firm.

Preheat the oven to 200ºC (400ºF/Gas 6). Line the pastry shell with foil, ensuring the side is also lined, fill with dried beans or pastry weights and bake for 10 minutes. Remove the foil and beans and bake for a further 10 minutes or until lightly golden. If any cracks or holes have appeared, they can be carefully patched with leftover scraps of pastry.

Reduce the oven temperature to 180ºC (350ºF/Gas 4). Using an electric mixer, (or in a bowl, by hand), whisk the eggs and the yolk with the sugar and some salt, add the cornflour, mix well then add the orange flower water and vanilla. Add the cream and stir to combine.

Spread the prunes evenly over the pastry shell, pour over the cream and egg mixture and place on the middle shelf of the oven. Bake for 30–40 minutes or until golden and the filling is just set. This flan is best when served lukewarm.

DREAM CHASER

From misty mountains to Sloane Square

DANY AT HOME, SYDNEY 1ST MARCH 1981, CELEBRATING

SHARED BIRTHDAY WITH TRISH.

IT WAS TO THE BLUE MOUNTAINS THAT I OFTEN ESCAPED WHEN I FIRST ARRIVED IN AUSTRALIA. I LOVED EVERYTHING ABOUT THIS DRAMATIC, BEAUTIFUL LANDSCAPE: THE HONEYCOMB-COLOURED ESCARPMENTS; THE BLUE-GREEN EUCALYPTUS FORESTS; THE TUMBLING WATERFALLS AND THE ECHOING CALL OF THE WHIP BIRDS. EVEN ON MISTY, MONOCHROMATIC DAYS, I FOUND THE MOUNTAINS TO BE A MAGICAL PLACE. THE PROSPECT, THEN, OF SPENDING A FEW MONTHS THERE WITH MONIQUE AND MICHAEL WAS REALLY QUITE APPEALING. THE RUGGED WILDERNESS SEEMED SO EXOTIC AND SO FAR REMOVED FROM SYDNEY AND, INDEED, FRANCE.

IT WAS NOVEMBER 1976 — NOT LONG AFTER I SOLD

Au Chabrol — that Michael and Monique lured me to stay at Glenella, their new Blackheath guesthouse, some 120 kilometres from Sydney. It had been six years since the three of us had opened Upstairs. How our lives had changed since those days of cooking trays of quiche Lorraine and giant pots of *boeuf Bourguignon*. Although I had no personal stake in Glenella, it was exciting to be involved in the set-up of what promised to be another great project. I warned Michael and Monique that I would only be staying for six months just to help them get up and running. I had *fourmis dans les culottes* (ants in my pants) and I was itching for adventure. After spending six months in Blackheath my plan was to hoist on my backpack and travel to the Aegean Islands for a bit of fun before going to live in London to study photography.

Although it was originally built as a family home in 1905, Glenella was extended to accommodate guests in 1915, when the tourist trade began to take off. The stately Federation-style homestead had established its reputation under George and Elizabeth Phillips. But when Monique and Michael bought the property it had been passed into the hands of a husband-and-wife team who had transformed it into a casual place meant for cheap and cheerful family holidays. The laidback couple, who ran the guesthouse with their innumerable children underfoot, both laughed at the chaos and enjoyed telling outrageous stories of all the disasters that had befallen them. Although the charm of the old building was still evident, the interior had been neglected and fallen into disrepair. The bedrooms featured a mishmash of odd furnishings and the paper-thin walls afforded no privacy whatsoever. I suppose it was therefore lucky that the bathrooms were all located downstairs in the basement!

It's fair to say Glenella had an air of eccentricity about it. On my first morning in the guesthouse I was awoken at six o'clock by a ghostly racket that sounded like rattling chains being dragged across the floor. By about 7 am, when I'd finally recovered from this rude awakening, an absolute giant of a man suddenly appeared in my room with a cup of tea. When I asked the former owners of the guesthouse what all the noise was, they laughed and told me that it was only 'Mr Enormous' feeding coal into the antique furnace in the basement to get the hot water going.

Although it was large, the kitchen at Glenella was very basic and, like the rest of the guesthouse, hadn't been touched since the 1920s. It wouldn't do at all for what Monique and Michael had in mind: instead of operating a guesthouse that served meals, Glenella would, instead, be a 'restaurant with rooms'. Michael was, of course, rather anxious and apprehensive about whether or not such a concept would succeed. At that time, the only other good restaurant in the Blue Mountains was Sophie's Fork 'n' View, which didn't offer accommodation. People travelled from Sydney to eat in Sophie's Katoomba restaurant because it was considered a fun outing. But would they travel 120 kilometres and stay longer? 'Of course,' we agreed. 'In France, we drive for hours to go to special restaurants, especially when there are rooms available to spend the night.'

Michael and Monique were looking for a lifestyle change. They now had a young son, James, to consider and they wanted to slow down, spend more time together as a family and fit in a bit more golf and gardening, too. They both agreed it was time to be a bit more 'grown-up' about running a good restaurant. It was a view shared by Sydney restaurateurs Gay and Tony Bilson, who, at the time, were also at the forefront of new and exciting ideas. In January 1977, after selling the cheerful, bohemian Tony's Bon Gout in the inner-city suburb of Surry Hills, the couple had relocated to Berowra Waters Inn, situated on the banks of the Hawkesbury River. The secluded architect-designed inn, set in bushland, is accessible only by boat and about an hour away from Sydney. Like the Bilsons, Michael, Monique and I were confident our customers would follow us no matter how difficult we made it for them.

On the grounds at Glenella was a pretty colonial cottage where I lived with Michael, Monique, James, and a big black dog named Fred who just turned up one day and moved in. Our first job was to renovate and modernise the kitchen. It felt great to start from scratch. Michael set up one enormous room solely for the purpose of making bread and pastry. It had special ovens and a large, white Formica table in the centre with shelving tucked underneath it. In the corner was the washing-up station – the domain of our dear Armand – who found accommodation a few doors away from Glenella. Armand was absolutely thrilled with his new station: it was a vast improvement over the black hole he worked in at Au Chabrol and even featured a massive industrial dishwasher.

Armand, who always had a cigarette attached to his bottom lip, took over from Mr Enormous as Glenella's 'Master of the Furnace'. To keep the hot water running, the poor fellow had to huff and puff down the stairs to the basement to shovel more coal into its maw. The thing used to break down all the time and Armand would moan to Michael, 'Eh, ça marche pas, ça marche pas.' We became accustomed to seeing Michael and Armand in the basement with their bums in the air, cursing the contraption they were constantly trying to fix. Oh, and then there were the fumes and the awful smell. No one missed the furnace when it was replaced with a functional gas heating system the following year.

Glenella also had a rather grand sitting room, which featured high ceilings and a huge fireplace at the entrance. Michael and Monique painted it red, so ever after it was known as the Red Room. Portraits of Glenella's original owners, the Phillips family, hung on the walls, giving it a nice sense of history and continuity. The original dining room, off to the right, was quite small, so when the restaurant was busy we would put tables in the Red Room. Although we cleaned and painted and polished the bedrooms, we pretty much left them as they were – full of mismatched furniture – because food was our main focus.

Before we opened, we placed an advertisement in the local paper seeking an apprentice. There we were painting and cleaning when there was a knock at the door. Michael and I opened it to find a plump fifteen-year-old country girl with apple-pink cheeks named Elise. 'I'm here for the apprentice job,' she announced.

We looked at her doubtfully: 'How much do you know about cooking?'

She calmly announced: 'I know everything!' Michael and I looked at each other in dismay. No one else had applied for the job. We had to hire her. When Elise started peeling and prepping for us, the poor thing realised she in fact knew very little about food. She was, however, a hard worker, and soon learned.

IT WAS NOT LONG BEFORE OUR FRIENDS AND OLD

customers started making the trek from Sydney to Blackheath to see what we were up to. Many of them were quite smart, stylish people, and they found it funny that they had to run downstairs to use the toilet, brush their teeth or take a shower. Before too long, Glenella became quite well known and staying the weekend became the thing to do. Although we had all moved on and matured from the days of Upstairs, Glenella was never formal and stuffy; it always had a fun, house-party feeling.

At the start, Michael was in charge of the main courses while I concentrated on the entrées and pâtisserie, which I soon taught Elise to do. One day Elise and I were making a *croquembouche* for a wedding. We had just finished baking two hundred perfectly round, golden little *choux*, which we then left to rest on trays in the kitchen. When we returned, we stood there in shock. There wasn't a single crumb of *choux* left in the room; every last one had vanished! I looked at Elise and cried: 'Oh Elise! What have you done with the *choux*? Did you eat them?'

'No!' she said, and pointed accusingly at Fred the dog, lying there whimpering, his stomach grossly distended. We had to start again.

At Glenella we were driven by our desire to use quality ingredients and so started to create 'exotic' dishes featuring duck and guinea fowl, which were now being bred by Australian farmers. We were completely in awe of *nouvelle cuisine*: Michel Guérard's *Cuisine Minceur* (Slimming Cuisine) and *Cuisine Gourmande* were our bibles and

Soupe laitue et amandes

LETTUCE AND ALMOND SOUP

SERVES 4–6

THIS IS A LIGHT SOUP SUITABLE FOR ALL SEASONS, EXCEPT DEEPEST WINTER. IT COMES FROM A FRIEND
IN PARIS. AS WELL AS BEING INEXPENSIVE, IT'S BOTH SIMPLE AND UNUSUAL.

80 g (2¾ oz) unsalted butter
80 g (2¾ oz) plain (all-purpose) flour
2 litres (70 fl oz/8 cups) chicken stock
freshly grated nutmeg, to taste
50 ml (1½ fl oz) Madeira
1 large firm iceberg lettuce
200 g (7oz) flaked almonds, toasted
150 ml (5 fl oz) cream

In a large saucepan, melt the butter over medium heat, mix in the flour and
reduce the heat, stirring constantly with a wooden spoon until it puffs up. Slowly
pour in the stock, stirring until it boils. Season to taste with salt, freshly ground
black pepper and nutmeg then add the Madeira. Let the soup simmer,
uncovered, for 15 minutes.

Cut the lettuce in half, then slice fairly thinly and add to the simmering soup.
Cook for only 5 minutes over very low heat to conserve the fresh-lettuce taste.
Add half the almonds to the soup and then remove from the heat.

To serve, add the cream, gently reheat (do not boil), ladle into a soup tureen
or individual bowls and serve sprinkled with the remaining flaked almonds.

Elizabeth David went back on the shelf. Our food processor was always on the go: if our ingredients weren't julienned or puréed they were made into a mousse. One of Michel Guérard's most influential innovations was to thicken sauces by making a demi-glaçe instead of the traditional flour-and-butter technique. To make it, you reduce the juices in the pan before swirling in a dollop of zero per cent *fromage blanc*. Zero per cent *fromage blanc* was unavailable in Australia at that time so we used full-fat cream in all those '*minceur*' recipes instead. It tasted delicious, and still looked light and lovely. Fish were stuffed with mousses, with little cream-filled flans as the garnish; and our seafood terrines were layered assemblages of puréed fish wrapped in seaweed. Though we embraced the art of *nouvelle cuisine*, we never went to the extreme of serving one scallop and a chive on a plate as an entrée.

My nephew James, on the other hand, proved to have a very picky palate. Now a cute blond toddler, he refused to eat anything except ham. He was very funny. He was always running around in the kitchen, usually minus pants. I would try to coax him to try something new. 'Look James, look at this beautiful chicken I've made. Won't you try some? A little taste?'

'*Non*!' he would say, stamping his foot. James had attended the *maternelle* in Sainte-Foy-la-Grande and spoke enough French to insist: '*Jambon, jambon, jambon*! I only want *jambon*!'

As James grew older he gradually became interested in what we were doing in the kitchen, and more adventurous with trying new things. He began to pester us constantly: 'Can I have this? Can I have that?' We'd be making something complicated, such as a layered mousse, which requires a lot of preparation, and we would say, 'No, no, James. Not now. This is for the customers.'

'Oh, all right,' he'd say, and then a minute later, he'd be back again, pointing to something else: 'Well, can I have that then?'

'No James. It's for the customers.' Everything he wanted seemed to be 'for the customers'.

One evening just before service, James disappeared into the cottage. We were busy getting ready and were wondering: 'Where's James? What's he got up to now?' Then Monique spotted him in the dining room. He was all dressed up in his best clothes, sitting at a table with some customers! Monique gasped and went running out, apologising profusely. 'Excuse me! I'm ever so sorry. This is my little son.'

'Oh yes, we know,' the couple said. 'He told us who he was. He said he wanted to be with us this evening. We're happy to have him.'

So, that night, James finally got to eat what the customers ate.

Armand was also well-fed and treated like a member of the family. He lived in a flat at the back of a neighbouring house where he had his own little garden. Although Armand didn't have many expenses, he also never seemed to have any savings and – apart from buying cigarettes – we could never work out what he spent his money on. James often accompanied Armand when he went to pick up extra supplies from the local shops. One day, when Monique and James were walking past the old-fashioned toy and sweet shop in

Blackheath, James begged his mother for a toy. 'Mum, Mum. Can I buy something?'

'No, I haven't got any money.'

'It's okay, Mum. Do what Armand does and just go into that shop next door to get money!' James pointed to the betting shop, unwittingly solving the mystery of where all Armand's money went!

Somehow the six months I planned to stay at Glenella turned into a year. I worked full time Thursdays to Sundays, when I would make the return journey to my home in Sydney. Monique often urged me to stay an extra night in Blackheath. 'Dany, don't go all the way home just to be alone. Stay with us and relax. We'll go for a bushwalk, meet with friends, cook a great dinner and have a chance to chat.' Artist Michael Ramsden lived nearby and on Mondays he and Michael played golf together. Michael was married to fashion designer Jenny Kee, who was based in Sydney, so he would often join us for dinner. We'd all sit around in the cottage until late at night, eating and drinking and solving the problems of the world. It was a wonderful way to wind down after the pressures of the weekend.

Monique didn't have to work too hard to persuade me to stay on Monday nights

I was thirty-six and often felt as if my life was finished; I had convinced myself that I would never find a new love.

too. Returning to Sydney often left me feeling depressed and emotional. Without Mimi, the place seemed so empty. I was thirty-six and often felt as if my life was finished; I had convinced myself that I would never find a new love. My sister constantly assured me it wasn't so; she was very kind, optimistic and supportive: 'Oh, don't worry, you'll find someone, you'll see!' She had a special knack of building me back up when I was feeling down.

After a while, it became apparent that Michael wasn't trying too hard to find a replacement for me. It was only after I let him know how desperate I was to leave that he began to do some serious research. He got in touch with George Perry-Smith back at The Hole in the Wall in Bath and asked if he knew anyone who might like to work at Glenella. George said he knew just the person for the job: his stepson Simon, a trained chef, and his wife Suzy, who were both keen to come to Australia. Simon and Suzy arrived in May 1978 and I worked with Simon for a month, easing him into his new job, while Suzy worked as a waitress.

It was during this time that our old Sydney friend Sandy Pearce brought Trish Hobbs up to Glenella for lunch. Trish was a well-known stylist who worked in advertising and magazines; she got her start as a stylist with a food photographer before freelancing on TV commercials and for magazines such as *Vogue Entertaining & Travel* and *Cosmopolitan*. I knew of her – she had often eaten at Au Chabrol – but apart from reading the riot act to her when she arrived late at the restaurant, we'd never really spoken. Sandy and Colette had bought shares in a remote farmhouse in the Ardèche and they were off to France for a few months to live the rural French dream. They urged Trish to take her two young sons out of school and join them. Trish thought this sounded very romantic and quickly agreed. Sandy then suggested Trish travel with Monique and James, who happened to be travelling to France at the same time. Monique and Trish had met a few times before and remembered liking each other, so Sandy arranged for her to go to Glenella so they could meet up again.

While discussing their shared travel plans, Trish pointed out to Monique that their flight to Paris in July landed in Athens on the way. 'Monique, why don't we have a little holiday in Greece with the children before going to France?' suggested Trish, who at the time, was mad on all things Mediterranean. Monique agreed: 'It does seem silly to land there and not see a few islands on the way.'

Monique knew that I would be backpacking around Greece in June and she liked the idea of travelling there, too. And that's how it turned out; in June, I travelled about in Crete, Rhodes, Santorini and Athens. The next month Monique and James, Trish and her two boys followed in my footsteps. They hired a convertible and had a wonderful time. Of course, James, who was five at the time, thought 'the big boys', Barney, then seven, and Stephen, thirteen, were the best fun in the world.

While Monique and Trish were gallivanting around Greece, I was back in Vélines, visiting my parents. I bought a square little Citroën LN so I could drive Monique and James around when they arrived in France and was therefore quite taken aback when, soon after arriving in Vélines, Monique said she wanted to go and visit Sandy, Colette, Trish and the boys in the Ardèche. I told Monique I wasn't sure if I wanted to go: 'That Trish is a bit snobby, isn't she? I think she's a bit much for my tastes.' 'Oh no, Dany! You're wrong!' Monique said. 'We had such a wonderful time together in Greece. You'll see!'

'Well, okay,' I said, thinking it wouldn't be too bad for just a few days.

Terrified that her daughters and grandson might starve to death once they'd left Vélines, Maman busied herself packing the car full of goodies from the Dordogne. The car was so crammed with hams, pâtés and trays of peaches that there was barely any room in the back seat for James. But James didn't mind a jot; all he cared about was getting back together with his new best friends, Stephen and Barney, as well as Sandy and Colette's children, Sebastian and Juliette, and countless other young cousins. We listened to his relentless refrains of 'Are we there yet? Are we there yet?' as we drove over the Massif Central and through the deep forest to the farmhouse.

'Pochon' was the name of the farmhouse, which was isolated and very difficult to find. Fortunately, Trish and Colette had gathered up a gaggle of children and spent the day putting up signs and symbols to guide us along the road. There was a big fuss made when we arrived to find Sandy surrounded by a bevy of women, including Trish. Sun-kissed after three weeks in Greece, she looked like a dark-haired beauty. 'You've met Dany before, haven't you?' Monique asked Trish. 'Oh, maybe once or twice,' Trish replied. Pochon itself was a big, old rambling farmhouse with a colourful past. It had served as a brothel for the Germans during the war and, because of the bad memories the house contained, the locals didn't want to have anything to do with it; it had been abandoned since 1945. It had no electricity and no running water so we relied on the flickering light from candles and a hand pump to draw water from the well. Sandy and Colette were looking forward to enjoying a simple, self-sufficient lifestyle on the farm; they had ducks, a goose and chickens clucking around the place. Of course, food was the first thing on my mind. There was a little camp cooker, an oven that worked off a gas bottle and an enormous fireplace with a huge black cooking pot hanging from a chain. It contained our supper. I sniffed at it. 'So what are we going to eat?' I asked.

'Trish has made us a great big pot of *boeuf Bourguignon*,' Sandy announced. I screwed up my face in disgust. 'Bah! I hate *boeuf Bourguignon*! Michael made this dish so often at

Those August days at Pochon were idyllic, with family and friends coming and going and happy children charging about. Every night there would be at least twenty of us gathered around the table to feast under the flickering light of the candles.

Upstairs that I can't bear to eat it.'

Trish put her hands on her hips. 'Oh, well, I hope you will like this one!' she said and I burst out laughing.

I had to admit Trish's beef stew was very good indeed. I told her it was the best *boeuf Bourguignon* I had ever eaten and she forgave my momentary lapse in manners.

Monique and I shared a room at the farmhouse. We each had half a single bed: I had the metal base that was minus a mattress and it was the most uncomfortable thing I'd ever slept on! Next door to us were our friends Tessa and Robert who had a big double bed made of metal. It was so rickety that every time they moved, the bed would make a screeching noise – '*Eeeenya, eeeeenya, eeeenya, eeeeenya!*' that tore straight through the walls. Monique and I would snort with laughter. I couldn't resist teasing them the next morning: 'Mmmm, sounds as if you two had a good time last night?'

'It's the bed! It's the bed,' they said. 'We can't even turn a page in our books without it squeaking!' Trish's room only had an *armoire* without doors, but she loved its *chapeau de gendarme* shape. She also had a bedhead, but no bed. Sandy mentioned to her there were some extra mattresses downstairs but Trish refused to use them. It was clear why Trish was sought after as a stylist: she had the romantic notion that because she was in rural France she should be sleeping on a bed of hay. It didn't occur to her that the hay she stuffed into bags should be dry; what she slept on was soon a freezing, slimy, green mess. Trish was definitely not a country girl, but she was mad about style and how beautiful things should look. Her two boys started out sleeping on air beds in her room but they soon joined the gang of children in the enormous attic. It truly was kid-heaven. The

Endive à la betterave rouge

BRAISED ENDIVE WITH BEETROOT

SERVES 4

THIS IS AN INTERPRETATION OF THE TRADITIONAL COLD BEETROOT AND ENDIVE SALAD, SERVED AS A HOT ENTRÉE; THE REDUCED CREAM BINDS TOGETHER THE SWEETNESS OF THE BEETROOT AND THE BITTERNESS OF THE ENDIVE AND GIVES AN AMAZINGLY BEAUTIFUL COLOUR TO THE SAUCE.

2–3 beetroots, trimmed

2 tablespoons rock salt

4 large endives (witlof)

50 g (1¾ oz) unsalted butter

juice of ½ lemon

1 tablespoon raw sugar

freshly grated nutmeg, to taste

200 ml (7 fl oz) chicken stock

100 ml (3½ fl oz) cream

40 g (1½ oz) prosciutto, diced into ½ cm
  (¼ inch) squares

1 small bunch chives, thinly sliced

Preheat the oven to 200ºC (400ºF/Gas 6).

Place the beetroot in a saucepan, cover with cold water, bring to the boil and parboil for about 15 minutes. Drain, roll the beetroot in the rock salt, place in a roasting tin and bake for 1 hour or more until a wooden skewer will pierce them easily. When cool, brush off the salt, peel and set aside.

Trim the endive, and arrange in a baking dish with a slice of butter on each, sprinkle with the lemon juice, raw sugar and season with salt, pepper and nutmeg (the same amount as pepper), and then add the chicken stock, poured in at the corner of the dish so as not to disturb the seasonings. Cover and bake for 40 minutes–1 hour or until they are very tender, particularly at the thick end. Remove from the oven, cool, and then remove with a slotted spoon, reserving the cooking juices.

Slice the beetroot into 5 mm (¼ inch) thick rounds (keep any off-cuts), cut the endives in half lengthwise, stopping at the thick end so that they stay in one piece. Sandwich the slices of beetroot between the endive halves. Place the endives carefully in a frying pan large enough to hold them in a single layer, along with some of their cooking juice, the cream and some off-cuts of the beetroot. Heat gently over a medium–low heat with a lid half covering the pan, until warmed through.

Meanwhile, fry the prosciutto in a separate small frying pan over medium–high heat until crisp and then set aside. When the endives are warmed through, remove to warmed serving plates.

Reduce the sauce in the pan over medium heat for 3–5 minutes or until deep red, then discard the beetroot off-cuts, and add more cream or cooking juices if necessary – the sauce should be quite thick. Spoon the sauce over each endive, then sprinkle the prosciutto and chives over the brilliant pink sauce.

Artichaut aux foies de volaille

ARTICHOKES WITH CHICKEN LIVERS

SERVES 4

THIS IS A VERY BEAUTIFUL DISH; THE INSPIRATION COMES FROM
A TRADITIONAL LYONNAISE RECIPE.

Preheat the oven to 200ºC (400ºF/Gas 6).

Place the artichokes in cold salted water in a saucepan and weight down with a plate. Bring to the boil, then reduce to a simmer and cook for 10–15 minutes or until the leaves pull off the artichokes easily. Remove the artichokes from the water and place upside down to drain. When they are cool enough to handle, open the artichokes out like flowers, remove and discard the hairy chokes in the centre and set the artichokes aside.

TO MAKE THE DRESSING: Combine the egg yolks, mustard, lemon juice and vinegar in a bowl and whisk to combine well, then gradually add the combined oils in a fine steady stream whisking constantly until thick. Set aside. You may need to add a little warm water for a pourable consistency.

Season the livers with freshly ground black pepper, toss with the olive oil and place on a baking tray. Roast for 5–7 minutes – they should still be pink on the inside. Cool and season with salt.

Thinly slice the avocado and squeeze over a little lemon juice.

Slice the livers and place inside the centre of the artichokes. Arrange the avocado slices between the leaves, cover generously with the dressing and sprinkle with the chives. Serve with a sprig of watercress to the side.

4 large globe artichokes, stems removed
250 g (9 oz) chicken livers
2 teaspoons olive oil
1 avocado
a squeeze of lemon juice
1½ tablespoons finely snipped chives
4 watercress sprigs

DRESSING
2 egg yolks
1 small teaspoon dijon mustard
juice of ½ lemon
1 tablespoon white wine vinegar
150 ml (5 fl oz) olive oil
150 ml (5 fl oz) grapeseed oil

ois.47   cal II

2 Paquet

1€50

main thing was they were happy, giggling and running about, without too many rules and regulations to hinder the fun.

Those August days at Pochon were idyllic, with family and friends coming and going and happy children charging about. Every night there would be at least twenty of us gathered around the table to feast under the flickering light of the candles. We drank bottles of wine and stayed up chatting and laughing into the night. This gorgeous country setting wouldn't have been half as much fun if we had had all the creature comforts.

Not long after arriving at Pochon I announced that I was going to drive down to see the Gorges de l'Ardèche, famous for its rugged limestone cliffs. Monique wasn't interested in coming along, but Trish piped up: 'Oh, I'd love to go!'

How intriguing! I had been getting a few romantic signals from Trish and a trip to the *gorges* seemed like the perfect occasion to determine if there was any real chemistry between us. Truthfully, I didn't hold out much hope. Trish was married with two children and famous for her good taste. I could hardly presume that good taste extended to me.

Colette, however, did her best to convince me otherwise. She, too, had detected that Trish was attracted to me and urged me to make a move. 'Go on, Dany,' she'd whisper. 'Can't you see the way Trish has been looking at you? I can! Now make a move!'

Any ideas I had about getting better acquainted with Trish on our trip to the Gorges de l'Ardèche were crushed when her son Stephen decided he wanted to tag along, too. Trish did her best to dissuade him. 'Oh no, Stephen. Don't you want to go horseriding instead? That would be much more fun! Or you could play a game outside with all your friends?'

But young Stephen insisted on coming with us. Although our thirteen-year-old chaperone was in the back seat, he spent the entire journey leaning forward, hanging off every word we said. When we stopped for a coffee mid-route, Trish sent her son off to buy croissants, hoping we'd have time for a quick chat. In typical teenage fashion, Stephen was back within minutes, determined not to miss anything that was going on.

Back at Pochon, Stephen and all the children would go off on long walks in the countryside to pick baskets of wild berries. One day, after trying to impress Trish with stories of my cooking ability, I said airily, 'Oh what should we make for dessert?' Trish surprised me: 'The children have picked all these lovely raspberries. Why don't you make us a raspberry soufflé?' 'Oh. What a lovely idea,' I replied, trying to sound confident. It was true they were the best kind of raspberries – tiny and wild and bursting with flavour – and, yes, I wanted to do the fruit justice, but I was also completely panicked by the idea of baking without a recipe. Of course, given I'd just been bragging about my culinary prowess, I had no choice but to rise to the challenge; fortunately, so did my two huge soufflés, which puffed up beautifully and were delicious. Trish was also very enthusiastic about some *écrevisses* (crayfish) she bought at the local market. After storing them in the *arrière cuisine*, she placed them in a bucket with a chopping board on top to ensure they wouldn't escape. Hours later, after way too much wine was consumed, we found the *écrevisses* had made a successful bid for freedom and we spent much time laughing and falling about with torches trying to track them down.

Sadly, our host Sandy was excluded from many of our late-night feasts due to the fact he'd picked up hepatitis in Thailand while en route to France. He was ill and jaundiced and the children, who couldn't pronounce hepatitis, said he had 'the potatoes'. Worst of all was the fact he couldn't over-indulge in food or drink while sharing his house with people who were wining and dining to excess every night. He'd sit up alone in his room banging the floor with his cane trying, unsuccessfully, to shut us up as we consumed bottle after bottle of red wine.

Most mornings Sandy and Trish would wander down to Annonay market to buy provisions for the Pochon crowd. It was a big effort to cater to about twenty people per day, so they'd often reward themselves with a post-market coffee and croissant.

One of the major highlights of my gastronomic pilgrimage to France was securing a reservation at Alain Chapel's superb Michelin three-star restaurant in Mionnay. Everyone spent the whole day primping and preening in preparation for the occasion: there was no electricity and therefore no hairdryers so there was a lot of studied hair-brushing in the sun. We also had to light the wood-chip boiler to heat the bathwater and take turns in the tub. Restaurant Alain Chapel was to be Trish's first three-star experience and she was very excited. She wore a wonderful black Sophia Loren dress cut low with spaghetti straps, which she hung in the bathroom in the hope the steam would ease out some of the creases. After Trish had stepped into her dress she asked me to fasten it at the back. Monique noticed and grinned. 'Ooh, la-la! You've gone bright red, Dany!'

'Oh, don't be silly,' I said, feeling even more embarrassed.

Sick as Sandy was, he was determined not to miss out on this experience. We had to take two cars – Sandy drove his little *camionette*; while I drove my Citroën LN – and we were really quite a sight. There we were, trailing out from a rustic rural farmhouse to one of the most famous restaurants in France!

Alain Chapel's restaurant was everything we had imagined it would be. Every dish was served under a *cloche*, which was very fashionable at the time, and each person was individually presented with what they had ordered. It was all so elegant and lovely. Adding to this uniquely French experience was the sight of a poodle dining at the table next to us; it had a napkin around its neck and was being served as if it were human!

The food at Restaurant Alain Chapel matched its reputation. Trish and I shared the master chef's signature dish, *poularde truffée en vessie* (chicken stuffed with truffles), enveloped in a pork bladder and cooked in a rich chicken broth. It was served in a gorgeous porcelain soup terrine, and, when the lid was lifted, its heavenly aromas engulfed us in a sensuous steam. We were impressed. We drank wonderful Burgundies and the waiters kept appearing with more and more perfect dishes. We were all abuzz with the excitement of it all, except for poor Sandy and his 'potatoes' who could only have little tastes of this and that, washed down with mineral water. For the rest of us, it was a wonderful introduction to three-star dining in France.

After saying goodbye to Sandy and Colette in Annonay, Trish and the boys and I went to stay in a hotel in Geneva. After three days I put Trish and her children on a train to Milan where they were off to meet their father. Monique, James and I then continued our journey back to Vélines, via Roanne. Our detour to Roanne was driven by the fact that we wanted to enjoy another Michelin three-star culinary experience, this time at Troisgros. Again, our meal was perfect; the legendary Troisgros brothers produced such imaginative and beautiful dishes that they left us breathless. Despite the distraction of such gastronomic delights, Monique began pestering me about Trish. 'Come on, Dany. Tell me what happened? You were in the hotel together for three nights! Do tell.'

'Oh no,' I said. 'My lips are sealed.'

IT WAS OCTOBER 1978 WHEN I LEFT FRANCE TO LIVE IN London and pursue my passion for photography. I had rented out my house in Sydney for twelve months and I was now free to see if what my old boss in the Paris photo lab told me was true: that London was far more exciting than Paris. Within a month or so of arriving in London, I managed to get a very smart sublet in Sloane Avenue in the borough of Chelsea.

In Australia I had been so busy in the restaurant scene that I had little time to do anything other than cook. Living in London would allow me to invest time in two of my other main interests: photography and listening to classical music. Although I signed up for a refresher course on photographic technique at the Polytechnic on Regent Street, I confess to being a bit of a dilettante: though diligent about doing my exercises, I never bothered taking the exams.

What I also discovered during that year in the UK was that London was completely lacking when it came to interesting *bistrots* and restaurants! I knew I could show those Brits a thing or two and at times was even tempted to open my own *bistrot*. Dining at Alain Chapel and Troisgros had been a huge inspiration. Trish, too, had been swept off her feet by the whole experience and when she came to Europe the following summer we went to another three-star restaurant and *auberge* in France: Michel Guérard's ravishing Les Prés d'Eugénie in Les Landes. It was the ultimate in French country charm. As well as being impressed by the impeccable service, Trish was in awe of the style and understated confidence that suffused everything. Even the neighbouring field had been garnished with one perfect stack of hay! As well as the fabulous food, we were seduced by everything from the silk sheets to the baskets of flowers and rustic country furniture. Although he had to leave town for a meeting, Michel Guérard had left instructions to spoil us. He remembered visiting my modest Au Chabrol restaurant in Sydney and he treated us to extra dishes and bottles of Champagne and Armagnac.

We tasted one fabulous dish after another and I couldn't help thinking to myself that, given the chance, I, too, could try to cook at this level. However, if my years at Au Chabrol had taught me anything it was that running a restaurant was really hard work. I had been there, done that. And now, I was going to make it as a photographer!

Of course, life doesn't always go according to plan. I'd been living in London for about nine months when Monique phoned to ask if I could return to Australia to run the Glenella kitchen for six weeks. Michael had made contact with the Troisgros brothers in France and was setting off to do a six-week stint in their fabulous three-star French restaurant. It was Monique and Trish that came up with the idea that I could return to Australia and cover for him. Michael's plan was to be back by November when Rothbury Estate would be hosting its Great Chefs' Dinner, which he also wanted me to be part of. 'Come on Dany. You could stay a bit longer and make the second dessert! The customers have been asking for you. Just think how fantastic it could be.'

Although I agreed to run the Glenella restaurant in Michael's absence, I demurred at the suggestion that I stay on to cook for the Great Chefs' Dinner. 'I don't have a restaurant any more! I don't want to be a chef. I want to be a photographer,' I told Monique. My stubborn little sister wouldn't take 'Non!' for an answer. It was all arranged and that was that. Monique and Trish had been conspiring for months to lure me back to Australia and it just so happened that around this time, I had to give up my London sublet, too. After leaving my possessions with a friend, I was, once again, bound for Blackheath. I never did return to my life in London.

After his six-week stint at Troisgros, Michael came back to Glenella bursting with new ideas on how to better manage a kitchen. He said he'd had enough of the informal Australian style and demanded a bit more respect be shown to him in the kitchen. He declared that he now wanted all staff to tie their hair back, wear white hats, and stop referring to him by his old childhood nickname, Neddy. Michael insisted the kitchen brigade should now say 'Oui, chef' whenever he issued a command. This worked for a few days until Monique couldn't help herself. She began mocking what we all thought was Michael's pompous behaviour and promptly shortened his title to an affectionate 'Cheffie'. I'm afraid this new title stuck and to this day we still call him Cheffie.

The Great Chefs' Dinner was organised by Australian winemaker, the late Len Evans and held on 24 November 1979. Len, who has been credited for putting the Australian wine industry on the map, owned a large Hunter Valley winery with a massive cellar, which he believed would provide the perfect setting for a splendid banquet. It was a remarkable and indulgent evening with a guest list that glittered. As well as a wonderful list of wines there was course after course of exquisite cuisine prepared by Australia's top chefs, each preparing food for 120 people.

As well as asking Michael to produce one of the main courses, Len had Stephanie Alexander making the sorbet, and Patrick Juillet and Tony Bilson each creating a special dish. One of the many special guests was one of the high priests of *nouvelle cuisine*, Roger Vergé, of Le Moulin de Mougins, who was in Australia to promote his classic *Cuisine du Soleil* cookbook. The Chefs' Dinner was an exercise in excess: there was a huge refrigerated trailer filled with bottles of Deutz Champagne that were delivered to both the dining room and the kitchen.

The atmosphere in the kitchen was fantastic. Even an incredible afternoon storm that temporarily knocked out the electricity was not enough to stop us; Stephanie Alexander was midway through making her Champagne and rose petal sorbet at the time and so the kitchen staff banded together to help her whip the mixture by hand and complete her 120 covers on time. My dessert, *gâteau Saint-Honoré*, was named after the patron saint of French bakers, so naturally I felt a certain amount of pressure to do him justice. The dish is a tour de force: first you make a base of *pâte feuilletée*, which you then top with a ring of choux and secure with spun caramelised sugar. You then fill the dough with *crème chiboust*. During the week leading up to the dinner, I had been making the dessert over and over again in order to refine and perfect the recipe. Trish and I pre-prepared the raw pastry the day before the dinner, but everything else had to be made on the spot. It was the first time Trish had ever worked with spun sugar, using forks to spin the hot toffee. Somehow, the dessert worked like a dream, which may or may not have had something to do with our steady consumption of Champagne. It seems the more Champagne we drank, the more artistic our spun sugar became! All up we made thirteen bases, hundreds of choux circles and thirteen basins of *crème chiboust* each containing eighteen eggs. This was *haute cuisine* on an industrial level and we were having great fun.

Then, the big moment arrived. Off went the lights! The feast was nearing its end and it was time for the grand finale, my *gâteau Saint-Honoré*. One by one the waiters picked up the waiting *gâteaux* and marched single file out into the dining room. Everything was going great until the twelfth man fell; his accidental rendition of a classic comedy routine could not have been choreographed any better. The cake went splat on the floor and the choux rolled off in all directions. The diners at the last table looked aghast until I casually

Then, the big moment arrived. Off went the lights! The feast was nearing its end and it was time for the grand finale, my gâteau Saint-Honoré. Everything was going great until the twelfth man fell; the cake went splat on the floor and the choux rolled off in all directions.

sashayed out of the kitchen holding up a thirteenth cake in triumph. As any experienced chef will tell you: it always pays to have an extra dish on the go.

After the Great Chefs' Dinner, it was Christmas. Monique didn't have too much trouble convincing me it was silly to go back to London alone. I was in love with Trish, so I stayed, determined to live in Sydney and give my career in photography a go. It was 1980 and because Trish was still working as a freelance stylist I was able to get a fair amount of work as a food photographer. I often used Glenella as the location and I had a lot of fun. Although I enjoyed the work, I didn't earn much and without my own studio I couldn't produce enough work to make my new career viable.

In 1981 I sold my Five Dock home in Sydney's inner-west and bought a lovely ground-floor flat with a garden in the eastern suburb of Bellevue Hill. To make ends meet, I started working part-time in the Glenella kitchen every weekend. But I wasn't the only one travelling to Blackheath on weekends; many of our friends had also started to buy houses in the region. Since returning from France, Sandy had bought a lovely little

Great Chefs of Australia
Inaugural Dinner

Saturday, November 24, 1979

Gâteau mon rêve

MY DREAM CAKE

SERVES 10

A LAYERED CAKE: ORANGE AND ALMOND BISCUIT, CHOCOLATE BAVAROIS AND LIGHT MERINGUE-WHIPPED CREAM.
I WOKE UP ONE MORNING AND TOLD MY SISTER THAT I HAD DREAMED OF A CAKE MADE WITH ALL THE INGREDIENTS
I LIKE BEST. I MADE IT STRAIGHTAWAY — AND FOR MANY YEARS AFTERWARDS.

TO MAKE THE ORANGE-ALMOND BISCUIT: Preheat the oven to 160ºC (315ºF/ Gas 2–3) and grease a 24 cm (9½ inch) round springform cake tin, lining the base with baking paper. Combine the sugar, almonds and flour in a bowl. Using an electric mixer whisk the egg whites with a pinch of sugar until stiff peaks form, then whisk in the orange zest and almond extract. Gradually fold through the dry ingredients a little at a time, using a metal spoon, being careful not to deflate the egg whites. Pour into the cake tin, smooth the surface and bake for 20–25 minutes. Cool on a wire rack. When lukewarm, open the ring, lift out the cake and remove the paper from the base. Return the biscuit to the tin, line the sides with a strip of baking paper then close the ring and set aside.

TO MAKE THE CHOCOLATE BAVAROIS: Bring the milk to the boil in a saucepan. Using an electric mixer beat together the egg yolks and sugar until pale and fluffy. Gradually beat in the milk and continue mixing for 1 minute. Return to the cleaned saucepan and cook over low heat, stirring constantly with a wooden spoon, for 20–25 minutes until the mixture thickly coats the back of a spoon; do not let it boil. Remove from the heat and transfer to a mixing bowl. Squeeze excess water from the gelatine and add to the milk mixture along with the chocolate and stir until smooth. Leave to cool. When lukewarm, and before it sets, whisk the cream to form soft peaks and fold it into the chocolate mixture. Pour into the cake tin over the biscuit, smooth the surface, cover and refrigerate overnight.

TO MAKE THE MERINGUE CREAM: Stir the sugar and water in a saucepan over medium heat until the sugar dissolves. Continue cooking, without stirring, until syrup reaches 110ºC (225ºF) on a sugar thermometer. In an electric mixer, whisk the egg whites with a pinch of sugar until stiff peaks form, pour over the syrup and whisk until cooled. Whip the cream to soft peaks and fold into meringue. Decorate the cake with clouds of meringue cream, remove from the tin and serve.

ORANGE-ALMOND BISCUIT

150 g (5½ oz) caster (superfine) sugar,
*   plus a pinch extra*
200 g (7 oz) ground almonds
30 g (1 oz) plain (all-purpose) flour
6 egg whites
finely grated zest of 1 orange
2 drops natural almond extract

CHOCOLATE BAVAROIS

750 ml (26 fl oz/3 cups) milk
9 egg yolks
150 g (5½ oz) caster (superfine) sugar
4 leaves gold-strength gelatine, softened in cold water
200 g (7 oz) dark chocolate, grated or finely chopped
300 ml (10½ fl oz) cream

MERINGUE CREAM

100 g (3½ oz) caster (superfine) sugar, plus
*   a pinch extra*
60 ml (2 fl oz/¼ cup) water
3 egg whites
300 ml (10½ fl oz) cream

wooden cottage called Summer Home. Colette, who was now separated from Sandy, bought in Blackheath, too: a very basic old guesthouse called Kubba Roonga. Granted, there was no 'Mr Enormous' to shovel coal into the furnace at Kubba Roonga, but you did have to put ten cent coins into a machine to get any warmth in winter. Although Colette's kitchen was always a bit chaotic, her Vietnamese-themed nights in Blackheath were a great success because, essentially, she was a great cook. Although Kubba Roonga was only a stone's throw away from Glenella, the two guesthouses were never in direct competition as their styles were so completely different.

———————

IN JANUARY 1983, *VOGUE ENTERTAINING* ASKED ME TO create a cake for the great Luciano Pavarotti, who was singing *La Bohème* at the Sydney Opera House. It was no surprise to be told the famous tenor loved rich cakes, and that chocolate was his favourite. The cake I created for Pavarotti was a supremely rich confection of layered chocolate, almond biscuit and chocolate-flavoured cream brushed with a raspberry/brandy syrup and adorned with chocolate curls and raspberries. This over-the-top creation was presented to Pavarotti at a gala supper after his opening night performance. The rotund Italian appreciated my efforts and, after eating three enormous portions, insisted I write out the recipe for him, then and there. *Vogue Entertaining* published the recipe, which Pavarotti had autographed with a flourish.

Not long after, Trish and I were strolling around the elegant boutiques in Double Bay when Joan Campbell, then food editor of *Vogue Entertaining*, spied me from the other side of the road and screamed: 'Dany! Dany! My readers say your cake recipe doesn't bloody work!' Oblivious to the startled looks from the chic shoppers, I yelled back: 'Then tell them they can't bloody cook!' Joan was a bit cool towards me after that.

For Christmas in 1983, Trish's lovely mum, Jane, or 'Nanna' as she was known, went to Glenella to care for Michael and Monique's dog and cat while they were away on holidays. Nanna had been searching for a small flat to buy in Sydney, but wasn't having much luck. So Trish made the decision for her: she found a place in Blackheath and bought it at auction one Saturday afternoon. Nanna took one look at her new home and burst into tears. Admittedly, it didn't look that great at first – it had a great big gaping hole in the roof – but Trish reassured her mum all would be okay. Trish then dedicated many months to lovingly restoring the rundown house into a beautiful home that Nanna adored. At this time I was working Fridays through to Sundays at Glenella before returning to Sydney, where I continued trying to forge a career path in photography. In all honesty, I was going nowhere fast and it was Sandy who finally gave me the wake-up call I needed: 'Oh come on, Dany, what the hell are you doing? Why are you wasting your time? You're such a wonderful cook. Why don't you go back to cooking and open a restaurant? You know you'll be successful.'

'Yes, I know. But … but … I want to do something different! I know I could run a good restaurant, but life is so short. Don't you think people should try different things?'

'Well, I think you should do what you do best and perfect it,' Sandy said. It was Sandy who encouraged me to open Au Chabrol; it was through Sandy that I met Trish; and it was Sandy who egged me on to open another restaurant. He has a lot to answer for!

Trish was also pushing me in the same direction. After our visit to Michel Guérard's Les Prés d'Eugénie in France, it had become Trish's dream to open an upmarket French *auberge*. As fabulous as her job was in fashion and advertising, she was fed up and wanted to do something different. Everyone told her she was stark raving mad: no one with any sense would give up a glamorous career as a stylist to work in hospitality. But Trish was determined: 'No, being a stylist has been a great career for me and I've enjoyed it immensely but I'm ready to do something new.'

As well as sharing the same birth date, another thing Trish and I have in common is that we are both perfectionists. The flipside to this is that once we have done something well, we are usually keen to move on and try something new. The advertising industry is very ephemeral, and Trish was keen to do something that would last 'forever'. She argued that nobody in Australia had yet done what she longed to do: open a lovely, chic, comfortable place that offered both stylish accommodation *and* outstanding food. She believed we were the perfect team to do it. She loved making things look beautiful and I loved to cook. Trish insisted it would be like cooking for a group of friends; I'd have the time and space to prepare interesting food for people who loved and appreciated it as much as I did. Add to this the fact that we would be living in beautiful surroundings and I was suddenly sold on the idea. Without the constant pressure of a crowded Sydney restaurant and the relentless day-in-day-out grind, this would be about making a lifestyle choice: we would only work on weekends; we would only cook for about ten guests; we would not offer a choice of menu. It would be like a wonderful house party where interesting people would come for a sybaritic weekend. And best of all, we would have lots of spare time for ourselves – for gardening, reading and enjoying a country lifestyle.

After searching for a suitable property in the Southern Highlands for a few months without much success, we happily accepted an invitation to spend the weekend at Kubba Roonga with Colette and Appley, a dear old friend of Trish's, who was an antique dealer. After enjoying a wonderful Sunday lunch, Trish and Appley and I opted to go for an afternoon stroll around Blackheath. It was then that we happened to look over a fence into the back garden of a most beautiful house, built in the classic colonial style of the 1880s. We'd walked these same streets a hundred times; why had we never noticed it before today? Even though it was located on the outer edges of the village, the house was surrounded by banks of rhododendron hedges and a stand of tall pine trees that gave the property an air of privacy. When we walked around the front of the house we found a gate that was chained shut and a sign that read: 'Trespassers Will Be Prosecuted'. Despite the stern warning, I found a passage through the hedges and Appley and I squeezed through the gap to have an illegal look around. At first, Little Miss Goody Two Shoes, Trish, stood back, saying, 'Look at the sign. You aren't supposed to go in!'

Eventually, curiosity crumbled her resolve and she snuck in for a snoop, too. The house was clearly empty. The shutters were closed tight and it was all very neglected and

DANY AND LUCIANO PAVAROTTI, SYDNEY OPERA HOUSE, 1983

overgrown and yet oh-so-romantic and beautiful. There was a large verandah that hugged three sides of the house and a mature garden that tumbled down for about a hectare next to an old clay tennis court. When we arrived back at Colette's we were still full of excitement. 'Oh there's the most beautiful house and garden only two streets away from you that we've never noticed before'.

As the weeks went by, Trish and I continued our search for a house in the Southern Highlands. Then, one morning, the phone rang at about eight o'clock, which was very early for us. It was Appley. 'Trish. Guess what?' she said. 'Your dream house is for sale!'

'Huh? What dream house?'

'The one we found at Blackheath!'

'Well,' said Appley. 'Do you have your copy of this month's *National Trust* magazine? I just opened mine and there it was. It's the house that we were looking at and it's for sale.'

After inspecting the property, Trish and I fell madly in love with it. But we thought, 'Oh, dear. It's in Blackheath of all places.' Yes, it would be good to be close to Nanna as she grew older, but it was far too close to Glenella. I wasn't at all keen to be competing for

Trish argued that nobody in Australia had yet done what she longed to do: open a lovely, chic, comfortable place that offered both stylish accommodation and outstanding food.

customers with my sister and brother-in-law. It would be like history repeating itself; like when I opened Au Chabrol near Upstairs. I also thought the property was too small for an *auberge*; it only had five bedrooms, so we'd never make any money. But truly, the house and garden were the most beautiful we had ever seen.

'Okay Dany,' said Trish, very reasonably. 'Let's do this. Let's put in a ridiculous offer way below the asking price and see what happens. If we can get it cheaply enough, we'll have money to expand it later on.' Somehow she managed to convince me and we duly put in a low offer; I was sure it was a waste of time. Much to my horror, however, we got the call: our offer had been accepted! It was now time to panic. After paying the deposit we thought, 'Oh my God, where are we going to get the rest of the money from?' Our finances weren't great. Neither of us had proper jobs as we both worked as freelancers and, in those days, no Australian bank would be prepared to lend money to two people without full-time work.

Trish turned to her solicitor Tony for advice and straightaway he said: 'I believe you'd do marvellously at anything you turn your hand to. I'll loan you the money myself.' So he gave us the money and in August 1983 the house was ours.

Tarte aux oranges confites

CANDIED ORANGE TART

SERVES 6

THIS MAKES A GOOD FRUIT TART IN WINTER WHEN NAVEL ORANGES ARE IN SEASON. YOU CAN COOK THE ORANGES THE DAY BEFORE AS WELL AS MAKE THE PASTRY IF YOU DON'T HAVE ANY READY MADE IN THE FREEZER.

CANDIED ORANGES

2 oranges

150 g (5½ oz) caster (superfine) sugar

250 ml (9 fl oz/1 cup) water

300 g pâte sucrée (sweet short crust pastry)
   (see recipe page 329)

3 large eggs

160 g (5¾ oz) caster (superfine) sugar

2 lemons

160 g (5¾ oz) butter, melted

160 ml (5¼ fl oz) cream, plus extra
   to serve (optional)

120 g (4¼ oz) ground almonds

TO MAKE THE CANDIED ORANGES: Slice the unpeeled oranges into 5 mm (¼ inch) thick slices and set aside. Combine the sugar and water in a saucepan over medium heat, stirring to dissolve the sugar. Bring to the boil and add the sliced oranges and simmer for 20 minutes or until tender. Remove from the heat and macerate the orange slices in the syrup until the next day if possible.

Roll out the pastry between two sheets of baking paper until large enough to fit the base and side of a 27 cm (10¾ inch) loose-based tart tin. Line the tart tin with the pastry and trim away any excess pastry. Cover with plastic wrap and refrigerate for at least 20 minutes or until firm.

Preheat the oven to 180°C (350°F/Gas 4) and place a heavy cast-iron tray (to fit the tart tin) in oven. Using an electric mixer, beat the eggs with the caster sugar and the finely grated zest of 2 lemons and juice of 1 lemon. When white and frothy, add the warm melted butter, cream and more lemon juice if needed, it should taste tart. Add the ground almonds and mix well. Pour into the prepared tart tin, place on the preheated tray and bake for 30–45 minutes or until dark golden and almost set. (Make sure the bottom of the pastry is cooked.) Cool the tart in the tin on a wire rack.

Drain the orange slices from the syrup and arrange overlapping on top of the cooled tart. Bring the orange syrup to the boil and cook until reduced by half. Use to brush over the oranges. Serve with whipped cream, if desired.

Gâteau pour Pavarotti

LAYERED CHOCOLATE AND RASPBERRY CAKE FOR PAVAROTTI

SERVES 10

THIS IS THE RICH CHOCOLATE CAKE I MADE FOR THE GREAT LUCIANO PAVAROTTI TO PRESENT TO HIM AT A POST-OPERA PARTY IN HIS HONOUR. HE LOVED IT AND — AFTER EATING THREE SLICES — ASKED FOR THE RECIPE. THE CHOCOLATE CURLS REQUIRE A BIT OF PRACTICE, BUT THE EFFECT IS WORTH THE EFFORT FOR A SPECIAL OCCASION.

Preheat the oven to 200ºC (400ºF/Gas 6) and grease a 24 cm (9½ inch) round springform cake tin, lining the bottom with baking paper and greasing the paper.

TO MAKE THE SPONGE CAKE: Beat 3 egg yolks with 1 whole egg and the caster sugar until the mixture is pale and fluffy. Sift together the almonds, cocoa and flour and mix well by hand. Fold the flour mixture into the egg mixture with a large metal spoon, alternating with the melted butter.

Using an electric mixer, beat the egg whites with the sugar until the mixture forms a thick meringue. Mix 2 or 3 tablespoons of the meringue with the chocolate mix and then fold into the remaining meringue. Carefully spoon into the prepared cake tin and cook on the centre shelf of the oven for 25–30 minutes or until a skewer inserted into the centre comes out clean. Remove from the oven, wait 5 minutes, then remove from the tin to a wire rack to cool completely.

TO MAKE THE CHOCOLATE CREAM: Combine the chocolate and cream in a bowl over a saucepan of gently simmering water, stir until just melted, then chill for about 20 minutes or until a spreadable consistency.

TO MAKE THE RASPBERRY EAU-DE-VIE SYRUP: Stir the sugar and water in a saucepan over medium heat until dissolved. Bring to the boil and cook for 2 minutes, cool then add the eau-de-vie-de Framboise, to your taste. Cool.

Slice the sponge cake horizontally into 3 using a sharp serrated knife. Place the bottom layer on the serving dish, brush with one-third of the raspberry syrup, then spread with half the raspberry jam, then spread with one-quarter of the chocolate cream. Place the second cake layer on top and repeat with the syrup, jam and chocolate cream. Place the final layer of cake on top, brush with

SPONGE CAKE

5 eggs, 4 separated and 1 whole

125 g (4½ oz) caster (superfine) sugar

100 g (3½ oz/1 cup) ground almonds

70 g (2½ oz) good-quality cocoa powder

50 g (1¾ oz/⅓ cup) plain (all-purpose) flour

50 g (1¾ oz) unsalted butter, melted and cooled

55 g (2 oz/¼ cup) sugar

CHOCOLATE CREAM

450 g (1 lb) dark chocolate, chopped

350 ml (12 fl oz) cream

RASPBERRY EAU-DE-VIE SYRUP

55 g (2 oz/¼ cup) caster (superfine) sugar

200 ml (7 fl oz) water

60 ml (2 fl oz/¼ cup) 'eau-de-vie-de Framboise', or to taste

2 tablespoons seedless raspberry jam

CHOCOLATE CURLS

450 g (1 lb) dark chocolate

the remaining raspberry syrup, and spread the rest of the chocolate cream over the top and sides of the cake. Refrigerate until the cake is firm. Meanwhile, prepare the chocolate curls.

TO MAKE THE CHOCOLATE CURLS: Gently melt the chocolate in a bowl over a saucepan of gently simmering water. Pour the melted chocolate over the back of a very flat, heavy baking tray, or over a plastic mat made for this purpose. The chocolate should be even and only 1 mm thick. Refrigerate for a few moments to set. Then, using a metal blade-like spatula, gently scrape the chocolate into curls. If it breaks, allow to soften slightly at room temperature, if it forms pleats rather than curls, return it to the refrigerator for a few minutes. A steady, cool hand is needed here and 'practice makes perfect'.

To serve, arrange the chocolate curls in circles on top of the cake and serve. If not serving immediately, cover and refrigerate. Remove from the refrigerator 1 hour before serving.

AN AUBERGE NAMED CLEOPATRA

Baguettes, boulangeries and Blackheath

THE AUBERGE NAMED CLEOPATRA IN ITS FULL GLORY.

'AND NOW FOR SOMETHING COMPLETELY DIFFERENT,' BEGAN LEO SCHOFIELD'S REVIEW OF OUR NEW VENTURE IN 'GOOD LIVING'. THE *SYDNEY MORNING HERALD* HAD SENT A PHOTOGRAPHER TO BLACKHEATH, SO WE KNEW TO EXPECT AN ARTICLE. MOMENTS AFTER WALKING OUT THE GATE ON HIS WAY TO SCHOOL ON THE MORNING OF 23 OCTOBER 1984, BARNEY SUDDENLY BELTED BACK UP THE STEPS AND THROUGH THE FRONT DOOR. 'IT'S HERE, MUM. IT'S HERE!' HE SHOUTED, WAVING THE NEWSPAPER.

WE HAD BARELY FINISHED READING LEO'S GLOWING

review when the telephone began to ring off the hook. That was the power Leo had as a food critic; by the end of the week we were booked out until Christmas and our waiting list spilled into the next year.

Trish and I had relocated to Blackheath exactly one year earlier, when the beautiful rhododendrons were just coming into bloom. When explorer George Evans (of Evans Lookout fame) built our Blackheath house in the 1880s, he named it 'Eirene' – from the Greek word meaning 'peace'. It described perfectly our secluded setting, which truly was an oasis of calm. Over its hundred-year history, Eirene had been owned by a string of high-profile people such as: William Henry Hargraves, one of the first big landowners in Blackheath; John Harris, five-time Lord Mayor of Sydney (who commissioned Paul Sorenson to design the once-beautiful garden); and Charles Morgan, a member of the House of Representatives. By the 1960s, many of the property's original outbuildings – such as the library, ballroom, stables, coach-house and outdoor kitchen – were so rundown they had to be demolished.

The doctors who owned Eirene before we did had used it as a weekend retreat and renamed the house 'Marnyong'. But as far as we could tell their only contribution to the home's 'improvement' was placing iron bars on the inside of every window so it felt like a prison. There were many beautiful mature trees in the garden, none of which had been pruned properly for years. Everything was overgrown. There were no flowers and lots of dense patches that were impenetrable to light. The indoor kitchen wasn't big enough to swing a cat, there was only one very outdated bathroom. In short, there was plenty of work to be done to transform Marnyong into the sybaritic *auberge* of our dreams.

Our architect friend Geoffrey, an expert on historic house restorations, helped us with the plans. We added a commercial kitchen, converted the attic into two bedrooms with a bathroom; created an apartment for ourselves with a sitting room/office; and raised the iron-clad roof to build an inside staircase up to a bedroom and a bathroom.

To help keep us afloat financially, Trish continued to work as a stylist in Sydney from Monday to Friday, leaving me to project-manage the build and keep on top of the paperwork. We knew we would be spending much of our lives in the kitchen and, because we were completely rebuilding it, we had a chance to make it both functional and beautiful. No ugly, industrial-style, window-less workplace for us, thanks very much! Trish, ever the romantic, would settle for nothing less than the ideal French country kitchen. We both wanted a lovely working environment that would be an expression of our happiness and therefore conducive to creating wonderful food. The design included enormous windows that would flood the space with natural light and allow us to look out over the garden while we worked.

BARNEY WAS NOW THIRTEEN AND, TYPICALLY, LIKED his independence; he refused to move into the house and lived in a room that had once been the garage. Barney, who attended a local school, also thought the renovations were a wonderful adventure and loved walking across the boards over the trenches. With Trish often away for work and her eldest son Stephen now living and working in Sydney, Barney and I kept each other company; after cooking his dinner, I'd help him with his homework. I wasn't much good at Latin, but French was another matter.

Trish would travel from Sydney to Blackheath every Friday night and despair at the lack of progress that had been made with the renovations. As someone who worked in the frenetic world of advertising, she was used to getting instant results. The kitchen looked like a battlefield, all trenches and pipes, without a floor or wall in sight! On the rare occasions that the builders had advanced at a pace that Trish found acceptable she would then give them reason to regress: 'Oh, no. I don't want that hand basin there! I want it on the opposite wall. And don't tell me it can't be done.' Trish found some lovely old doors, too, which, because they were so crooked, caused further complications for the builders. The mundane practicalities of drains, sewerage lines and placement of power points were of no interest to Trish, as long as it 'looked right'.

When she wasn't working, Trish spent her time sourcing the fittings and furnishings that would make the house a home. We literally bought everything: from Persian rugs to light fixtures to toilet-roll holders and a reclaimed staircase. Trish's dream French country kitchen also demanded: lace curtains; large, white, porcelain Limoges cups and saucers; brass racks for the pots and pans; tiny moulds for making *petits fours*; three cookers (a Godin woodstove, electric ovens and a big professional propane gas cooker); fridges; a beautiful old French pâtisserie table and a black-and-white tiled floor. We spent months tracking down the company that imported the same blue-and-white wall tiles that Maman had in her kitchen in Vélines. Trish had spent the past fifteen years gathering props for photo shoots and the many contacts she made paid off handsomely for us. For our dining room, Trish found white damask antique tablecloths and napkins; a silver candelabra with ivory-coloured candles; porcelain fruit stands and vases; Limoges plates; and classic crystal glasses.

Trish also set to work furnishing the five bedrooms. Each room was named after a French flower and featured an eclectic mix of antiques, *objets d'art* and paintings that didn't cost a fortune. Some walls were even upholstered with a seventeenth century document-print French fabric that came direct from the Palais Royal in Paris. The French specialist we found to do the job had just finished upholstering some walls in the Palace of Fontainebleau in France and we were suitably impressed. The beds were adorned with French white-cotton embroidered quilts and, as one reviewer put it, 'were like sleeping on powder puffs'. Loveliest of all were the two 'blue rooms' in the attic that shared a sky-lit bathroom. The classic-styled bathrooms all had brass fittings and old-fashioned tubs with clawed feet, bath oils, Roger Gallet soaps and that essential French invention – the bidet! To keep with the spirit of romantic escape, we decided the rooms would have no telephones and no televisions, but plenty of fresh flowers.

Trish persuaded a set painter she knew to come up and stay for a month to decorate the walls downstairs. Though a bit of a madman, he was a true artist. After arriving with his three-legged dog, he would wake up at about noon and drink every drop of wine in the house before finally getting into his groove by about ten o'clock each evening. Despite his often bizarre behaviour, he gave Trish exactly what she wanted: delicate sponged 'Rosé in the Sunshine' for the dining-room walls; 'Eau de Nil' in the hallway; and 'Sun-drenched Yellow' in the sitting room. When he went to Blackheath to have a beer, the locals – a mostly rough bunch of miners and truck drivers – wondered what to make of the unusual artist with the three-legged dog, camp Scottish accent and anarchist views.

It's fair to say that the two of us often went a teeny bit over the top with our attention to detail and that our shared penchant for perfection often proved pricey; in order to complete our auberge we had to borrow another $25,000. At one point, after finding some antique pillowcases she adored, Trish decided that we simply must have big, square, French-style pillows for the beds. Trish asked an industry contact who was a crack seamstress to replicate the pillowcases – which were pure cotton with intricate ruffles and Swiss lace – and she ordered about forty, enough for all the beds. Although they cost a fortune, they looked wonderful.

As our auberge began to take shape, Trish and I had started toying with names for our new venture. I couldn't even pronounce its current name, Marnyong, so that wasn't an option. In the end, it was the neighbourhood children – James, Barney, Sebastian and Juliette – who christened the house. The children, who were already firm friends after our August in the Ardèche, all had remarkable radars for treats and used to tear around from house to house looking for food. They knew just where to find a slice of cake or fresh-baked bread and they'd hang around waiting for it to emerge from the oven. Being asked to do a chore, such as chopping the wood, was the signal to quickly hop back on their bikes to see what was cooking at the next house. While Trish and I struggled to settle on a name for the house, the kids started calling it 'Cleopatra', after the name of the

Ragoût d'asperges en tartelette

ASPARAGUS, SPRING ONION
AND CHERVIL TARTLETS

SERVES 4

THIS IS A VERSION OF THE ASPARAGUS RAGOÛT ONE FINDS ON THE TABLE OF EVERY HOME IN THE BORDELAIS
AND THE DORDOGNE DURING THE WHITE ASPARAGUS SEASON IN SPRING. I FIND GREEN ASPARAGUS ARE BETTER
FOR THIS RECIPE AND I ALWAYS COOK AN EXTRA PASTRY SHELL IN CASE OF BREAKAGE.

PASTRY SHELLS

10 g (¼ oz) butter, melted

250 g (9 oz) pâte brisée (short crust pastry)
   (recipe see page 328), chilled

ASPARAGUS FILLING

2 bunches thin green asparagus

10 g (¼ oz) butter

2 tablespoons olive oil

40 g (1½ oz) piece of prosciutto, finely diced

4 spring onions, finely diced

60 ml (2 fl oz/¼ cup) duck demi-glaçe or
   2 tablespoons reduced chicken stock

1 small bunch chervil

160 ml (5¼ fl oz) cream

2 tarragon sprigs, leaves picked

TO MAKE THE PASTRY SHELLS: Brush the insides of four 10.5 cm (4¼ inch) loose-based tartlet tins with the melted butter. Roll out the pastry on a lightly floured work surface to 3 mm (⅛ inch) thick and use to line the tins, trimming any excess. Place on a baking tray and refrigerate for 20 minutes.

Preheat the oven to 200°C (400°F/Gas 6). Line the base and sides of the pastry shells with aluminium foil, fill with dried beans or pastry weights and refrigerate for 10 minutes. Bake the pastry shells for 10 minutes, then remove the foil and weights. Reduce the temperature to 180°C (350°F/Gas 4) and bake for a further 5–10 minutes or until evenly coloured and light golden. Cool a little, before carefully removing the shells from the tins. Place them back on the baking tray. Turn the oven temperature down to 160°C (315°F/Gas 2–3).

TO MAKE THE ASPARAGUS FILLING: Trim 1 cm (½ inch) from the asparagus bases and, using a vegetable peeler, peel from the base to about halfway up the spears. Cut off the tips, at about 7 cm (2¾ inches) long, and set aside. Cut the remaining asparagus stems into 2 cm (¾ inch) lengths.

Melt the butter and oil in a medium–large frying pan over medium heat. Add the prosciutto and spring onion and sauté for 1 minute. Add the asparagus stems and cook, stirring, for 2–3 minutes. Add the duck demi-glaçe, reduce the heat to very low, cover and cook for 2–3 minutes.

Reserve some of the chervil sprigs for garnish and finely chop the remaining sprigs. Add the cream, chopped chervil and tarragon to the asparagus stems and cook for 10–15 minutes or until reduced to a creamy consistency. Meanwhile, place the asparagus tips in a steamer basket placed over a saucepan of simmering water and steam for 3–4 minutes. Fill the pastry cases with the asparagus cream, top with the steamed asparagus tips and garnish with a sprig of chervil.

Artichauts farcis à la Barigoule

STUFFED ARTICHOKES

SERVES 4

ARTICHOKES MAKE AN EXCELLENT ENTRÉE AND THIS RECIPE IS TYPICAL
OF COUNTRY HOME COOKING OF THE VERY BEST KIND.

4 violet artichokes (see note)

1 onion, finely diced

1 carrot, finely diced

1 tablespoon olive oil

200 ml (7 fl oz) white wine

1 thyme sprig

200–400 ml (7 fl oz–14 fl oz) chicken
    stock or water

STUFFING

1 tablespoon olive oil

50 g (1¾ oz) prosciutto, lean and fat, very finely diced

1 onion, very finely diced

200 g (7 oz) button mushrooms, chopped

1 walnut-sized piece of day-old bread, crust removed,
    soaked in chicken stock

1 large garlic clove, crushed

1 heaped tablespoon chopped flat leaf
    (Italian) parsley

1 egg yolk

4 thin slices of pancetta, to cover each artichoke

Cut the stems from the artichokes, slice off the top one-third from each artichoke and remove any tough outside leaves. Blanch in boiling salted water for 5 minutes. Drain upside down. When cool, remove the hairy choke from the centre of each artichoke to make enough space for the stuffing.

TO MAKE THE STUFFING: Heat the olive oil in a frying pan, add the prosciutto and sauté quickly, add the onion, brown lightly, then add the mushrooms and stir-fry for 2–3 minutes. Remove from heat. Squeeze the liquid out of the bread and add to the pan along with the garlic, parsley and egg yolk. Check the seasoning and mix well. Divide stuffing between artichokes, cover with a slice of pancetta and secure with kitchen twine.

Preheat the oven to 180ºC (350ºF/Gas 4). In a heavy-based roasting pan, just big enough to hold the 4 artichokes, place the onion and carrot in the olive oil. Place over medium-high heat and arrange the artichokes on top. Season with salt and pepper and let the onion start to colour, then add wine and thyme. When this has reduced by half, add enough stock or water to come halfway up the artichokes. Bring to the boil, cover and transfer to the oven to bake for 20 minutes. Remove the lid and return to the oven for a further 8 minutes or until the pancetta has browned. Remove from the oven, and remove and discard the kitchen twine. Check seasoning and serve in the roasting pan, or place each artichoke on an entrée plate surrounded by vegetables and cooking juices.

NOTE: Violet artichokes are a variety of globe artichoke that originated in southern France where they are loved for their exceptional flavour and tenderness. If unavailable, subsitute with any other variety of globe artichoke.

Huitres aux épinards, champignons farcis

POACHED OYSTERS WITH STUFFED MUSHROOMS

SERVES 4

I TOOK THE CRÉPINETTE WITH OYSTERS FROM BORDEAUX ON A TRIP TO THAILAND AND VIETNAM. THIS RECIPE
DEMANDS SOME EXPERIENCE IN THE KITCHEN AND IT IS NECESSARY TO WORK QUICKLY AT THE END.
IF YOU HAVE A MEAT GRINDER, IT IS PREFERABLE THAT YOU DO YOUR OWN MINCING. IF YOU DON'T HAVE
A MEAT GRINDER AT HAND, BUY FRESH UNSEASONED PORK MINCE FROM YOUR BUTCHER.

TO MAKE THE STUFFED MUSHROOMS: Wipe the mushroom caps dry, break out the stems, then clean and dice the stems. Brush the caps with oil and set on a baking tray, cover and place in the refrigerator. Sauté the stems quickly in some grapeseed oil or until tender and set aside to cool. Drain the cèpes and finely dice and add to mushroom mixture, reserve their juice.

Combine the pork mince, crab meat, mushroom stems, egg, fish sauce, wine and pepper and mix well. Stuff the mushrooms using a soup spoon, the mix should be very heaped up and smooth. Refrigerate until needed.

Open the oysters, discard the shells, put them and any juice from the shells in a strainer over a small saucepan. Measure the juice obtained and add fish stock to make up to 250 ml (9 fl oz/1 cup), if necessary. Add the vermouth and 50 ml (1³/₄ fl oz) reserved cèpes juice, then cook over medium heat for 15–20 minutes or until reduced by half then set aside. Keep the oysters in the refrigerator if you are not finishing the dish at once. You can prepare ahead up to this point.

Half an hour before serving, preheat the oven to 200ºC (400ºF/Gas 6) and drizzle the mushrooms with a little grapeseed oil. Bake for 15–20 minutes or until they are slightly brown on top. Set aside and keep warm. In a frying pan quickly wilt the spinach, drain well and keep warm. In another frying pan, gently warm the reduced sauce and then add the oysters and cook for only 1 minute to warm through.

Spread the spinach on four warm entrée plates. Arrange 6 oysters (per plate) on the spinach. Place the sauce back on the heat and reduce a little more, whisk in the butter and a few drops of lemon. Spoon about two tablespoons of sauce over each serving of oysters, place a mushroom on each plate and serve.

2 dozen large oysters in their shells, not open
250 ml (9 fl oz/1 cup) fish stock, if needed
100 ml (3¹/₂ fl oz) dry white vermouth
400 g (14 oz) English spinach, stalks trimmed
1 small knob butter
juice of ¹/₂ lemon

STUFFED MUSHROOMS
4 large (about 6–7 cm/2¹/₂–2³/₄ inch diameter)
    cap mushrooms
grapeseed oil, for cooking
2 g dried cèpe (porcini) mushrooms soaked in 80 ml
    (2¹/₂ fl oz/¹/₃ cup) tepid water for 30 minutes
240 g (9 oz) pork belly, minced (or pork mince)
160 g (5³/₄ oz) raw crabmeat, coarsley chopped
1 small egg, beaten
2 teaspoons Thai fish sauce
2 teaspoons dry white wine
1 pinch ground pepper

a. Cèpe. — *b.* Morille. — *c.* Mousseron.
d. Champignon de couche.

street. We mulled it over for a millisecond: why not just keep calling it Cleopatra? When Leo Schofield called one night to say he had heard the rumour that the *auberge* was to be called Cleopatra he told us he thought it was camp and dreadful and so, of course, that's what cemented our decision. What fun! What we didn't know, then, was that there was another notorious 'Cleopatra' in Sydney, which was a massage parlour for gentlemen. Had we known that, we might have come up with another name to avoid many confusing phone-calls.

In readiness for the opening of Cleopatra, I planted a geometric garden of herbs behind the kitchen; we had thyme, parsley, basil, chives, rosemary, sage, verbena, dill, lettuce, sorrel, tarragon and – two of my particular favourites – chervil and savory. Before the sun went down each day, I would go out to pick all the fresh herbs I needed, right there at the back door.

I wanted our bread to taste exactly the way that little bakery in Vélines smelled and, in order to achieve this, I needed to find just the right combination of flours... It took me weeks and weeks of trial and error... to come up with a great baguette …

When we opened Cleopatra there weren't any bakeries to speak of in Blackheath. And there certainly wasn't any French country bread on the market, so, from the day we opened, we resolved to make our own. While we were still in Sydney I had started reading everything I could about the art of making bread. I had advanced beyond *Le Guide Marabout de la Pâtisserie et des Desserts* and onto the far more precise measurements and directions in *Gaston Lenôtre*, one of many French cookbooks from the 1970s. Although my friends in France also sent plenty of bread recipes, they weren't much help, as they always required the use of flour that was simply unavailable in Australia at the time.

One of my most enduring memories of France is the lingering smell of country bread. There was a tiny, old-fashioned *boulangerie* in Vélines run by a baker named Platon, who was always dusted in a fine coat of flour. Platon's *boulangerie* was, essentially, a house with woodstoves out the back and scales hanging from a ceiling. I loved visiting Platon each day and breathing in that aroma of freshly baked country bread.

I wanted our bread to taste exactly the way that little bakery in Vélines smelled and, in order to achieve this, I needed to find just the right combination of flours. I mixed and mixed, using various proportions of buckwheat and semolina (to make the crust crunchier) and rye. It took me weeks of trial and error and a lot of taste tests to come up with a great baguette, made from four different flours. When we eventually opened, we would bake the bread in the Godin woodstove which we named Marcelline after

Cleopatra
is a country house.

To come and stay at Cleopatra
is the feeling of
staying with good friends.

And to enjoy,
once more, the fabulous cooking of
Dany Chouet.

You arrive at Cleopatra
on a Friday evening (dinner will
be served from 8 p.m.).

As Cleopatra is not a
restaurant there is no choice of
dishes. (Unless by special
arrangement.) The menu is
decided entirely by the season
and Dany's imagination.

The house itself is classic
Australian colonial – one of the
first six houses built in
Blackheath, circa 1880.

There are five double
bedrooms for guests – decorated
by Trish Mullene – named
Jasmin, Lilas, Glycines, Narcisse
and Jonquille.

As the names suggest, the
rooms have a warm country
feeling. With old country
furniture, crisp white linen and,
of course, fresh flowers.

And in the spirit of Cleopatra's
relaxed hospitality, breakfast
will be served in your room.

Curl up with a book in front of
an open fire, walk in our
hectare of wonderful garden
or chase a ball around our
old tennis court.

But apart from that there
is not much else for you to do at
Cleopatra.

Except eat and sleep.

THE FIRST BROCHURE FOR CLEOPATRA, 1984

Soupe de moules à l'orange

MUSSEL SOUP SCENTED WITH ORANGE AND SAFFRON

SERVES 6

I HAVE MADE THIS RECIPE TO SERVE SIX BECAUSE YOU WON'T BE SORRY IF THERE IS ANY LEFT THE NEXT DAY, THAT IS, IF YOUR GUESTS DON'T WANT SECONDS.

Scrub the mussels thoroughly under running water but do not soak them or you will lose their precious liquor. Place them in a pot with one-third of the shallots and the wine. Cover and cook, shaking and stirring, as they open transfer to a colander above a deep bowl. Discard any mussels that do not open.

Remove the mussels from their shells, removing their hairy beards, and discard the shells. Place the mussels in a bowl and strain the cooking juices into a separate bowl and set aside. Rinse out the saucepan.

Sauté all the vegetables and garlic except the tomatoes in the olive oil over medium heat. Stir often with a wooden spoon and do not let it colour. After 3–4 minutes add the tomatoes, cook for another 3–4 minutes then add the hot fish stock, reserved mussel juice and saffron. Cook for 30 minutes over medium heat until the vegetables are very tender.

Now you can either blend the soup in the pot with a hand-held blender, or pass it twice through a mouli, first using the largest holes and then through the fine holes, so as to keep all the flavours and the consistency.

You can prepare ahead to this point.

To finish the soup, steam the extra leek for 4 minutes and set aside. Heat the soup, when simmering, add the cream and the orange zest and juice. Season with salt and freshly ground black pepper. Let it simmer for only a few minutes. Place 8–10 mussels in each soup plate, ladle over the boiling soup and place the steamed leeks in the centre of each.

1 kg (2 lb 4 oz) mussels
3 French shallots, diced
100 ml (3½ fl oz) dry white wine
2 carrots, diced
2 small onions, diced
1 large celery stalk, diced
1 small leek, white part only, thinly sliced, plus
*   1 large leek, extra, cut into julienne*
3 garlic cloves, chopped
2 tablespoons olive oil
1 x 400 g (14 oz) tinned Italian peeled tomatoes,
*   drained and chopped or 250 g (9 oz)*
*   chopped fresh tomato*
2 litres (70 fl oz/8 cups) fish stock, heated
2.5 g (20–25) saffron threads
120–150 ml (4–5 fl oz) cream
finely grated zest of ½ orange
juice of 1 orange

my great-grandmother. The bread, which we cooked in a 200°C oven, had to be baked in batches, four loaves at a time, and we had to be on hand to turn it so it didn't cook more on one side than the other. In the beginning, mixing the dough was Trish's job, but sometimes she was so tired she'd forget all about it. After falling into bed around midnight Trish would suddenly sit bolt upright and groan: 'Oh no, I haven't done the bloody bread mix!' So back to the kitchen she'd go. Despite the effort involved to cook fresh bread daily, the results were worth it. We presented the baguette whole on a breadboard with a knife – as you would expect in a home in the French countryside. Our lives were made simpler when we finally received proper baguette moulds from France.

We also made the flaky mini-croissants and *petits pains au lait*, which we served for breakfast, along with a selection of our home-made jams. I didn't want to make the more traditional brioches, which I found too rich and sweet. Instead, we served the *pains au lait* halved and buttered with jam; they were often more popular than croissants.

Brillat-Savarin, the late, great eighteenth-century gastronome once said: '*Convier quelqu'un, c'est se charger de son bonheur pendant tout le temps qu' il est sous notre toit.*' (When we invite someone, it means we are responsible for their happiness the entire time they are under our roof.) That was our vision at Cleopatra: we wanted people to come to our place to relax and enjoy. We didn't want them to have to make any decisions or worry about anything. Everything would be looked after. It was a philosophy expressed in our very first brochure, designed and printed by Gary, one of Trish's old advertising friends. It was an elegant and simple cream-coloured card entitled *L'art de vivre*, with elegant tissue-paper-lined envelopes that we posted around to our friends, former customers and media types. When Trish asked Gary how much we owed him, he just shook his head. 'No, no. It's a gift. I think you have a great idea and I really want you to succeed.' We were blessed to have such wonderful friends.

On a practical level, our plan for Cleopatra went like this: we'd offer weekend packages for ten friends who would arrive in time for a low-key Friday night dinner of, say, soup, fish and a fruit tart. We'd then turn up the charm for breakfast which would be served either on the verandah or on a tray beside the bed. The Saturday lunch, weather permitting, would be served exclusively to hotel guests in the garden and then we would reach the weekend's crescendo for the Saturday dinner. Sunday lunch would be a lazy affair and, depending on the season, would be either enjoyed al fresco or in front of a crackling fire. Our ten guests would then make their way back to Sydney, relaxed and refreshed after a weekend of pure indulgence. Some guests chose to arrive for Sunday lunch and then leave after breakfast the next day, giving us the rest of the week to unwind. Running Cleopatra wouldn't be taxing. Oh, no. It would be fun! We'd be nestled in the Blue Mountains with a beautiful garden backdrop, living in a beautiful house with a beautiful kitchen, making beautiful food to serve on beautiful plates in a beautiful dining room. We would enjoy this idyllic existence for five years and then reassess our plans. It seemed like a splendid idea.

My friend Yvette, from the old Au Chabrol days, came to Cleopatra for a few months to help us get started. She did everything from painting and hanging curtains to setting up and serving, making breakfast, making beds, tending to the fireplaces and washing the lettuce. We also had her sleeping in a different room each night to report on the comfort of the bed, the lighting, the effectiveness of the curtains and the view of the plumbing from the bathtub.

Cleopatra opened on 27 July 1984 and was filled for the first two weekends by our closest friends. Trish lavished so much tender loving care on each detail that our friends felt as if they had stumbled onto a romantic film set; it was infused with *calme, luxe et volupté*. Trish spent hours doing fresh flower arrangements for the rooms and Caravaggio-esque fruit bowls to decorate the tables. We spent a fortune on candles and fruit alone! Trish also wrote all the menus out by hand in beautiful black ink; they, too, were works of art.

Once we had opened, Yvette would stay at Nanna Jane's house every Friday to Sunday, and then take the train back to Sydney. As well as being lovely for Trish and Barney to have Nanna in Blackheath, it helped us out immensely as a boarding house for our staff. Luckily, Nanna Jane was very sweet and didn't mind this arrangement one bit.

Despite living in Australia for years, Yvette had retained her cute French accent and even agreed to dress up like the archetypical French maid – in a black dress with an antique, frilly, white-lace apron. Yvette's uniform had Trish's advertising friends in hysterics: 'You just can't resist, can you? You even art-direct the staff.'

On the morning after our official opening night I was on duty to help with breakfast. After that it was agreed that I would never work that shift again; I was far too grumpy! It's true. I wasn't much of a morning person and neither was Trish. I need a quiet cup of coffee and time to slowly wake up before I start rushing about. By the end of the second week we had hired a girl to come over and help Yvette make breakfast, which consisted of freshly squeezed juice, home-made jams, flaky mini-croissants and the *petits pains au lait*.

At first it was just the three of us making the lunches and dinners. I did most of the cooking, Trish made the desserts and bread and served the food, and Yvette was there to assist Trish. Trish would help me garnish the entrées before whipping off her apron and teetering out in high heels to the dining room with the dishes; she'd then tie her apron on again to help create the main courses. Having never worked in a restaurant before, Trish was happy to have Yvette on hand for the first few weeks. As well as showing her how to set up and serve, Yvette taught her a few golden rules, such as: 'Never go back to the kitchen empty-handed.' Up until this point Trish only understood how restaurants worked from a customer's perspective; so it was all new to Trish – as were the shooting pains she felt in her lower back by the end of the first weekend.

I will never forget our first two August weekends at Cleopatra; we were run off our feet. Then, suddenly, not long after we opened, the bookings dried up. Trish's immediate response was to panic, but I told her: 'Calm down. You don't know what's coming. I've been through all this before. Don't worry; just enjoy it!' So she'd potter about the garden, digging up bulbs, before separating them and arranging them in an artistic pattern. She even remembers thinking at the time: 'Yes, I must remember this day when I could spend

Le cassoulet

DANY'S CASSOULET

SERVES 8–12

IN SOUTH-WEST FRANCE, THE CASSOULET, SYMBOLIC DISH OF OCCITANIE, HAS ACHIEVED NATIONAL STATUS AND HAS MANY VARIATIONS. IT IS A COMPLETE MEAL, DOES NOT NEED ANYTHING BEFORE AND VERY LITTLE AFTER, EXCEPT MAYBE A SMALL GLASS OF ARMAGNAC. THE CASSOULET, ONE OF MY FAVOURITE MEALS TO COOK, GATHERS TOGETHER ALL THE INGREDIENTS I LOVE. MY CASSOULET IS FAR FROM BEING *CATHOLIQUE* AS WE SAY IN FRENCH AND IS NOT MADE IN THE TRADITIONAL WAY, BUT AS PROSPER MONTAGNÉ (AUTHOR OF THE *LAROUSSE GASTRONOMIQUE*) SAID: 'ONLY BADLY INFORMED PEOPLE SAY THERE IS ONLY ONE WAY TO MAKE CASSOULET.'

½ garlic bulb, finely chopped

1 bunch flat-leaf (Italian) parsley, finely chopped

1.5 kg (3 lb 5 oz) neck of pork (scotch fillet)

1 kg (2 lb 4 oz) lean pork belly

800 g (1 lb 12 oz) pork skin, without fat

1.5 litres (52 fl oz/6 cups) dry white wine

1 tablespoon black peppercorns

1 large bouquet garni (12 thyme sprigs,
   2 bay leaves, 20 parsley sprigs)

1 kg (2 lb 4 oz) dried white Great Northern or
   cannellini beans

1 brown onion, unpeeled, studded with 2 cloves

1 bay leaf

250 g (9 oz) speck, diced

60 g (2¼ oz) duck fat

3 medium carrots, diced into 1 cm (½ inch) cubes

3–4 large onions, finely diced

4 large very ripe tomatoes, peeled, seeded and chopped
   (or 800 g (1 lb 12 oz) tinned Italian
   peeled tomatoes)

½ garlic bulb, extra, chopped

1.5 litres (52 fl oz/6 cups) chicken, pork or duck stock

bones reserved from the pork belly

THE DAY BEFORE SERVING: Combine the garlic and parsley and season to taste with salt and pepper. Remove excess fat from pork neck and trim. Pierce holes along the meat and insert one-third of the garlic and parsley mixture deep into the meat. Tie up with string like a roast. Leave the skin on the pork belly, remove the bones and reserve them for later.

Arrange the pork skins flat on the work surface, season with salt and pepper and spread thickly with the remaining garlic and parsley mixture. Roll up like a thick sausage and secure with string at 1.5 cm (⅝ inch) intervals.

Place the three cuts of meat in a large container. Cover with wine, sprinkle over the black peppercorns and immerse the bouquet garni. Cover and refrigerate. Ensure you turn the meats around in the marinade once during the 24 hours.

TO PREPARE THE DISH: Place the beans in a large stainless-steel stock pot, cover generously with cold water, add the studded onion and the bay leaf. Bring to the boil and cook until they are only half-cooked and swollen, just a bit more than blanched.

Strain the beans into a colander and refresh under cold water. Discard the onion and bay leaf and leave the beans to drain.

Preheat the oven to 200ºC (400ºF/Gas 6). Remove the meat from the marinade and place the pork neck only in a roasting pan with a little marinade and place the other meats in a bowl covered in refrigerator until needed. Strain the marinade (reserving the bouquet garni) and set aside. Roast the pork neck, basting often with a little of the marinade. Cook for about 1 hour and 15 minutes, then remove and set aside. Then collect the roasting juices and set aside.

In a 15 litre (3.9 gallon) stainless-steel heavy-based saucepan, fry the speck with the duck fat until golden. Add the carrot and onion and sauté gently for about 15 minutes without browning. Add the tomato and reduce to a nice, thick consistency. Season with freshly ground black pepper only. Add the drained beans, pour in the reserved marinade from the meat, and bring gently to the boil. Bury the pork belly and pork skin-roll, reserved bouquet garni, pork belly bones and garlic in the beans. Add enough stock to cover the beans by 2 cm (³/₄ inch).

Do not stir the mixture any more. Simmer, covered, for at least 1–2 hours or until the pork belly is tender (checking with a skewer to see if it is done) and beans are soft but still holding their shape.

Remove the pork belly and pork skin roll from the pot. Set aside with the roast pork neck to cool. If they are to be used the day after, cool and keep well covered in the refrigerator. Pour beans out of the pot into a bowl and stir to distribute the flavours. Discard the bouquet garni and the pork bones and check the seasoning.

SERVING THE CASSOULET: Preheat the oven to 200ºC (400ºF/Gas 6). You need two 4-litre (1 gallon) earthenware or cast-iron pots for this. Divide the beans between the pots so that they come halfway up the side of each pot. Thickly slice the roast pork neck and the pork belly, then remove the string and thinly slice the pork skin roll. Chargrill the pork sausages on one side only (or cook under the grill/broiler). Remove the duck legs from their fat.

Divide the duck legs, pork neck slices, pork belly slices, pork skin slices and sausages between each pot, pressing the meat and skin so that most of it is covered by the beans and some of the meat is still visible so that it will brown during cooking. Pour over the reserved roast pork juice.

Mix together the breadcrumbs, garlic and parsley and sprinkle generously all over the top. Drizzle a little liquid duck fat on top of the breadcrumbs to crisp them. Bake in the oven for 30–40 minutes or until golden brown on top, very hot, and sizzling around the edges.

6 thick pork Toulouse-style sausages,
  halved lengthways
12 confit duck legs (see recipe page 320)
80 g (2³/₄ oz) dry breadcrumbs
1 large garlic clove, crushed
1 bunch flat-leaf (Italian) parsley, chopped
melted duck fat, to drizzle

the whole time in the garden.' It was true! After Leo Schofield's review appeared in the *Herald*, Trish wouldn't have another weekend like that in the garden for seventeen years.

Before too long, it became clear that our original plan to host parties of ten was not going to work. Some of our customers would phone, dying to come, but agonise that they couldn't get together enough people at the same time. Others would say: 'I know the accommodation is booked out but can we please come to eat?' Finally, we relented, rearranging the restaurant until we eventually catered to about fifty people, ten of whom would be accommodated in our beautifully restored guest bedrooms. Business really snowballed when we lifted the cap on numbers and the telephone was always ringing! We never suspected that just taking bookings would take up so much time and, because we lived on the premises, we never had a break. Even when we put the answering machine on, we felt compelled to take the call.

The magnificent eighty-year-old garden that cocooned us from the rest of the world really helped to give Cleopatra its special magic. Included in Paul Sorenson's design were plantings of exotic trees from Europe that grew well in the cooler climes of the Blue Mountains. There were dogwoods, magnolias and maples, rare conifers, birches, elms, apples and even an Irish strawberry tree, all surrounded by enormous rhododendrons that, every spring, put on a display that verged on being gaudy. In autumn, after the rains, I often found *cèpes* or slippery jack mushrooms under the trees to garnish the week's menu. At first no one would eat them, but by the mid-1990s I'd converted many of my customers, who even started requesting them.

In the morning mists of winter, Cleopatra had a special poetry about it. While I tended my herb garden, the flowers and shrubs were mostly Trish's domain. She knew

Aldo later told us that the dining room was bathed in the aroma of the bouillabaisse, *and that when the soup was served everyone fell into complete silence, broken only by the sounds of slurping and little moans of pleasure.*

little about gardens when we bought the place, but after studying up on the subject she got quite carried away redesigning the flower beds. Although we hired a gardener, Trish loved to work out there on weekdays and plant new beds of rare and interesting plants as well as a pretty array of forget-me-nots, bellis perennis, lupins, dianthus, delphiniums and roses. There were lots of roses – enough to supply the house with vases of cut flowers and attract a variety of birds. For our city guests it was a novelty to be woken up by a chorus of birdsongs from the kookaburras and parakeets. We even had an iridescent blue satin bowerbird that Trish catered to by planting blue flowers for it to line its nest. This was back in the days before everyone had a mobile phone, so Trish would stretch the phone cord as far as it would go on the verandah and balance it on the front steps next to the reservations book. When the phone rang Trish would throw down the secateurs, take off her gardening gloves and race back to the house, struggling to catch her breath so she wasn't panting when she lifted the receiver; it just wouldn't do if one of our customers thought they had mistakenly called a phone sex line! Trish would take the booking, walk back to the garden, put the gloves back on and pick up the secateurs. It was 'snip, snip, snip' then 'ring, ring, ring' over and over again. Often Trish would race to the phone only to find that the call was actually coming from the lyrebirds, mimicking the sound of a ringing telephone!

Trish and I often brought extra work on ourselves; in our efforts to source the best ingredients we would make the drive down to Sydney on Thursday with a lengthy shopping list. As well as schlepping all over town to buy provisions, we'd try to squeeze in lunch and dinner at a restaurant, and fit in a film or concert, too. In those early days I once found such an exciting selection of fish at the markets that I decided to make *bouillabaisse* for our Friday night guests. Because the soup is quite labour-intensive to make, it wasn't offered very often, so Trish rang a few of our regulars to let them know what was cooking. Before she knew it we had twenty-eight orders for *bouillabaisse*. The tables of four quickly grew to tables of eight so it was a bit of a nightmare in the kitchen. One diner that night was Aldo Zuzza, an Italian restaurateur friend and celebrated elder of the Sydney restaurant world. As usual, I *moulinéed* the soup at the last minute and there was poor Trish, racing to and from the kitchen with the big porcelain tureens of *bouillabaisse* and all the trimmings and heaving platters of fish for six to eight people. Aldo later told us that the dining room was bathed in the aroma of the *bouillabaisse*, and that when the soup was served everyone fell into complete silence, broken only by the sounds of slurping and little moans of pleasure.

'Trish and Dany, you need me to advise you,' Aldo told us that night. 'You need to enclose the verandah in glass. You need to have more space, more tables, more covers! You need to make more money!' We thought about it – for exactly two seconds – we weren't going to ruin our beautiful colonial house for mere money; aesthetics would always come first.

Right from the start, Cleopatra attracted fantastic customers. The Ryans were among our first regulars; they were a wonderful couple from the country who stopped to stay with us on their way to the Easter Show. During the dinner service, Mr Ryan kept getting up to go outside, telling Trish: 'I'll just be a couple of minutes. I'll be back soon.' We had no idea what was going on. We later found out that he had an enormous cattle truck parked outside and that he was popping out to check on his cows. The Ryans returned around Easter time for many years afterwards.

Then there was the guy who pulled up one day in an enormous Rolls Royce with his wife, who was dripping in diamonds. They only stayed one night, but he handed Trish a $100 tip, which, back then, was about half of what it cost to stay at Cleopatra for the entire weekend. 'I'm sorry,' Trish said, 'you are very generous, but I couldn't possibly accept this …' But he insisted. 'You are doing something so fabulous that you won't be able to keep it up for too much longer. And besides, you're certainly not charging enough.'

Mr Ryan agreed. 'We are really enjoying this, but you won't be doing this for long. It won't last.' We laughed, determined to stick it out and prove them wrong.

Originally we had a large refectory table that seated ten in the dining room, as well as two other tables for the extra people who came for Saturday dinner. When we started having parties of four, or six or just couples, Trish would set the big table accordingly and make artful divisions between the groups out of pumpkins and candelabras or her arrangements of fruit.

One Saturday evening, a man and a very beautiful woman were the last to arrive for dinner. The only places left were the two in the centre of the big table. Trish took their coats, opened their wine and escorted them in but the woman took one look at the table and stumbled backwards out of the room. 'No, no. I can't sit there,' she said with a wild look in her eyes. 'But what's the matter?' asked Trish, who was feeling very embarrassed. 'Once you sit down you'll see you actually have more space than you would have at a table for two. It's actually very comfortable,' she said. Before turning on her heel and storming out of the restaurant the woman turned to Trish and said: 'Sitting next to my ex-husband and his girlfriend will certainly not be comfortable!' And that was the end of the refectory table.

Despite this awkward one-off incident, thrusting perfect strangers together at the large communal table also meant many new friendships were forged. The atmosphere was wonderful, like being at a house party. After spending the afternoon chatting, our guests would often arrange to meet for a bushwalk or a game of tennis or *pétanque* and then request to sit together for dinner, too. A lot of these friendships endured well beyond the confines of Cleopatra.

It wasn't long after Leo's review was published that our original plan to cater to ten to twelve people went out the window. People would ring up and say: 'We're coming up on Saturday to Leura. Can't I please bring everyone over for dinner on Saturday night?' Trish would somehow find a spot for an extra table, and, before we knew it, Saturday nights were very busy. To help us cope, we had to hire a local girl, Jill, who helped me in the kitchen prepping vegetables and washing up.

As a chef I was probably most renowned for my Perigourdin/Bordelaise dishes. But I certainly didn't limit myself to that corner of France and I was always looking for recipes from other regions, too. Provence was a favourite – I was immersed in Jacques Médecin's *La Cuisine du Comté de Nice* and *La Cuisine Provençale* written by J.B. Reboul in the nineteenth century. Instead of giving precise measurements, the recipes suggested a handful of this and a bunch of that, which was fine by me. La Mazille's *La Bonne Cuisine du Périgord*, of course, was still a great reference book, but I also loved *La Cuisine Lyonnaise* by Félix Benoit and Henri Clos-Jouve.

Some of the early entrées I made included: a classic dish from Bordeaux called *crepinette aux huitres* (a little flat sausage that I served hot with natural oysters); and a Provence dish, *artichauts à la barigoule farcis* (baby artichokes stuffed with a *mirepoix* of vegetables). I also made a *ragoût d'asperges* served in a tartlet pastry shell, a *crépinette* with rabbit and *tourin Périgourdin* (garlic and onion soup with eggs) and octopus *sétoise*.

Very few restaurants make their own puff pastry – either because it is too much hard work or because they were never taught to do it properly. But I believe that fresh puff pastry makes all the difference to a dish and I used it in two of my most popular starters – a *feuilletée aux moules et épinards* and a *feuilletée aux asperges*.

Maman also inspired a stunning dish that I modelled on a traditional salad she made using witlof and cooked beetroot, two ingredients that marry very well together. It became my braised endive stuffed with beetroot, served with a hot-pink sauce, thickened with cream and garnished with crisp prosciutto.

Some of the main courses in those early days included: baby lamb persillade, *the way Maman used to do it at Easter time;* barramundi *beurre blanc;* noisette d'agneau, *a little loin of lamb stuffed with crushed pistachios and basil and wrapped in caul fat; and roast duck with apple and prunes.*

Some of the main courses in those early days included: baby lamb *persillade*, the way Maman used to do it at Easter time; barramundi *beurre blanc*; *noisette d'agneau*, a little loin of lamb stuffed with crushed pistachios and basil and wrapped in caul fat; and roast duck with apple and prunes. Finding plump juicy prunes was difficult, so I would soak the dried ones in tea (for desserts), port or a little cognac and then heat them in the oven until they released their flavour. When combined with a duck demi-glaçe, the sauce was rich and sweet and, when partnered with roast duck, it was perfect. Guinea fowl was another favourite, which I baked under a slice of pork fat to keep moist and served with braised red cabbage cooked with apples and chestnuts and a guinea fowl demi-glaçe. Every weekend there would be four freshly made pots of stock and reduced demi-glaçe on the stove. Many chefs who made their own stock and demi-glaçe prepared just one pot of veal stock to use with every dish. That was not good enough for me; I made individual pots of stock specifically designed to complement each meat dish: be it lamb, beef, chicken or guinea fowl.

In my La Mazille cookbook, *La Bonne Cuisine du Périgord*, I also found a lovely recipe for chicken cooked in *verjus* with grapes. *Verjus* was not readily available in Australia at that time and cannot be made from table grapes so, after a quick ring-around, Trish and I headed off to the Hunter Valley at dawn to pluck the last remaining grapes from the vines after the mechanical harvester had passed through and collected the fruit. Len Evans was as generous as ever – donating us buckets of grapes and treating us to lunch and Champagne, too. We made enough *verjus* to keep the dish on the menu for a month.

As well as the hits, there were a few misses, one of which was *pochouse Bourguignonne*,

Pintade aux choux rouge et châtaignes

GUINEA FOWL WITH RED CABBAGE
AND CHESTNUTS

SERVES 4

A GREAT MAIN COURSE FOR WINTER — THE APPLES IN THE RED CABBAGE ADD A LOVELY 'ZING'.

BRAISED CABBAGE AND CHESTNUTS

150 g (5½ oz) dry chestnuts, soaked overnight or 400 g (14 oz) tin chestnuts or 300 g (10½ oz) cooked fresh chestnuts

3 white onions, thinly sliced

2 tablespoons duck or goose fat

½ small red cabbage (about 500 g/1 lb 2 oz), thinly sliced

250 ml (9 fl oz/1 cup) dry white wine

1 bouquet garni (10 parsley sprigs, 1 clove stuck in 1 bay leaf, 3 thyme sprigs)

juice of ½ lemon

2 granny smith apples, peeled, cored and cubed

250 ml (9 fl oz/1 cup) chicken stock (or more)

1 large guinea fowl, 1.5 kg (3 lb 5 oz) or, 4 baby guinea fowl, one per person, (about 450 g/ 1 lb each)

4 thyme sprigs

8 thin pancetta slices

2 tablespoons grapeseed oil

45 ml (1½ fl oz) Madeira or port

300–400 ml (10½–14 fl oz) guinea fowl or chicken stock

TO MAKE THE BRAISED CABBAGE AND CHESTNUTS: If using dry chestnuts, boil them in lots of cold water for about 1 hour or until soft. Strain and set aside. If using tinned or ready-cooked chestnuts, they need to be added 5 minutes before the cabbage has finished cooking.

Meanwhile, sauté the onions in the duck fat for 8 minutes, without colouring, add the cabbage, stirring to combine and cook for about 8–10 minutes or until the cabbage softens. Add the wine, bouquet garni and lemon juice and season to taste with salt and pepper. Simmer, covered, for 30 minutes. Add the cooked dried chestnuts, the cubed apples and enough stock to keep moist. Simmer, covered, over medium–low heat for about 1 hour, checking the liquid level at the bottom of the pot and adding more stock if necessary, until the cabbage is soft and melting – like a compote. Cool down and remove the bouquet garni.

You can prepare ahead up to this point.

Preheat the oven to 220°C (425°F/Gas 7). Clean the bird(s), season inside and out with salt and pepper and place the thyme inside. Drape the pancetta across the breast and secure with kitchen twine. Place the bird(s) in a roasting pan, drizzle with a little grapeseed oil and bake for 18 minutes for baby guinea fowl. The flesh will still be pink (cook for a further 5–7 minutes if you prefer them less rare). If you are cooking a large guinea fowl allow 30–40 minutes cooking time. Remove and turn the bird(s) breast side down and rest covered in a warm place.

At this stage the cabbage should be heating up, keep checking it does not dry out or catch, add more stock if necessary.

Discard the fat from the roasting pan and deglaze with the Madeira. Add the stock and bring to the boil then reduce it by one-third to one-half until a tasty sauce. Strain through a fine sieve into a saucepan ready to reheat.

Cut the twine from the guinea fowl, remove pancetta and keep warm. Cut the legs and breasts from the bird(s) and arrange on a serving dish along with the pancetta and cabbage, spoon some sauce over the guinea fowl and serve.

Poussin au verjus et raisins

SPATCHCOCK WITH GREEN GRAPES, GARLIC AND PARSLEY

SERVES 4

THIS IS AN AUTUMN DISH. IF YOU ARE LUCKY ENOUGH TO LIVE NEAR A VINEYARD, THERE ARE ALWAYS BUNCHES
OF GRAPES LEFT AT EACH END OF THE ROWS. UN-RIPE ACIDIC GREEN GRAPES ARE BEST BUT, OF COURSE,
YOU CAN USE ORDINARY TABLE GRAPES COMBINED WITH A LITTLE LEMON JUICE.

4 spatchcocks (about 500 g/1 lb 2 oz) each)

4 thyme sprigs

6 large garlic cloves

1 tablespoon olive oil

2–3 kg (4 lb 8 oz–6 lb 12 oz) seedless green grapes
(acidic and not too ripe) or wine grapes

250 ml (9 fl oz/1 cup) strong chicken stock

50 g (1¾ oz) unsalted butter

juice of 1 lemon

40 g (1½ oz/ 1⅓ cups) finely chopped flat-leaf
(Italian) parsley

Preheat the oven to 220ºC (425ºF/Gas 7).

Clean the birds, then place a sprig of thyme and a half clove of garlic, crushed, inside each, then season inside and outside with salt and pepper. Finely chop the remaining garlic and set aside.

Drizzle the spatchcocks with olive oil and roast for about 20 minutes or until the skin is crisp and golden. Rest, covered, in a warm place. Reserve any of the roasting juices.

Meanwhile, reserve 4 handfuls of the best looking grapes. Juice the remaining grapes in an electric juicer to obtain about 250ml (9 fl oz/1 cup) of grape juice. Combine the grape juice with the stock in a saucepan over medium heat and cook for 15–20 minutes or until reduced by half. Set aside.

When ready to serve, reheat the sauce, add the reserved chopped garlic and cook for 3–4 minutes. Whisk in the butter, add the lemon juice to taste and the chopped parsley. Skim any fat from the roasting juices and add to the sauce. Warm the reserved whole grapes in the sauce for only 1 minute, then either cut the spatchcocks in half, or leave whole, and pour the sauce and grapes around them, and serve.

Saumon, à la purée d'olives noires

SALMON WITH BLACK OLIVE PURÉE, ON A BED OF SPRING ONIONS

SERVES 4

SIMPLE AND DELICIOUS, THIS MAKES A GOOD MAIN COURSE FOR SUMMER,
SERVED WITH A GREEN SALAD AND CRUSTY BREAD.

Half cook the spring onions in extra virgin olive oil over medium–low heat for 5 minutes, very gently and without colouring. Stone the olives and purée very finely in the food processor with the olive oil and a little freshly ground black pepper.

Preheat the oven to 210°C (415°F/Gas 6–7). Season the salmon with pepper only and sprinkle with thyme, then spread 1¹/₂ tablespoons of the olive purée very carefully onto the flesh side of each fillet. Place on a baking tray, skin side down, surround with the spring onions, cover with aluminium foil and cook in the oven for 8–10 minutes.

When cooked, divide the spring onions equally between some warmed serving plates and sit the salmon on top. Deglaze the pan with lemon juice, whisk in about 2 teaspoons of olive oil, check the seasoning, then drizzle over and around the salmon.

1 bunch large spring onions or 4 white onions, very thinly sliced

350 g (12 oz) Kalamata black olives, with stone

2 tablespoons extra virgin olive oil

4 salmon fillets (about 200 g/7 oz each), skin on, cleaned

1½ tablespoons lemon thyme leaves

juice of 1 lemon

LEFT: DANY AND STAFF UNPACKING THE VEGETABLE DELIVERY AT CLEOPATRA.

RIGHT: THE FRONT VERANDAH AND GARDEN OF CLEOPATRA GLOWING IN THE MIST.

a fish stew from Burgundy. This delicious fish dish was made of carp, eel and trout and cooked in red wine. I had eaten it in France and did a lot of research into how I could replicate it. Right from the start, the dish was doomed; it turned out that the carp was studded with a million bones that were impossible to pick out and that Australian eels had a much stronger flavour than French eels. I cooked it for some regulars who, much to my dismay, didn't enjoy it and were spitting out bones, left, right and centre. That was the end of my relationship with *pochouse*. Although I often managed to get very close to re-creating the tastes and smells of certain French dishes, with others, it was just impossible. It was also sometimes the case that the cultural divide was too wide to bridge. The classic *tête de veau* was a case in point. The huge calf's head staring up at the staff as it soaked in the sink didn't make me very popular in the kitchen. And, despite it being one of my preferred dishes, I couldn't convince my customers to try it.

One of my many successful desserts was my own recipe: a grilled nectarine tart. After precooking the *pâte brisée sucrée* (sweet short crust pastry) and then allowing it to cool, I would put in a layer of *crème pâtissière*, and, on top of that, nectarines, sliced in two, cut-side up. I would then hide all the pastry under foil, sprinkle the nectarines with sugar and grill the tart until the nectarines were warm, soft and caramelised.

I also made Paris-Brest and a Périgourdine speciality: *tarte aux noix au chocolat* (walnut tart with chocolate). Trish and I had loved eating this dish in the Dordogne, although every chef had their own way of doing it. After finding a version at a pâtisserie that we especially loved, I asked *la patronne* if she would give me the recipe. She was horrified and chased us out of the shop! Finally an old friend sent a couple of recipes that Trish and I amalgamated and then reinvented to create the ultimate *tarte aux noix*. The dessert became Trish's speciality. It was so rich that even a small slice was too much after eating a large main so we later served it as a petit four — a lovely mouthful.

Another dessert that we adored, from La Mazille was *crème aux trois parfums* – a delicate little pot of cream with three flavours that we would serve with deep-fried *merveilles*, a crisp speciality eaten at carnivals in France. The *merveilles* were fried at the last minute so they could be served hot and then sprinkled with sugar. I loved them but our customers were starting to get calorie-conscious and often left them, untouched, on their plates.

On 12 April 1986, Trish and I made a spectacular cake to honour the appearance of Halley's Comet which was set to sweep across the sky that night. The cake was shaped like a comet and covered with sparklers and it was a much bigger sensation than the actual comet itself. We thought we could see it from the tennis court but apparently we were looking in the wrong direction!

In France, Sunday lunches are for getting together with family and friends to savour good food, wine and conversation. We wanted to replicate this tradition at Cleopatra and so served a range of classics – hearty, warming and satisfying food – which also provided the perfect fuel for an afternoon bushwalk. I made *cassoulet*, brain and sweetbread pie, *potée Bourguignonne*, *choucroute*, *petit salé* with lentils, and when it was warmer, aioli *garni*. Because most of our clients weren't French and didn't know the history and tradition behind each dish, they might behold a *pot au feu* and say: 'What's this? Boiled chook and veggies?' This prompted me to add little flourishes to each dish to make them seem more elegant. For example, I made an individually wrapped cabbage parcel to accompany the *potée* and a mustard or mushroom sauce to go with the *pot au feu*. In France, however, these dishes are celebrated for their simplicity.

In winter, I loved roasting a huge leg of pork for Sunday lunches. I would cook the meat very slowly until it was tender in the oven. I was never an early riser so I'd leave instructions for the staff doing the breakfast shift to put the pork in at eight o'clock so that it would be nicely underway by the time I came into the kitchen.

On Sundays we also cooked for many Sydney chefs who came to talk shop; we'd sit around and grumble about suppliers; praise to those with a professional approach; and use our networks to find staff. Some chefs would also send their apprentices up for lunch with their partners or to stay Sunday night as a 'reward'. That was always fun; we would serve extra dishes 'to taste' as we wanted them to give us a glowing report.

In 1984, the *Good Food Guide* awarded Cleopatra two chef's hats; it was the only restaurant outside the Sydney metropolitan area to receive that rating, which we retained

Because most of our clients weren't French and didn't know the history and tradition behind each dish, they might behold a pot au feu *and say: 'What's this? Boiled chook and veggies?' This prompted me to add little flourishes to each dish to make them seem more elegant.*

until we closed. Over the years Trish and I received many great reviews, not only in the Australian press, but in London and New York, too. The *New York Times* correspondent Johnny Apple waxed lyrical about Cleopatra and we also featured in the Courvoisier *Book of the Best* featuring restaurants around the world. When it came to matters of wine and food we wanted our customers to share in our sense of sheer enjoyment. 'I have just floated back to work after spending two days at a hedonistic retreat called Cleopatra ...' Stephanie Alexander wrote in the *Epicurean* in February 1986, which we thought expressed exactly the experience we were striving for.

Television, too, helped to build our profile; we were often invited to appear on cooking programs to highlight our approach. My first 'how-to' segment was very funny. The producer asked me to do a step-by-step demonstration of how to make rabbit pie, a recipe inspired by my grandmother. It was a very grim experience: the lighting was horrid and the voice-over was a monotonous drawl, as if I were a scientist describing a laboratory experiment. I wasn't even supposed to smile. Somehow my television debut still made an impression. Not long after the segment went to air Trish and I were out in the garden shovelling a mountain of manure in preparation for our new plantings. It was a Tuesday and Cleopatra was closed, so we were quite startled when a shiny stretch limousine full of Hong Kong businessmen sidled up to the kerb. It's safe to say we didn't look terribly presentable when one of the men approached us and said: 'We're here for the rabbit pie we saw on television.'

It took some time to convince the men that: firstly, we were closed and simply could not serve them; secondly, we did not have a fridge full of rabbit pies ready to pop into the oven; and, thirdly, a phone call would have saved them the two hours' drive each way.

Every week the menu at Cleopatra changed. Trish was never able to re-use any of her lovely handwritten pages, so every Friday she'd sit down to write out a whole new set. The menus were so beautiful that clients would ask to take them home, however we were quick to snatch up those that artist John Olsen had drawn on to add to our own souvenir collection. Because we didn't offer any choices about what would be served at Cleopatra, we would field endless phone calls during the week from customers wanting to know what we were serving and what wines to bring.

After a few disastrous weekends we discovered that certain would-be diners had the habit of booking tables at both Glenella and Cleopatra, often for groups of ten, before making a last-minute decision about where to eat. This often meant the difference between making a profit or a loss that weekend. Of course, there is no passing trade on top of a mountain lost in the swirling mist, but we usually had a waiting list of at least ten tables every Saturday night. So Trish and Monique developed a system where they checked with each other to see if there were any double bookings. They then called the culprits and informed them sweetly that their booking had been cancelled because we knew they had a booking at the other restaurant under the same name on the same night. As Trish and Monique both made the same calls, these 'charming' people were then left with nowhere to eat that night, which meant the practice soon stopped.

As the pace picked up at Cleopatra we needed extra storage space and so asked to use a shelf in the large Glenella coolroom. Although we were grateful to have the extra space, the arrangement was not very practical as Glenella was about one kilometre away. I would rush over in my car promising to be 'just five minutes' but inevitably get sidetracked and persuaded to stay for a coffee and chat with Monique and Cheffie.

One day, while down in the coolroom ticking items off my list I noticed a pot I had never seen before on a shelf just over my head. Curious, I tipped it over ever-so-slightly so I could have a peek at its contents. I had a reputation for being nosy and unable to resist 'having a look'. The next thing I knew I was splattered with a sudden shower of liquid duck fat and coated from head to foot. I slipped out the downstairs door and hurried home to take a shower. 'That will teach you!' said Trish. Not even the sound of the shower was enough to drown out her laughter from the kitchen.

As my cooking evolved and became more refined, I needed more help in the kitchen. We had more customers, too. By 1985, we were serving about twenty guests every Saturday night. I hired my first apprentice, who took on some of the bread-making and dessert duties, which really helped take the pressure off. We also hired a French waiter named François and an assistant to help make the breakfast, clean the rooms, change all the bed linen and iron the Swiss lace pillowcases.

Tourte de lapin

RABBIT PIE

SERVES 4

THIS WAS ALMOST AS POPULAR AS THE CASSOULET, ALWAYS IN DEMAND AND, WE WERE TOLD, 'WORTH THE JOURNEY'. THIS IS REALLY A DISH FOR ALL SEASONS, USING LUSCIOUS FARM-BRED RABBITS.

Roll the pastry out to 3–4 mm (¹⁄₈ inch) thick, enough to cover a 32 cm x 22 cm (12¹⁄₂ x 8¹⁄₂ inch) 1.5 litre (52 fl oz/6 cup) capacity oval pie dish. Place on a tray and refrigerate. Preheat the oven to 140ºC (275ºF/Gas 1). Cut the legs from the rabbit and chop the body into large chunks, season, then brown the rabbit pieces in about 2 tablespoons of the duck fat in a frying pan. Transfer to a flameproof roasting pan, sprinkle the flour all over the rabbit and place in the oven for 5 minutes. This is to cook the flour while cooking the pancetta, onion and shallot.

In a heavy-based saucepan, fry the pancetta in ¹⁄₂ tablespoon duck fat, add the onion and shallot and cook, stirring, until light golden. Remove the roasting pan, hot from the oven, and over medium heat flambé with the cognac, then place the rabbit into the saucepan and toss with the onion mixture. Deglaze the roasting pan with a little of the stock, scraping all the browned bits, and add to the pot. Add the wines and garlic, let it reduce for about 3 minutes, then cover with stock up to the level of the meat. Simmer gently for 40–50 minutes until the meat is tender.

Meanwhile, sauté the mushrooms in 2 teaspoons of the duck fat then set aside to cool. Brown the baby onions in a saucepan in a little more duck fat, add 250 ml (9 fl oz/1 cup) of the stock, cover and cook until tender. Set aside to cool.

When the rabbit is cooked, remove the rabbit pieces to a tray and cool. Strain the liquid into a saucepan, remove about 50 ml (1³⁄₄ fl oz) and refrigerate to set. Add the cream to the remaining liquid in the saucepan and cook for 15 minutes or until reduced and has become velvety. Check seasoning, then set aside.

Preheat the oven to 220ºC (425ºF/Gas 7). Remove the bones from the rabbit pieces and cut the meat into large cubes. Arrange the rabbit in the pie dish, spreading the onions and mushrooms evenly amongst the meat. Add the reserved braising liquid. Brush the edge of the pie dish with egg wash, cover the pie with the pastry, press around the edge with a fork, and trim any excess. Cut a hole in the centre and make a little aluminium foil 'chimney' to let the steam escape. Brush the pastry with egg wash and bake for 15–20 minutes or until the pastry is cooked and golden. Heat the sauce in the saucepan. When ready, remove pie from the oven. Remove the 'chimney' and pour in a ladleful of the hot sauce.

300 g (10¹⁄₂ oz) good-quality puff pastry (pâte feuilletée)
1 large rabbit (about 1.5 kg/3 lb 5 oz)
3–4 tablespoons duck fat
1 tablespoon plain (all-purpose) flour
100 g (3¹⁄₂ oz) pancetta, diced
2 onions, sliced
1 large French shallot, sliced
2 tablespoons cognac (or armagnac)
1 litre (35 fl oz/4 cups) rabbit or chicken stock, or to cover
250 ml (9 fl oz/1 cup) dry white wine
50 ml (1³⁄₄ fl oz) sweet white wine (Monbazillac or Sauternes type)
1 large garlic clove, chopped
20 small button mushrooms
15–20 baby onions (pickling size or spring onions)
125 ml (4 fl oz/¹⁄₂ cup) cream
egg wash (1 egg whisked with 1 tablespoon milk)

Crème aux trois parfums

PÉRIGOURDINE THREE-FLAVOURED
CUSTARD CREAM

SERVES 4

INDIVIDUAL POTS OF CUSTARD CREAM FLAVOURED WITH ANISE, ALMONDS AND ORANGE
FLOWER WATER, SERVED COLD AND INSPIRED BY LA MAZILLE WHO USED PERFUMES FROM
NATURE WHICH ARE UNAVAILABLE IN AUSTRALIA. I EXPERIMENTED TO GET A SIMILAR RESULT.

50 g (1¾ oz) caster (superfine) sugar

4 egg yolks

400 ml (14 fl oz) cream

¾ teaspoon sweet anis liquor (Anisette, Sambuca)

½ teaspoon dry anise aperitif (Casanis, Pernod)

1 teaspoon natural almond extract

2½ teaspoons orange flower water

¼ teaspoon natural vanilla extract

Preheat the oven to 160°C (315°F/Gas 2–3). Place four 8 cm (3¼ inch) diameter, 140 ml (4¾ fl oz) capacity ramekins (dariole moulds) in a high-sided roasting pan, lined with a thin cloth folded at the bottom (to prevent the ramekins moving).

Whisk together the sugar and egg yolks until pale and frothy. Gradually add the cream and all the 'perfumes' (alcohols, almond and vanilla extracts and orange flower water). Leave them to stand a while for the flavours to develop, then skim the froth from the top. Boil water. Pour the custard into the ramekins and cover each loosely with aluminium foil. Pour enough boiling water into the roasting pan to come halfway up the sides of the ramekins, and bake for about 50 minutes. The *crèmes* are cooked when they do not wobble any more in the centre. Remove from the bain marie and cool completely on a wire rack.

In 1985 – the same year my Papa sadly passed away – Trish and I had the house listed with the National Trust. That same year I also gave up the concept of not giving my customers any choice. It was just too restrictive. As well as catering to the dreaded vegetarians and those with dietary requirements, I realised that, for all my proselytising, not everyone was ready to eat tripe, brains or tongue. So, on Saturday nights, I started offering two entrées, two main courses and three desserts to make sure everyone could find something they liked. Saturdays became such a big deal that people stopped coming on Fridays, which meant we were forced to extend the options on both nights. It was only on Sundays that we stuck to a set menu.

Trish became an expert at balancing orders. She hated having to say we had run out of something on the menu, so, using her winning powers of persuasion, she orchestrated the orders, making things easier for us in the kitchen. Trish also had great fun 'out front' with her favourite waiter Michael Robertson; their shared sense of humour helped the pair breeze through even the busiest service. Our Sunday lunches were a waiter's worst nightmare, especially when served in the garden with the tables spread apart under the trees. Michael said it felt like running a marathon: 'If this was a city restaurant, those tables would be a block apart from each other!'

One night, Trish fell into the kitchen, helpless with laughter. 'That woman on table three just said to Michael, "Oh, you are such a funny, handsome boy. I hope there's a lovely girl waiting at home for you".' Without missing a beat Michael had replied: 'No, but there's a lovely boy.' Everyone laughed.

The 'lovely boy' was, of course, Sean Moran – a great cook – who I often called upon to come to my rescue when a member of staff was sick or away. Sean, who went on to open Sean's Panaroma, in Sydney's Bondi, would arrive full of energy and raring to go.

We were lucky to find some excellent staff over the years, especially considering most of our trade was on weekends. We rarely advertised for help, relying instead on industry contacts. Nevertheless, it was hard to keep waiters and assistants for more than a few months. We needed staff to be flexible, available to work part-time, and willing to give up their weekends. Hospitality staff traditionally enjoy going out on the town to unwind after work. But Blackheath was no place to party and after a few months of social isolation, the novelty of working for us would often wear off.

We gave one sweet French-speaking boy a job waiting tables after he told us he had trained at Club Med. Originally from Mauritius, our new waiter was very handsome and full of enthusiasm. Although he could clear a table of eight in one go, his English wasn't great. He'd appear in the kitchen, saying: 'Lady on table two she want order something. The word, it start with a "ch".' Trish would then have to rush out and translate. One night, one of our regular customers, a woman in her sixties, called Trish over. 'Do you know what your waiter just said to me? He said: "Many ladies like to go to the bushes with young men. You like I meet you in bushes near tennis court in ten minutes? I like ladies like you".'

'So sorry,' started Trish, but the woman interrupted. 'No, my dear, it is years since I have had an offer like that! It's wonderful.' Meanwhile, her husband was helpless with laughter: 'Come on, old girl, I'm looking at you in a new light tonight!' Unfortunately, we felt that not everyone would be amused by such an offer and so we had to let our new staffer go. Maybe a Club Med-trained waiter wasn't quite what we needed, after all.

Many of the staff that we managed to retain long-term at Cleopatra lived locally in Blackheath. Blanche, who was in her early sixties when she applied for the role of kitchenhand, had been working as a housemaid since she was eleven. She was the most reliable, wonderful, sweetest helper you could ever imagine. Every day she would arrive early for work and don her special rubber gloves. I'd only ever have to show her how to do something once. She was worth her weight in gold and could do the work of three apprentices.

But Blanche did have a curious idiosyncrasy, which was an obsession with directions. You couldn't even mention the possibility of going somewhere without Blanche launching into a long monologue about the best route to take. 'After five minutes, Dany, you'll see an enormous tree and you'll know that you have to keep on going ...' She wouldn't stop until she had, in her mind, got us there safe and sound. Of course, we used to egg her on. 'So Blanche, we're thinking of going on holiday next year to Queensland ...' The kitchen staff would then hide in the pantry and listen, trying to smother their laughter, while Blanche, the human GPS, started telling us in excruciating detail how to get there.

When Blanche eventually bid us farewell it was to follow her partner, who had decided to live in outback Western Australia. Blanche was very upset and came to us in tears. She said: 'I have to go but I just want to tell you that I've never been happier in my life than since I have been here working with you all.' We certainly missed Blanche.

One of my star cooks, Gary, began work at Cleopatra while Blanche was still with us. Gary was a handsome man who had been adopted by a rural family. Gary and Blanche came from the same country background, so they shared a common bond; he would sometimes whip up a batch of scones and jam just to please her. Like Blanche, Gary was a natural in the kitchen. He absorbed everything like a sponge and we worked together like clockwork. After a while I hardly had to tell him anything; he was intuitive and knew what was required. It was like having a second pair of hands. We have a video made by Doug Livermore, a filmmaker friend of ours, which documents *A weekend in Cleopatra*. The footage shows a kitchen that is a study in calm; there is classical music playing in the background and Gary and I glide about effortlessly, as if our movements have been choreographed. With just a few nods and quiet words we manage to communicate with complete accord and complicity.

Gary performed well even when tackling the most painstaking tasks. He loved pâtisserie and was always asking me to show him new skills. His *feuilletée* pastry became a marvel and elevated our hors d'oeuvres to little works of art. As well as having a wonderful attitude, Gary's quest for knowledge was relentless; no matter how labour-intensive my ideas were, he would be there, by my side, ready to go.

Staff dinners were always held after service, where we'd often sit around eating and drinking until about three o'clock in the morning. We had one very good customer named Bernard who always phoned ahead to find out what I was cooking. He would then send a

Beignets de dattes, glace au miel

DATE AND PISTACHIO FRITTERS
WITH HONEY ICE CREAM

SERVES 4

THIS IS AN UNUSUAL AND DELICIOUS DESSERT. THE HONEY ICE CREAM CAN BE MADE WITH YOUR FAVOURITE HONEY. YOU'LL NEED TO START THIS RECIPE 24 HOURS BEFORE YOU WISH TO SERVE IT.

TO MAKE THE HONEY ICE CREAM: Heat the milk and honeys in a saucepan, stirring to dissolve the honey. Using an electric mixer (or by hand), whisk the egg yolks and sugar together until the mixture is pale. When the milk and honey is boiling, gradually add to the whisking egg and sugar mixture. Transfer to a clean saucepan and cook over a low heat, stirring constantly with a wooden spoon until the custard thickens and coats the back of the spoon. Do not boil. As soon as it is thick, strain into a bowl and cool. Freeze in an ice-cream machine (sorbetière) according to the manufacturer's directions.

TO MAKE THE CRÈME PÂTISSIÈRE: Boil together the milk, vanilla and sugar. In a mixing bowl, combine the cornflour and a pinch of salt, stir in the egg and yolk and mix well. Add the hot milk, whisking constantly. Transfer the milk mixture to a clean saucepan, cook over a medium heat, whisking constantly, until thick and bubbling. Remove from the heat and immediately stir in the butter. Cover the surface of the crème pâtissière with plastic wrap. Cool. Add the pistachios and the kirsch and mix well.

Stuff the dates generously with crème pâtissière, using a large teaspoon, and set them aside. Prepare the batter at least one hour before use. It can be done a few hours before. Separate the eggs and refrigerate egg whites. Place the flour and a pinch of salt in a bowl, then stir in the combined egg yolk, beer and melted butter and thin the mixture to the consistency of thick cream, if necessary, with water. Cover and stand for at least 1 hour.

To serve, heat the oil in a deep-fryer or deep wide saucepan to 180°C (350°F). Beat the egg whites and a pinch of sugar until stiff and fold this gently into the rested batter. Coat the dates in batter, one at a time, and cook in the oil until light golden, drain on paper towels. Serve the dates dusted with icing sugar and accompanied with the honey ice cream.

12 large dates, stones removed
oil, for deep-frying
icing (confectioners') sugar, to serve

HONEY ICE CREAM

500 ml (17 fl oz/2 cups) milk
100 g (3½ oz) leatherwood honey
100g (3½ oz) yellow-box honey
6 egg yolks
2 tablespoons caster (superfine) sugar
150 ml (5 fl oz) cream

CRÈME PÂTISSIÈRE

250 ml (9 fl oz/1 cup) milk
2 drops natural vanilla extract
25 g (1 oz) caster (superfine) sugar
45 g (1½ oz) cornflour (cornstarch)
1 whole egg, plus 1 egg yolk
30 g (1 oz) unsalted butter
40 g (1½ oz) shelled pistachios, roasted, chopped
1 tablespoon kirsch

BATTER

2 eggs
200 g (7 oz/1⅓ cups) plain (all-purpose) flour
200 ml (7 fl oz) warm beer
60 g (2¼ oz) melted butter

courier to Cleopatra with wonderful $300-a-bottle wines for the weekend with detailed instructions on which ones to decant and when. Then, after service, when we'd all be sitting around the kitchen table, eating and laughing, the door would suddenly burst open and there he'd be. 'So this is where the party is, I see! What are you eating?' Often it would be something that Trish had made, such as a Thai green curry with chicken, and Bernard would say: 'May I have some, too?' He would then sit down and join us for our meal, which was usually accompanied by cheap Beaujolais!

In later years, when staff numbers had increased even further, we shared our dinner at six o'clock every evening, which was a much more sensible time. We always ate well. Trish would make everything from homemade ravioli filled with pumpkin to a spicy hot curry. I then decided that everyone working in the kitchen should take turns cooking the staff dinner. It became a bit of a contest to see who could turn out the best food. I had to remind the staff not to spend hours and hours on preparing these dinners and inform them that the more expensive ingredients were off-limits. We had a glass or two of wine with dinner – after all, this was a French kitchen – but I had to keep an eye on the apprentices to make sure it was just a small glass.

At one point, some of our waiters and apprentices decided to rent a nearby house to share, so that poor Nanna had a bit of space. When they clocked off for the night they'd head back home to party on, which went a long way towards keeping a lot of our staff. We just had to promise the real estate agent that the rent would get paid. Although we would have loved to sell wine, Cleopatra was limited to being BYO due to licensing

Most nights there was a 'fete' atmosphere; far removed from the description of scenes played out in fiery, testosterone-driven kitchens run by some chefs. At Cleopatra, we could do without the violence, shouting and swearing. That is not to say that everyone was not absolutely aware of who was 'the boss' in my kitchen.

regulations that specified we had to provide separate men's and women's toilets with two stalls in each; of course, there wasn't the space for that inside our historic house. But, in stark contrast to the standard of wine that was often quaffed at Upstairs and Au Chabrol, our Cleopatra customers had developed a taste for superb, world-class wines. Some of our other committed wine buffs would also phone ahead to see what was on the menu and bring wines to match what I was cooking. Often, during service, when it was all hands on deck, we'd get well-meaning customers sending back glasses of wine to the kitchen. 'This is for the chef,' they'd say to the waiter. Sometimes they'd even march into the kitchen themselves, proudly proffering a glass of Margaux or Pomerol: 'Try this, Dany, and let me know what you think!' I was always polite but the glass would remain untouched until after service. Getting the food out required all my concentration. After the service was another matter entirely. Most often, there'd be plenty and, while winding down after work, everyone would pour themselves a glass and then lend a hand, polishing silver and glasses and preparing the bread mix for the next day. Gary and I would perch on stools preparing our to-do lists and, little by little, the restaurant would again be clean and tidy. Most nights there was a *'fete'* atmosphere; far removed from the description of scenes played out in fiery, testosterone-driven kitchens run by some chefs. At Cleopatra, we could do without the violence, shouting and swearing. That is not to say that everyone was not absolutely aware of who was 'the boss' in my kitchen.

In 1986, one of our staff mentioned that she knew an Italian woman in Blackheath named Luciana who grew lovely flowers. Trish, who was always on the lookout for beautiful blooms, went to meet Luciana and her husband, who had both retired. Trish offered Luciana money to grow and cut a certain amount of flowers for us each week. She also noticed that Luciana had a very nice kitchen garden with beautiful baby vegetables grown from seeds that had been sent over from Italy. She even had *mâche* (a salad green with velvety leaves and a rich flavour), which my grandfather used to grow in Sainte-Foy-la-Grande. And so we came to an agreement with Luciana that she would supply us with fresh salads and herbs and huge bunches of flowers. Although she was in her sixties, Luciana launched headfirst into her new career as a market gardener. She had her long-suffering husband dig up their lawn and replace it with neat and tidy rows of vegetables. For several years, it was a brilliant arrangement for both of us. Being Italian, Luciana also thought she could teach this French cook a thing or two and so, after delivering her produce to Cleopatra, would often insist on giving me cooking lessons, too.

Someone else who was getting along in age was Armand. Armand was still at Glenella, happily washing up and gambling away. He'd sometimes come over to Cleopatra, too, to lend a hand and try and earn a bit more cash. Monique often worried about what would happen to Armand if they sold Glenella – which they did in Easter 1989. Armand was old and tired and he would not have coped with the pressure at Cleopatra, but Monique and Cheffie promised to take care of him.

It sounds like a tidy end to a novel, but the truth is that Armand died on the day the Glenella contract changed hands. He was buried where he was happiest. We had a little ceremony, buried his ashes and planted a tree in his honour.

Glace à la verveine, tartelette citron

ALMOND-LEMON TARTLET WITH LEMON VERBENA ICE CREAM

SERVES 4

THIS DESSERT WAS OFTEN ON THE MENU AND PROVED TO BE VERY POPULAR. THE SCENTED LEMON VERBENA BUSH GREW SO WELL IN THE MOUNTAIN AIR.

200 g (7 oz) pâte sucrée (sweet short crust pastry)
   (see recipe page 329)
1 large egg
20 g (¾ oz) caster (superfine) sugar
zest and juice of 1 lemon
30 g (1 oz) ground almonds
1 drop of almond extract
30 g (1 oz) melted butter
30 ml (1 fl oz) cream
250 g (9 oz) mixed red berries, such as strawberries,
   raspberries, or redcurrants
1 tablespoon icing (confectioners') sugar
juice of ½ lemon

LEMON VERBENA ICE CREAM
15 fresh leaves lemon verbena (if you aren't fortunate
   enough to have a lemon verbena bush, buy a small
   plant from a nursery)
250 ml (9 fl oz/1 cup) milk, heated
4 egg yolks
40 g (1½ oz) sugar
125 ml (4 fl oz/½ cup) cream

TO MAKE THE LEMON VERBENA ICE CREAM: Make the ice cream the day before, you want to serve this dessert. Infuse all the leaves in hot milk for at least 15 minutes, then strain the leaves out.

Whisk the yolks and sugar until pale, pour the hot milk over this and keep whisking until well mixed. Transfer to a clean saucepan and cook over low heat, stirring constantly with a wooden spoon until the custard thickens and coats the back of the spoon. Do not let it boil. As soon as it is thick, strain into a bowl and cool.

Freeze in an ice-cream machine (sorbetière) according to the manufacturer's directions. Transfer to individual moulds or in one container to serve.

Preheat the oven to 200ºC (400ºF/Gas 6). Roll out the pasty to 3 mm (⅛ inch) thick and line four 8 cm (3¼ inch) long boat-shaped tartlet moulds, place them on a baking tray and refrigerate for at least 20 minutes or until the pastry is firm.

Using an electric mixer, whisk the egg, sugar and half the lemon zest and juice. When pale, add the ground almonds, almond extract, melted butter and the cream. Pour into the prepared tartlet moulds lined with pastry and cook for 8–10 minutes or until the filling is set and the pastry is light brown. Cool on a wire rack.

Mix the fresh red berries of your choice, icing (confectioners') sugar and the remaining lemon juice, to taste. Just before serving, take the ice-cream moulds from the freezer to soften a little. Arrange the fruits and the almond tartlet on serving plates and unmould or scoop the ice cream last.

Gâteau moelleux, chocolat et orange

CHOCOLATE, ORANGE AND WALNUT CAKE

SERVES 8

A DENSE, RICH CHOCOLATE CAKE FLAVOURED WITH ORANGE
AND GROUND WALNUTS WITH A SHINY CHOCOLATE ICING.

Preheat the oven to 160°C (315°F/Gas 2–3).

Grease a 22 cm (8½ inch) springform cake tin and line the base with baking paper, even if the tin is 'non-stick'.

Melt the chocolate in a bowl over a small saucepan of simmering water. As soon as the chocolate melts, remove and keep warm so that it does not set. In a food processor finely grind the walnuts, but not too fine (as they will form a paste), set aside.

Using an electric mixer, combine the egg yolks and sugar, whisk until very pale. Add the melted chocolate and mix until just incorporated. Fold in the ground walnuts, orange peel, coffee and vanilla, and mix well.

Whisk the egg whites with a pinch of salt until very stiff, then fold into the cake mixture delicately, using a metal spoon, try not to deflate the egg whites. Pour the mixture into the prepared cake tin and bake for 35 minutes or until cooked when tested with a skewer. Cool on a wire rack for 5 minutes before carefully removing the sides of the tin, and remove the paper on the base while still warm.

TO MAKE THE CHOCOLATE ICING: Heat the cream in a saucepan over medium heat and when hot, remove from the heat and stir in the chocolate. Keep stirring until the chocolate has melted and the mixture is smooth, then stir in the liquid glucose, if desired. (This can be omitted, but the glucose gives the icing a high glossy finish.) Keep stirring from time to time until the icing feels cool to the touch – using the back of your little finger. When cool and getting thick, pour over the cake and spread with a palette knife. If the temperature is correct it will be shiny and smooth, and show no traces of the knife. Decorate around the edge with walnut halves and slices of candied orange peel.

1 teaspoon nut butter, for greasing

100 g (3½ oz) dark chocolate
  (70% cocoa solids), chopped

80 g (2¾ oz) walnut halves, plus extra
  for decorating

4 eggs, separated

80 g (2¾ oz) caster (superfine) sugar

100 g (3½ oz) candied orange peel, diced, plus extra
  slices for decorating

2 teaspoons best-quality instant coffee granules,
  finely ground

1 teaspoon vanilla extract

CHOCOLATE ICING

150 ml (5 fl oz) thick cream

200 g (7 oz) dark chocolate, chopped

1 large teaspoon liquid glucose (optional)

HATS OFF TO FRENCH CUISINE

An artisan in the kitchen

MAMAN AND DANY WITH SPOILS FROM THE SARLAT MARCHÉ

EVERY YEAR TRISH AND I TOOK OUR HOLIDAYS IN FRANCE TO VISIT MAMAN IN
VÉLINES AND SEEK OUT FRESH INSPIRATION FOR CLEOPATRA. IN PARIS, I HIT THE
BOOKSHOPS AND SPENT MANY HAPPY HOURS ALONG THE QUAYS OF THE SEINE,
PORING OVER COOKERY BOOKS IN THE *BOUQUINISTES*. MY FAVOURITE BOOKSHOP
WAS LOCATED ON THE LEFT BANK AND SPECIALISED IN ALL THINGS CULINARY.
I BECAME VERY FRIENDLY WITH THE OWNER WHO WOULD SEND ME HER LIST
OF NEW TITLES AND THEN SHIP THE VOLUMES I REQUESTED TO AUSTRALIA.

I STILL SUBSCRIBED TO *CUISINE ET VINS DE FRANCE*
magazine, keeping my eye open for anything new and interesting. That is how I kept
up with culinary developments in France and where I first read about new and talented
chefs, such as Alain Ducasse.

From 1987 onwards, the main research that Trish and I conducted was at Michelin
three-star restaurants; we'd have to make our booking well in advance to secure a table.
We learned a lot gallivanting about as gourmands: sometimes we felt the food wasn't
good enough; other times we were dazzled and inspired, but we always left feeling
refreshed and excited about returning to Cleopatra. Of course, some of our enthusiasm
was tempered by the knowledge that ours was an isolated weekend retreat that would
never have the same impressive turnover or the same impressive number of kitchen staff
and apprentices.

One great idea I picked up at Michel Trama's three-star L'Aubergade, in Puymirol,
in the Lot et Garonne, was curing my own duck breasts to make *magret de canard seché*.
Luckily, the cool mountain air was perfect for the job. After covering the outside of the
pantry windows at Cleopatra with fly screens, I used to hang the *magrets* (which were
individually wrapped in muslin (cheesecloth) from the ceiling. Customers often stood
outside the pantry window, wondering what in the world the *magrets* were, dangling there
like mummified bats.

At first we went to France during the Australian winter, which was our busiest
time at the restaurant. Many of our budget-minded friends thought we were bonkers.
And I guess we were! We'd say: 'But it's summer in France!' Eventually, we realised the
number-crunching types were right, and so went in January instead. And besides, winter
in France was actually the perfect time to go because the restaurants would be serving

winter menus, which is what we served in Blackheath for most of the year. Nevertheless, I simply had to return to France for Bastille Day on 14 July 1989 during the bicentenary of the Revolution. I wasn't going to miss the celebrations! We collected a rental car in Paris and mapped out our itinerary: after visiting Monet's garden in Giverny, we would drive to Vézelay to visit two more Michelin-starred restaurants – Georges Blanc's Vonnas and Marc Meneau's L'Espérance.

Having lived in Australia for so long, the distances in France seemed quite insignificant while we were planning the tour from afar. On the day we set out, the weather was hot, humid and oppressive. And, as we soon discovered, it's actually a long drive from Normandy to Burgundy. We had reserved a table at Marc Meneau months in advance and were due there that evening. But by the time we arrived, my head was thumping from the heat and I felt violently ill. As we checked in, I said: 'Look, I don't think I can eat dinner tonight. All I want is a bath and some painkillers. I'm so disappointed, as I'm you sure you will be all booked out for tomorrow night.' *Mais non, Madame,* the man at the desk said. 'We had a cancellation. It's no problem. I'll book you in right now.' Then he looked at Trish. *'Et, vous, Madame?'*

'Oh, this Madame is feeling just fine,' Trish quickly said. 'A table for one, *s'il vous plait.'*

So Trish dressed and went down to the dining room where she ordered a glass of Champagne and studied the menu. Knowing she'd be returning for dinner the next evening, she ordered a light meal: she had oysters *naturale*; a wonderful water jelly on a watercress purée; and a fish course – *rouget au jus de betterave rouge* and a half-bottle of white wine. Although she thought she'd skip dessert, the staff plied her with amazing trays of *petits fours* and more Champagne. *En bref,* Madame knew restaurants from the inside out and therefore had no qualms about dining at her table for one, while I suffered alone in silence.

Seated next to Trish was an American couple who spoke no French at all. Because of their lack of knowledge about the language, they couldn't detect her accent and, assuming she was French, gossiped about her the whole time. 'Who is that woman? Where's her husband? How can she be so glamorous and not be with a man?' Much to Trish's amusement, they dissected every little thing she did: from the way she was dressed to what she ordered. Trish warned the waiters what the couple were doing so they were in on the joke, too.

The next morning I woke up feeling much brighter and joined Trish in the garden for breakfast. The tacky Americans happened to be seated next to us and turned beet-red as soon as they heard us speaking in English. They pushed their chairs back and scurried out of the garden; that was the last we saw of them. We couldn't stop laughing. Hopefully they learned an important lesson: never assume others speak only one language.

That night at dinner I had the *crêpe de maïs au foie gras* – a dish that I re-worked for the Cleopatra menu. I made a parfait of chicken or duck livers instead and also cooked ordinary large duck livers 'à la maniere de foie gras, en terrine'.

Gary and his partner Steven took advantage of us closing Cleopatra that July and conducted a 'tour de France', too. The pair hired a little convertible Citroën and we arranged a rendezvous in Vélines. Maman was very excited and decided to show us all off by inviting the neighbours over for an aperitif. All our guests dressed up for the occasion and arranged themselves around the *salon* and adjoining *salle à manger* with plates and forks and linen napkins. Most of those in attendance were members of the Vélines church choir and so arrived with briefcases full of sheet music. There was an elderly man playing the piano, which, as always, was out of tune, and the group all took turns to recite poems and sing songs. Maman, as usual, was busy giving orders: who would sing what, and with whom. Gary and I did all the cooking while Steven and Trish served our guests. Yvette, who happened to be in Bergerac visiting her parents, also helped out running to and from the kitchen; it was a natural response for the five of us to automatically slip into work mode. It was as if we were back at work; we produced and served trays and trays of elegant little pastry hors d'oeuvres, cakes and Monbazillac. Because of our professional approach, Maman's elderly friends started behaving like difficult customers, snapping their fingers and demanding our attention: '*Oh pardonnez-moi, garçon, encore du gâteau?*' In the dining room, Maman was glowing with pride; in the kitchen we were all in hysterics trying to keep up with the relentless requests made by Vélines' elderly villagers. Boy, could they eat and drink.

AFTER VÉLINES WE WENT TO A FABULOUS FORMAL

event in the Gardens of Versailles. Placido Domingo was singing and it was all very glamorous. There was Trish, in her gorgeous, black-taffeta Linda Jackson creation, taking it all in: the floodlit château; beautiful people; vintage Champagne; Lenôtre hors d'oeuvres and dazzling floral displays. I dreaded to think what new and extravagant ideas Trish would try and emulate at Cleopatra after being so inspired by the experience.

Our flight departing Paris was at eight o'clock the next evening, which meant we had to be at the airport by about five o'clock. I wanted to leave France on a high note so I made a lunch booking at the most beautiful restaurant in Paris, if not the world: Le Grand Véfour in the Palais Royal. The restaurant was established in the eighteenth century at the time of Louis XVI. Back then, it was called Café de Chartres and had tables on different levels; nowadays there are plaques commemorating all the famous people who have eaten there, such as Victor Hugo, Napoleon and artist Jean Cocteau. Although she does not have a plaque engraved in her honour, the French writer Colette, a passionate foodie, used to live in the Palais Royal district and dined regularly at Le Grand Véfour when Raymond Oliver was head chef.

Everything about Le Grand Véfour was perfect. In fact, we were so enamoured with the place that we decided to share the experience with Gary and Steven, who were staying on in Paris for a few more days. When we asked the maître d' if we could pay for their dinner in advance, he said: 'Well, if you trust us with your credit card!' 'Of course we do,' I said. 'But please make sure they don't order the most expensive wines!' It was a precious and unforgettable experience for all of us.

Tian de coquilles Saint-Jacques au basilic

SCALLOPS WITH TOMATO AND BASIL OMELETTE

SERVES 4

THIS WAS INSPIRED BY AN ENTRÉE I HAD IN HAUTE PROVENCE IN THE LATE 1980S WHILE STAYING IN A LONELY 'MAS', WHERE FINDING INVENTIVE AND TASTY FOOD OF SUCH A HIGH STANDARD WAS A PLEASANT SURPRISE.

5 large eggs

100 g (3 1/2 oz / 1/2 cup) tomatoes concassé (about 2 tomatoes peeled, seeded and coarsely chopped)

20 g (3/4 oz / 1/3 cup finely shredded basil

1 garlic clove, crushed

olive oil, for drizzling

16–20 fresh scallops (with roe), depending on size

100 ml (3 1/2 fl oz) fish stock (or dry white wine)

200 ml (7 fl oz) cream

TO MAKE THE OMELETTE: In a mixing bowl, beat together the eggs, 80 g (2 3/4 oz/4 tablespoons) of the tomato concassé, the basil and garlic, and season with salt and pepper.

Heat a 12 cm (4 1/2 inch) blini pan with a drizzle of olive oil. When hot pour one-quarter of the egg mixture into pan and cook, until just set. Remove with a spatula and place on a flat baking tray and cool. Repeat the process until you have four omelettes.

Place the scallops in a colander over a saucepan to gather any juices they may give, clean the scallops, separate the roe from the scallops and set both aside. Place any scallop off-cuts in the saucepan, add the fish stock, cream and remaining tomato, bring to the boil over medium heat, then reduce the heat to low and cook until reduced by half. Season with salt and pepper. Strain the sauce into another saucepan and set aside.

When the omelettes are cold, thinly slice scallops into 3 mm (1/8 inch) thick rounds and arrange in an overlapping circle around the edge of each omelette, place the pieces of roe in the centre in a rose pattern, and season with salt and pepper.

You can prepare ahead up to this point. Keep in refrigerator until needed.

Preheat the oven to 200°C (400°F/Gas 6) 10 minutes before serving. Drizzle a little olive oil over the scallops and cook for 4–5 minutes; any longer and they will shrink and become chewy. Meanwhile reheat the sauce over a very low heat. Place the scallop 'tians' on warm entrée plates and ladle over the sauce to serve.

Crabe en feuille de choux

CRAB AND CABBAGE PARCEL WITH SCALLOPS

SERVES 4

MY FAVOURITE CRUSTACEAN, WITH THE BEST CRAB SAUCE INSPIRED BY MICHEL GUÉRARD.
WE COULD NEVER MAKE ENOUGH OF THIS ENTRÉE AT CLEOPATRA.

Brush the crabs clean under cold running water. Remove four claws and refrigerate. Remove the body shells, cut the crabs in half and clean thoroughly. Extract the crab flesh, place in a bowl and refrigerate. Crack the remaining crab legs and refrigerate with all the crab-body shells.

Carefully separate the cabbage leaves without breaking them. Choose four large pale green leaves without holes, cut them in half, discarding the ribs, and steam for 2 minutes. Refresh under cold water, drain well and set aside in a cool place.

To make the crab sauce, heat the butter and 2 teaspoons of the olive oil in a heavy-based saucepan, sweat the onion, carrot and shallots for 5 minutes. In a separate frying pan, heat the remaining olive oil over medium heat and fry the reserved crab legs and bodies until they turn red, then add to the pot with the vegetables, crushing the shells with a pestle or kitchen hammer. Add the cognac and port, cover and reduce the liquid by half. Add the tomato, tomato paste, bouquet garni, garlic, cayenne pepper, wine and 150 ml (5 fl oz) water and season with salt and freshly ground black pepper. Cook for 10–15 minutes, or until reduced by one-third. Allow to cool a little, discard the bouquet garni. Pass the mixture through the large holes of a mouli, and then pass again through the fine holes, extracting as much liquid as possible. Place in a saucepan over medium heat. Add the cream to the sauce; simmer for a few minutes until you get a nice, rosy, unctuous sauce. Set aside.

To make the crab parcels, season the reserved crabmeat with salt and pepper and a few drops of lemon juice. Spoon onto the steamed cabbage leaves then wrap the leaf to form a parcel. Meanwhile, heat the crab sauce over low heat. Steam the parcels over gently simmering water for 6 minutes. At the same time, steam the scallops and reserved crab claws for about 4 minutes or until the scallops just turn opaque and crab claws are bright pink.

To serve, place a crab parcel on each plate, pour a ladleful of sauce around and arrange scallops and decorate with a crab claw. Serve very hot with a fresh crusty baguette.

4 large blue-swimmer crabs, uncooked
1 small green savoy cabbage
2 teaspoons butter
2½ tablespoons olive oil
1 onion, finely diced
1 carrot, finely diced
3 French shallots, finely diced
60 ml (2 fl oz) cognac (or brandy)
60 ml (2 fl oz) port
3 tomatoes, coarsely chopped
2 teaspoons tomato paste (concentrated purée)
1 small bouquet garni (lemon thyme)
1 large garlic clove, crushed
1 pinch cayenne pepper
300 ml (10½ fl oz) dry white wine
200 ml (7 fl oz) cream
12 scallops, cleaned
juice of 1 lemon

These three-star research trips totally revolutionised my style of cooking. But despite being suitably inspired by Georges Blanc's restaurant and books, sourcing ingredients to do his dishes justice in Australia was not always easy. The only supplier that sold proper, corn-fed chickens lived interstate, which meant we had to have the birds sent to us by courier. And there was only one farmer in Australia who sold beautiful, white, milk-fed (*sous la mère*) veal and he lived 4000 kilometres away in Perth! But the cost of transporting the goods was worth it; how else could I make roast veal with a Périgourdine mushroom sauce or tender veal cutlets with horseradish cream and home-made noodles?

It was largely thanks to our friend French-Canadian chef Serge Dansereau that the quality of goods being sold on the Australian market began to improve. Serge was working at Sydney's Regent Hotel at the time and because he had the backing of a major hotel chain, was able to apply a bit of pressure on the farmers and demand a higher standard of produce. No one was interested in selling ten plump, corn-fed chickens to us at Cleopatra; but they were certainly interested in selling dozens per week to a major hotel chain. After adding our small order to his, we would then drive 125 kilometres to Sydney to collect our chickens and ducks from the Regent Hotel's kitchen door.

In 1990, we slipped away for a short holiday to Thailand, leaving Barney, then nineteen, in charge. Soon after we left, the hot water tank exploded like a geyser, soaking all the freshly ironed and starched linen. Although it was a Sunday, Barney managed to find a plumber and get a new heater installed. Thankfully, he didn't tell us about it until we got home. He said: 'All's well now. I didn't want to worry you!' In spite of the scary explosion and the stress of having staff not turn up to work, Barney coped remarkably well. It was character-building stuff.

Like Barney, Trish was very calm under pressure. During a trip to France later the same year, I decided to stay on for a bit longer in Vélines to keep Maman happy. She had been playing the guilt card, complaining and pulling strings: 'I never see enough of you! We need to discuss your inheritance. You're always going off with Trish and having fun and going to restaurants while your own mother is going to die tomorrow. Ha! Then you'll be sorry!' Another time it was: 'Look, it's Sainte Madeleine's Day, my name day. You'd better come and visit now because, by next Sainte Madeleine's Day, I'll be dead.' So of course I rushed to be at her bedside, even though she was as strong as an ox.

To help Trish cope at Cleopatra in my absence, we hired a chef who, little did we know, was a perfect idiot. All our bookings for that weekend had been made long in advance and I had left him explicit instructions along with ordering lists and menus. We were doing a wedding on the Saturday with salmon being the only main course on offer. The numbers had been confirmed and it all seemed pretty straightforward. But it just so happened that on the Thursday and Friday nights before the wedding we were exceptionally busy, with forty people turning up for dinner both nights. When Trish came in with an order for salmon on the Friday night, the chef said: 'No, no, we're out of salmon. You'll have to give them the other main course.'

'Oh dear,' said Trish. 'Can't we take some salmon from the wedding supplies then?'

'There isn't any more.'

Trish couldn't believe her ears. 'Wait,' she said, trying to stay calm. 'We're having a wedding tomorrow for fifty people and salmon is the main course. Surely that's still in the fridge?'

'No. I've used it all.'

Trish's jaw dropped. She went back to the dining room and, in her own charming way, convinced everyone to change their order. She then had to get on the phone and find someone who was prepared to bring up enough salmon for the Saturday. The wedding was saved. In fact, at three o'clock the next morning, after all the staff had gone home, Trish was still there by herself, bringing the guests more and more Champagne, ice buckets and beer. It soon became apparent that the guests were going to party all night and even though she longed to lock up, Trish felt she had to stay up to keep an eye on proceedings. Unfortunately, she also had to deal with a group of sleazy, drunk men who seemed inordinately interested in the fact that she was all alone. Over the years, Trish and I had become accustomed to people speculating about our sleeping arrangements. But while all alone and dealing with drunks making lewd innuendos, Trish hit a low point; this was not fun.

I like to ease into my day and wake up slowly and so, for me, all that smiling and being chatty early in the morning was hell; I simply do not like to speak until after I've had a quiet morning coffee.

Living on the premises at Cleopatra began to drive me bananas, too. I could never just open the door to the kitchen in the morning to have a cup of coffee in silence. There was always someone there; someone you had to talk to. If it wasn't the breakfast people, it was the kitchen people. I like to ease into my day and wake up slowly and so, for me, all that smiling and being chatty early in the morning was hell; I simply do not like to speak until after I've had a quiet morning coffee. Although Trish and I tried setting up a tea tray and kettle in the flat, it wasn't the same. We soon came to the realisation that we had strayed far from our original plan, which was to work on weekends and then enjoy living in the splendour of the house for the rest of the week. Because all our own things were crammed into our flat, we tended to stay there; it was easier. We had a fireplace to sit and read by, so it was cosy enough, but the lack of privacy proved to be a never-ending source of stress. I began to have strange nightmares involving toilets and Trish was developing asthma.

One Tuesday, which was the day we usually slept in, we woke up to find Cleopatra shrouded in an incredibly thick mountain mist. It was so thick that you could only see about two feet in front of you. Trish padded downstairs in her slippers and dressing gown to put on a pot of coffee. But as she pottered about in the kitchen she suddenly realised there was a group of people at the windows staring in at her! It was horrible. She opened the door and said: 'Look, I'm really sorry but we're closed.' Evidently, that wasn't enough; there was a frightful woman at the door who gave her a five-minute lecture: 'I say, do you know what time it is? I think it's disgraceful that you're still in your dressing gown at eleven o'clock in the morning ...' and so on.

Trish told her where to go in no uncertain terms; I could hear the shouting from upstairs. Trish was, understandably, furious. But it's fair to say her comments would probably not feature in a guide to customer relations. That dreadful woman actually forced Trish and I into admitting how bad things had become; we had to do something to alleviate our stress levels.

My nightmares stopped in 1991 when we bought a house just down the street. As well as moving into our own private space, we could rent out our apartment at Cleopatra, too. The fact that Australia was in the throes of an economic crisis meant we were also forced to rethink our financial situation. Our accountant said: 'Look, you're paying the mortgage every day. Maybe you should try to make money every day?' So we began to open every weeknight and Cleopatra became more and more like the restaurant I never wanted it to be. We knocked down the wall between a bedroom and the dining room so we could squeeze in a few more tables and accommodate an extra ten people. Of course, all of these refurbishments cost a fortune. Trish decided a whole new look was in order and had gorgeous triple-lined curtains made. Her talented son, Stephen, who had recently moved up to the mountains to live, also lime-washed the walls in a gorgeous pale-yellow. On the very first weekend we re-opened for business a customer managed to tip a whole bottle of red wine against the wall. Stephen had to then lime-wash over the stains, which became an almost weekly task for him. As well as the food, the décor at Cleopatra was ever-evolving.

Because Trish and I were working for ourselves, we never had to work towards a strict budget; and therefore there was never any great pressure to make a big profit. But we weren't silly; if there were expensive ingredients in one dish, we would balance that out with a more economical option. For us, taste and quality was paramount. We were never driven by cost; only by desire and inspiration. The pleasure of cooking for others and pleasing our guests was everything; we simply wanted others to enjoy the same things we enjoyed. But in business, however, we found that people eventually ground us down and forced us to become less inventive. One of my foibles – which can drive Trish crazy – is reading menus, as that is where you can really tell if a chef has put thought and imagination into the offerings. Balancing a menu is an art, and it is unfortunate when the customers take charge. It was with a big sigh of regret that we acquiesced: from February 1992, Cleopatra began to offer five entrées, five mains and five desserts at every sitting. We weren't the only ones who regretted the change; even today people visiting us in France are nostalgic about those early days at Cleopatra. 'Oh, don't you remember when you used to offer a special set Sunday lunch menu? That was so lovely.'

Cleopatra always served hearty portions. But unfortunately, once we started offering more options on the menu, the customers often ignored Trish's suggestions about what to order. For instance, if she knew they were going to order the *cassoulet* (which is very rich and filling with braised beans, duck and pork), she would suggest they have a light entrée, such as the celery *rémoulade* and a sorbet for dessert. But, oh no. They wanted to start with de-boned pig's trotters and chicken *farce* in a *crépinette* and end with the rich Dôme *chocolat-velours*. And then they'd complain that my food was too rich!

Another downside of giving people so much choice meant they were far less likely to try something new. Often, over the course of a weekend, guests would order the exact same thing two or three times, saying it was so delicious they just had to have it again. My ideal customer would say: 'Hmmm, I've never had that, but why not? I'll give it a go!' That's one of the reasons I've always loved to cook. And I've always admired Australians for their enthusiasm and openness to new experiences. But when there were five dishes to choose from for each course, it became that much harder to winkle out their sense of culinary adventure.

How I wish we had a dollar for every time a customer complained: 'Oh, I can't have that. I'm allergic to it.' What they really meant was: 'I don't like it.' Harder nuts to crack were people who claimed to be allergic to onion and garlic. There's onion and garlic in almost every French dish, or at least in the stock, and there were times when I screamed inside: 'Idiot! If you don't eat onion and garlic, why are you in a French restaurant?'

Worst of all were customers who would look at the menu and say: 'Oh dear. I am a vegetarian and there's nothing here I can eat. Could you get the chef to whip up something special for me?' They obviously had no idea how a kitchen works; we didn't have time to concoct something 'special'. And, besides, to me, everything on the menu *was* 'special'. I had invested hours planning and balancing the dishes I would serve and hated sending out dishes that weren't interesting. So when customers requested 'just a quick pasta with basil' I felt like throwing in the towel. It was my opinion that people should come to Cleopatra because they wanted what we had to offer and what we had poured our time and effort and talent into. If there was a huge list of ingredients they couldn't, or wouldn't, eat, they shouldn't bother to come. It's like going into a French dress shop and complaining that they don't sell kimonos. When people calling to book declared they were vegetarians or vegans, they would become extremely angry when Trish suggested they try a vegetarian restaurant instead. The *Sydney Morning Herald Good Food Guide* would get bristling three-page letters from outraged vegetarians, saying that we had served them something with a trace of anchovies in it. I have no patience with the 'well-done-meat' or 'vegetarian-because-I-feel-sorry-for-the-animal' brigade. Perhaps because my childhood was spent watching animals get butchered in an abattoir and the fact that I'd always eaten meat.

Even when I first started cooking, I never made anything too extreme, such as offal, without offering an alternative. There are people who adore tripe, and who'd return to the restaurant a few weeks later, salivating for more of the same. After driving all the way from Sydney, such customers would then be crushed to learn that tripe wasn't on that week's menu. But as much as I loved offal, it was hard to justify the cost, knowing we'd only sell four or five portions. At maximum capacity, Cleopatra only served fifty-four

Crépinette de pied de porc, sauce échalote moutarde

PIG'S TROTTER AND CHICKEN SAUSAGE

MAKES 6 (10 x 5 CM) CRÉPINETTES

THIS IS A VERY COUNTRY-STYLE, GUTSY AND WARMING ENTRÉE FOR COLD WINTER MONTHS.
YOU'LL NEED TO START THIS RECIPE 24 HOURS BEFORE YOU WISH TO SERVE IT.

2 pig's trotters, 400 g (14 oz) each

1 onion, studded with 2 cloves

2 carrots

1 celery stalk

1 leek

1 small turnip

1 small bouquet garni (thyme, parsley, bay leaf)

10 peppercorns

200 g (7 oz) crépine (caul fat) soaked in cold water
for 1–2 hours until clean and white

6 handfuls of bitter salad leaves (baby endive, baby
radicchio, curly endive)

½ bunch chives, finely chopped

CHICKEN FARCE

4 French shallots, thinly sliced

grapeseed oil

150 g (5½ oz) cleaned white button mushrooms,
thinly sliced

5 g (⅛ oz) dry cèpes (porcini), soaked for 1 hour in
warm water (optional)

1 garlic clove, crushed

2 tablespoons chopped flat-leaf (Italian) parsley

300 g (10½ oz) cleaned chicken meat, about
2 large legs

1 small egg, beaten

1 tablespoon cream

freshly grated nutmeg, to taste

Wash the trotters thoroughly, scrape any hard skin and singe to remove any hair. Place them in a saucepan and cover with cold water, bring to the boil, skim and add all the vegetables and seasonings. Boil slowly for 2½ hours at least, or until a wooden skewer will pierce them very easily at the centre. Let the trotters cool down in their stock, but not get completely cold.

Meanwhile, soak the crépine in cold water for 1–2 hours until clean and white. When the trotters are lukewarm, remove from stock, then strain stock and reserve (this is a marvellous gelatinous stock which can be saved to use in soups or stews). While still warm place the trotters on a board and with your hands remove all the bones, feeling every piece of meat and making sure there are no little bones left. Chop the meat into 1 cm (½ inch) pieces, season with salt and pepper and set aside in the refrigerator if using the next day.

TO MAKE THE CHICKEN FARCE: Take the trotter meat from the refrigerator and place in a warm area to loosen so it is easier to handle. In a small frying pan, sauté the shallots in a little grapeseed oil for 2 minutes, set aside in a bowl. In the same frying pan fry the mushrooms for 3–4 minutes then add to the shallots. If using cèpes, then drain, roughly chop and add to the bowl, with garlic and parsley.

Chop the chicken meat in a food processor, not too fine, and scrape out into another bowl. Place shallot and mushroom mixture in food processor and process until quite fine. Add to chicken mixture. Add the beaten egg, cream, nutmeg and season with salt and pepper and mix thoroughly.

Preheat oven to 200ºC (400ºF/Gas 6). Spread the crépine as thinly as possible over a chopping board and cut into six 20 x 25 cm (8 x 10 inch) rectangles. At 7 cm (2¾ inches) from narrow end, spread 2 tablespoonfuls of chicken farce into 10 x 5 cm (4 x 2 inch) rectangles and arrange 2 tablespoons of trotter meat on top, then spread another 2 tablespoons of chicken farce on top of that. Then wrap up the crépine, making a parcel in the shape of a fat sausage and place on a baking tray. When you have the six parcels lined up, not touching, bake in the oven for 15–20 minutes. They should be golden on both sides.

TO MAKE THE MUSTARD SAUCE: While the crépinettes are cooking, place the shallots, spring onions, vinegar and white wine in a saucepan over medium heat and reduce by half. Add the cream and 2 tablespoons of the reserved trotter stock. Cook for 10–15 minutes or until reduced to a coating consistency, if too thick add a little more trotter stock. Keep warm.

To serve, arrange the salad leaves on plates. Whisk the mustard into the sauce and check seasoning. Ladle a small amount of sauce onto each plate, sit the crépinette on the sauce, sprinkle with chives and serve very hot.

MUSTARD SAUCE

2 French shallots, chopped

2 spring onions, chopped

50 ml (1¾ fl oz) white wine vinegar

250 ml (9 fl oz/1 cup) white wine

150 ml (5 fl oz) cream

1 tablespoon dijon mustard

Brandade de morue en feuilletée de courgette

CREAM OF SALT COD LAYERED WITH

ZUCCHINI SLICES

SERVES 4

VISUALLY ATTRACTIVE AND A LIGHTER WAY OF EATING BRANDADE. ITS RICHNESS IS WELL BALANCED BY THE CRUNCHY ZUCCHINI AND THE ACIDITY OF THE TOMATOES. IT IS BETTER IN SUMMER MADE WITH RIPE JUICY TOMATOES. YOU'LL NEED TO START THE BRANDADE FOR THIS RECIPE THE DAY BEFORE SERVING.

1 large zucchini (courgette)

olive oil, for deep frying

50 g (1¾ oz/⅓ cup) plain (all-purpose) flour

TOMATO CONCASSÉ SAUCE

750 g (1 lb 10 oz) any variety of ripe tasty tomatoes

1 very large French shallot, finely diced

2 tablespoons olive oil

1 bouquet garni (1 bay leaf, 2 parsley sprigs, 2 thyme sprigs, 1 celery stalk)

2 garlic cloves, crushed

1 tablespoon tomato paste (concentrated purée)

1 tablespoon sugar

BRANDADE

500 g (1 lb 2 oz) very white, thick piece salt cod

½ small onion, sliced

1 bay leaf

2 mashing potatoes, (such as desiree), peeled and sliced

200 ml (7 fl oz) olive oil

2½ tablespoons cream and 2½ tablespoons milk, mixed together

freshly grated nutmeg, to taste

1 large garlic clove, crushed

finely grated zest and juice of ½ small lemon

TO MAKE THE BRANDADE: The day before serving, place the salt cod skin-side up, place the colander in another dish and add enough cold water to cover. Make sure the fish is not in contact with the bottom of the dish where the dissolved salt from the fish is stagnating. During the first 24 hours, change the water at least 4 times. Place in the refrigerator if the weather is very hot.

TO MAKE THE TOMATO CONCASSÉ: Peel and seed the tomatoes, chop roughly and set aside. Sweat the shallots in a saucepan for 5 minutes in the olive oil or until just beginning to turn golden, add the tomato pulp, bouquet garni, garlic, tomato paste and sugar, and season with salt and pepper. Cook slowly for 20 minutes. Remove the bouquet garni squeezing out the juices. Then put the tomato mixture through a mouli or blend, but not too fine. Set aside.

TO FINISH THE BRANDADE: Drain the salt cod, rinse under cold water, place in a saucepan and cover with cold water. Add the onion and bay leaf, bring to the boil slowly. As soon as it boils, remove the saucepan from the heat and cool a little.

Meanwhile boil the potatoes until soft, drain, crush with a potato masher and set aside in a warm place.

You must make the brandade while the fish is still warm but cool enough to handle – drain, remove the bones and break into small flakes. In a small saucepan warm the olive oil, in another small saucepan warm the combined cream and milk with a grating of nutmeg.

In a heavy-based saucepan, heat 45 ml (1½ fl oz) of the olive oil and garlic over low heat. Allow it to sizzle but do not let it colour, then add the cod quickly and work with a wooden spoon until the fish is reduced to a fine paste. At this point it is also possible to transfer it to an electric mixer fitted with a paddle. (Recipe continued page 233.)

Continue to beat, slowly adding the remaining warm olive oil, alternating with the warm milk and cream mixture.

Now add the mashed potatoes and keep mixing until the mixture is creamy; then stir in the lemon zest and juice. Season with nutmeg, white pepper and salt if needed. The brandade should be white and light, and kept warm, covered, above a bowl of simmering water (bain marie).

Gently heat the tomato sauce in a saucepan. Slice the zucchini (courgette) into 3 mm ($\frac{1}{8}$ inch) thick rounds, allowing about 10 per person.

Heat the olive oil in a deep-fryer or wok to 180ºC (350ºF). Roll the slices of zucchini in plain flour to lightly coat and deep-fry in batches until cooked through and crisp. Drain on paper towel. Keep warm on a tray in oven at 120ºC (235ºF/Gas $\frac{1}{2}$).

To serve, spread out four warm entrée plates, place 3 zucchini rounds on each plate, top each with 1 tablespoon of warm brandade, another zucchini round, another tablespoon of brandade and finish with a round of zucchini on top.

NOTE: Left-over brandade will keep if well sealed, in the refrigerator for a couple of days, reheat over a bain marie.

Petits farçis du vieux Nice

STUFFED BABY SUMMER VEGETABLES
WITH FRESH TOMATO SAUCE

SERVES 4

A PERFECT WAY TO ENJOY BABY SUMMER VEGETABLES, EACH WITH ITS OWN STUFFING AND A FRESH BASIL
AND TOMATO SAUCE. VISUALLY THIS IS A LOVELY DISH. MADE IN LARGE QUANTITIES FOR A PARTY (IF YOU CAN
FIND SOME WILLING HELPERS), THESE VEGETABLES ARE STUNNING. THEY CAN ALL BE PREPARED UP TO THE
STAGE OF PUTTING IN THE OVEN, THEN THEY CAN ALL BE BAKED TOGETHER.

STUFFED TOMATOES

4 Roma tomatoes, about 6.5 cm (2¾ inch) long

1 very large tomato, or two medium tomatoes

1 onion, very finely diced

1 tablespoon olive oil, plus extra for drizzling

1 large garlic clove, finely chopped

80 g (2¾ oz) fresh pork, minced

40 g (1½ oz) pancetta, minced

40 g (1½ oz) parmesan cheese, grated

1 small egg, beaten

1 tablespoon chopped flat-leaf (Italian) parsley

1 tablespoon sliced basil

STUFFED BABY SQUASH

4 baby squash, about 6–7 cm (2½–2¾ inch)
   diameteror 4 baby zucchini (courgette), extra

1 small zucchini (courgette)

1 tablespoon olive oil, plus extra for drizzling

1 small spring onion or white onion, finely diced

1 small tomato, peeled, seeded and chopped

1 very small clove garlic, chopped

1 small egg yolk

2 teaspoons dry breadcrumbs

2 teaspoons finely grated parmesan

1 teaspoon chopped chervil

1 teaspoon finely sliced basil

TO MAKE THE STUFFED TOMATOES: Slice off the 'hat' from the Roma tomatoes,
two-thirds from the top, hollow them out and reserve the flesh in a bowl.
Sprinkle salt inside each, turn them upside down in a baking dish with 'hats' to
the side. Set aside.

Peel and seed the remaining tomato, chop the flesh and add to the reserved
tomato flesh in the bowl. In a frying pan over medium heat, sauté onion in half
the olive oil and add tomato flesh and garlic.

At the same time, fry the minced pork and pancetta in remaining olive oil
over medium heat, add to tomato and cook for 15 minutes, stirring often. Cool.
Preheat the oven to 180ºC (350ºF/Gas 4).

When the stuffing is lukewarm, add parmesan, egg, parsley, basil and season
with salt and pepper if needed. Fill tomato shells with stuffing, replace their 'hats',
drizzle with olive oil, and bake for 20–25 minutes. Watch carefully to see they
do not split or break.

STUFFED BABY SQUASH: Preheat the oven to 180ºC (350ºF/Gas 4). Blanch the
squash or zucchini for 2 minutes, then drain. On the stem side, cut a little 'hat' off
the squash so you can hollow them with a teaspoon. Alternatively, halve the
zucchini lengthways and hollow them out with a teaspoon and set aside on a
baking tray. Chop the flesh finely together with the zucchini. Heat half the olive
oil in a frying pan over medium heat, sauté the squash and zucchini mixture for 5
minutes. Place into a bowl and set aside.

In the same frying pan, sauté the onion gently in the remaining olive oil until
softened, then add the tomato, garlic and season with salt and pepper. Add
to the squash mixture and set aside to cool. When lukewarm, stir in the egg yolk,
1 teaspoon of the breadcrumbs, the parmesan, chervil and basil. Mix well and

spoon stuffing into the squash shells, mounding with a tablespoon. Sprinkle with the remaining breadcrumbs. Put the 'hats' on top and drizzle with olive oil. Bake for 15–20 minutes.

STUFFED BABY EGGPLANT: Preheat the oven to 200ºC (400ºF/Gas 6). Cut the eggplants in half lengthwise, place on a baking tray, criss-cross the flesh side only with the tip of a small sharp knife, drizzle half the olive oil all over and season with salt and pepper. Bake for about 20–30 minutes. When the flesh is soft remove from oven and cool.

Meanwhile, in a frying pan over medium heat, sauté the mushrooms in the remaining olive oil, very quickly so they have just lost their water. Remove pan from the heat and set aside, with the mushrooms still in the pan.

In a mixing bowl beat egg, add parsley, mint and garlic, olives and half the breadcrumbs.

Turn the oven down to 180ºC (350ºF/Gas 4). Scoop out the flesh from the eggplant, chop the flesh, add to the frying pan containing mushrooms and cook over high heat stirring constantly for 2–3 minutes to dry them out. Remove from heat, cool a little then add to the egg mixture, season with salt and pepper and mix well. Fill the eggplant shells with the stuffing, sprinkle with remaining breadcrumbs, drizzle with a little extra olive oil and bake for 15 minutes until light brown.

To serve, arrange one of each vegetable on serving plates with a sprig of basil and the fresh tomato sauce (see recipe page 230).

STUFFED BABY EGGPLANT

2 small eggplants (aubergines) about 10 cm
  (4 inch) long
2 tablespoons olive oil, plus extra for drizzling
120 g (4¼ oz) button mushrooms, finely chopped
1 small egg
2 teaspoons chopped flat-leaf (Italian) parsley
4 mint leaves, finely sliced
1 small garlic clove, finely chopped
12 Kalamata olives, pitted and finely chopped
2 tablespoons dry breadcrumbs

basil sprigs, to serve

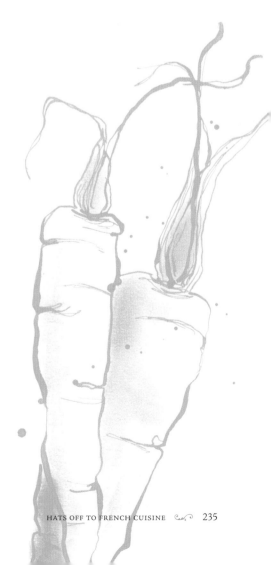

covers, which meant we just didn't have the turnover. You cannot cook just a tiny bit of tripe; you have to cook a big pot so it was a waste of time, money and gas.

As the menu grew, it took forever to take people's orders. 'But we can't decide! We want everything. It all looks lovely.' If the customers were good eaters and really loved the food, Trish would send out an extra entrée or two for them to share because we loved the fact they appreciated our efforts. In order to cope with our manic schedule, we also adjusted our weekends; eliminating the Sunday lunch as part of the package was a subtle way of raising the price to cover our growing costs without too many people noticing. We had found that guests often had other things to do on Sundays and were keen to rush back to Sydney. The new mid morning checkout time also eliminated the problem of people sneaking back to their freshly made-up beds on Sunday afternoons for a postprandial snooze. This caused chaos when the Sunday night customers arrived early and forced us into a frenzy of cleaning and remaking the beds with clean, fresh linen.

NOT LONG AFTER WE MADE ALL THESE CHANGES TO our menu, our gorgeous Gary left in a sudden and incomprehensible flurry. We were devastated. But if there is one lesson his unexpected departure taught us it was that 'no one is irreplaceable'. We coped. And in his place arrived Ken Gomes, a great cook and a great support who remains a close friend to this day.

At last, our beloved kitchenhand Roso, who used to despair over ever finding her Mr Right, found him. Over the years, Roso had witnessed all the ensuing dramas in the kitchen when staff had stood us up or left with only a week's notice. So when she became engaged she seriously asked us if a year's notice would be enough before she married and moved away. We had to agree that a year would probably suffice, but we were sad to see her go; she was like family. As well as being by our side for years she had seen Barney grow up, take his final exams and graduate from high school. On a busy Friday night Roso would often sigh and say: 'Hey, remember Friday nights with soup, fish and tart? Home and in bed by midnight? What the hell happened to that good idea?' Naturally we gave her a dishwasher as a wedding present.

To celebrate my fiftieth birthday, Trish and I closed Cleopatra one Sunday in March 1992. We had 110 people on the guest list, including many old friends from Upstairs and Au Chabrol. Before the economic crisis we had planned to go to Seville. Instead, we held a party *à la* flamenco. Ken cooked a wonderful Spanish feast and my fiftieth was a lot of fun.

Cleopatra continued to evolve in the 1990s. We painted the house in muted lime-washed shades of blue and yellow. Trish planted new azaleas and scented rose beds and terraced the lawn which elevated the whole al fresco dining experience. The bulk of our trade was always in winter, when our customers – especially those with a European background – liked to feel the change of season, which was most dramatic in the mountains. They'd go for bracing walks in the bush, sit by the open fire, eat hearty dinners, and wear all their gorgeous cashmere winter coats and beautiful boots that were unsuitable in balmy Sydney.

Spring was also hectic. It was when the crowds converged to look at the mountain gardens in full bloom and it culminated in Blackheath's rhododendron festival in November. It was the perfect time for special events; we'd do glamorous birthday parties and garden weddings and serve up to 150 guests in giant marquees. We never did Christmas or Boxing Day; we simply couldn't afford to pay staff triple wages. But we did host a couple of cracking New Year's Eve parties.

In the 1980s we seldom had any business in the summer. All that changed in the 1990s as more and more upmarket hotels and restaurants began sprouting up in the area. Worth mentioning was the opening of the charming, five-star Lilianfels, in Leura, in 1991; perched on a cliff's edge overlooking a valley, Lilianfels was one of many such luxury hotels that helped revolutionise tourism in the region and lure more and more people to the mountains. Increasingly, many Australians were ready to admit they hated baking on Bondi beach and much preferred eating lunch in the cool, mountain air. Of course, the presence of a luxury hotel with eighty-five rooms made it economical for new subsidiary industries to open (such as laundries). Hospitality workers also began migrating to the mountains, making it much easier to both hire and retain staff. It also became feasible for wholesalers to now travel from Sydney; suddenly, we could get daily deliveries of fresh fish!

Lilianfels often rang us to book dinners for their guests and our restaurant was the only one they would recommend. The hotel also put the taxi drivers on notice, which resulted in our customers getting a lot better service. It used to be a nightmare trying to convince a Blackheath taxi driver to pick up clients after midnight because they'd all gone off to bed!

Although we remained open every day, Trish and I stopped working Monday, Tuesday and Wednesday nights. We now had a very reliable staff of twelve and I had total trust in Ken running the kitchen. Trish further freed up her time when she discovered the joy of photocopying her handwritten menus. Along with all the new laws on hiring and the labyrinthine list of rates for apprentices, our accounts became increasingly complicated. To help us better manage our finances we hired a young woman who came in one day a week to do all our bookkeeping on the computer and pay staff directly into their accounts.

If ever anything went wrong, Trish and I were only a few doors down. But even when we weren't at the restaurant we still took bookings, ordered ingredients, conducted research, planned menus and worked in the herb garden at our house. Old habits die hard. I often made surprise visits to the kitchen during service. 'Just checking,' I'd say. It was difficult to believe that just the two of us, Trish and I, had ever managed to run the restaurant on our own.

Ken – who had promised to work for us full-time for two years – gave us plenty of notice when he felt it was time to leave. But even when he was back working in Sydney, he was still a great support to us. Ken was always cheerful and good-natured and if I ever had a problem and phoned him, he could tell by the tone of my voice what was up. All he would say was: 'Hello, Dany. When?' Meaning when did I need him. I could always count on him for what we came to call his 'guest appearances'. Of course sometimes he would tease me: 'Oh, Dany, I just don't know …' Then there'd be an agonising wait before he said: 'Is the 5.30 pm train all right for tonight?'

If Ken wasn't busy, we'd talk him into staying the night and cooking dinner for us over at our house. Trish often said: 'Ken, if ever I become really, really rich, I'm going to employ you as my personal chef.' Ken could cook a range of different cuisines – French, Italian or Asian – and do so extremely well.

> *The mains became more elaborate and labour-intensive, too. My rabbit with garlic received a lot of attention. The dish was a rearrangement of my grandmother's very country concoction of rabbit and potatoes cooked in a cocotte.*

A visit to Cleopatra became almost de rigueur for actors and filmmakers visiting Sydney and needing to be entertained. They would be sent up to us on Sundays by their handlers for a long, lazy lunch in the garden. Sometimes, they'd stay the night. I remember one spring when the garden was at its peak, everything flowering at once, and a famous film director was standing on the front steps in his dressing gown. 'Look at this!' he thundered, waving his arms about like a conductor. 'Just look at this! This is paradise! Absolute paradise!' Just at that moment, Trish made an entrance carrying a tray laden with coffee and treats. 'Mind you,' he said, pausing rather theatrically and giving Trish a sidelong glance, 'it's an expensive paradise but paradise nonetheless!'

Now that I had enough staff to support me in the kitchen, I was able to further develop my own style of cooking. We also had time to produce elegant *mises en bouche*, which were just that: small perfect mouthfuls to awaken the appetite. The point of the serving being so small was so it didn't dull the appetite for the courses to come.

Among the new entrées were a *ballotine* of cabbage, filled with chestnuts and celeriac; mussel soup with saffron; crab tartlets with a crab claw on the side and an oyster and mushroom soup with a *brochette* of deep-fried oysters balanced over the soup dish. Our cheese soufflé with tarragon sauce was very successful and the fresh crabmeat in a cabbage parcel was so scrumptious that it was a challenge for Trish to convince people not to order it, so we wouldn't run out. A table of eight would all order the crab, and Trish would start shaking her head. 'No, no, no, you can't do that. Since there are eight of you, and there are four entrees, why don't you order two of each of the entrées, and I'll bring you two extra crabs so you can all have a taste.' It always worked.

The mains became more elaborate and labour-intensive, too. My rabbit with garlic received a lot of attention. The dish was a rearrangement of my grandmother's very country concoction of rabbit and potatoes cooked in a *cocotte*. I de-boned the rabbit in advance and pre-fried the potatoes in duck fat before arranging them into a little galette. Next I placed the rabbit on top of the galette with garlic and parsley so the juices seeped into the potatoes. For service, I'd slice the rabbit, arrange it on the potatoes and then drizzle the sauce on top. The result was a far more elegant version of Grandmère Rachel's stew.

I also made *poulet sauté à la lyonnaise*, a potato pie that originated in the region of Berry; and a *tourte de volaille* (chicken and salsify pie) inspired by La Mazille. (Salsify was non-existent in Australia at that time so I substituted them with parsnips, which also worked well.) I also made my version of *canard Montmorency*, which is duck breast roasted until pink and served with cherry sauce; the legs are made into a little *pâté en croûte* and served on the side. Another favourite was my roasted milk-fed lamb sliced into *noisettes* with a baby tartelette of double-peeled broad beans surrounded by slivers of artichoke and finished with lamb jus.

At this point we had a full-time pastry chef to help us produce our pastry dishes, which were always in high demand. Every single person who came to work in the kitchen wanted to learn how to make pastry. Even the chefs!

Another one of my signature flourishes was the fact that I served a generous dollop of sauce on the plate instead of the little 'comma' on the side that had become so fashionable. A good sauce is a lot of work and I can't see the point of going to all that trouble if you don't serve enough to really get a good taste of it. You should also be able to mop it up with bread at the end of the meal. I even had a special ladle to ensure the right amount was added. I wanted sauces that were light not gluggy or thickened with flour and never bubbling away in a bain marie. Instead, I heated up for each portion *à la minute*, or even *à la seconde* in a little saucepan, sometimes *montée au beurre* – with the butter whisked in at the last minute.

AS WELL AS RELYING ON MY INTUITION IN THE KITCHEN, I also conducted a lot of research that would help further develop my technique when cooking different dishes. Salmon was one ingredient that I really studied up on. Because Tasmanian salmon was always of such a high quality, I used a lot of it; I always had two fish dishes on the menu, which could be ordered either as entrées or mains. One of my favourite ways to celebrate salmon was to cure it and serve the gravlax in a tartelette with sheep milk's yoghurt or baby blinis. Alternatively, I'd top a slice of salmon with a black olive purée and bake it on a bed of sweated spring onions. Realising that many of our customers weren't prepared to do battle with the raw French-style *plateau de fruits de mer*, I made an *assiette de fruits de mer* instead: it included a crab salad, baby mussel salad, and cooked prawns and oysters served with a lemon mayonnaise.

A typical Sunday lunch in the 1990s included *a potage aux perles du Japon* (made from the bouillon of the *pot au feu*) and a *pot au feu* with baby vegetables followed by a

Canard aux cerises et petit pâté en croûte

ROAST DUCK WITH CHERRIES
AND LITTLE DUCK LEG PIES

SERVES 4

IN FRANCE WE WOULD USE NANTES OR ROUEN DUCKS FOR THIS DISH; IN AUSTRALIA AND ENGLAND THE SPECIALLY
BRED WHITE AYLESBURY DUCKS HAVE THE BEST TENDER BREAST MEAT AND TASTE.

Cut the legs from the ducks, keeping 2 legs for another use. Season the duck buffets inside and out with salt and pepper and place them in a roasting pan and set aside.

TO MAKE THE LITTLE DUCK PIES: Gently poach 2 legs of the duck in enough stock to cover them for 30 minutes or until tender. Meanwhile, roll the puff pastry out to 3 mm (⅛ inch) thick and line four 8 cm (3¼ inch) pie dishes. Cut rounds from remaining pastry for lids, place on a baking tray and refrigerate until firm.

Remove the poached duck legs from stock, reserve stock. Remove meat from bones and finely dice, place in a bowl with the duck livers and mix well. Add the cream, parsley, and season with salt and pepper. Fill the pie dishes with the duck mix, brush the edges of pastry with the egg wash and stick on their lids. Brush the lids with egg wash and refrigerate.

Preheat the oven to 220ºC (425ºF/Gas 7). In a saucepan over medium heat, reduce wine by half, add the port or Banyuls bring to the boil and flambé. Reduce the heat to a simmer, and poach the cherries in this liquid for 2–3 minutes maximum. Using a slotted spoon, remove cherries and set aside to cool. Add the stock to the cherry poaching liquor, reduce, taste and season with salt and pepper. Set aside and keep warm.

Roast the duck buffets for 15–20 minutes. Turn breast downwards and place in another oven at 80ºC (165ºF/Gas ¼) for 10–15 minutes to keep warm if you have one (or cover tightly with aluminium foil and rest on top of the stove). The duck meat will relax, the juices will go down into the fillets and they will be uniformly pink.

Reduce the oven temperature to 210ºC (415ºF/Gas 6–7). Cook the pies for about 15 minutes or until they are golden. Heat the sauce, add the Guignolet and cherries. To serve, slice the duck fillets from the breastbone and serve with the sauce, cherries and a little pie.

2 white Aylesbury or Muscovy ducks, 1.5–1.8 kg
   (3 lb 5 oz to 4 lb) each
400 ml (14 fl oz) cabernet sauvignon wine
75 ml (2½ fl oz/⅓ cup) Port or Banyuls
300 g (10½ oz) dark cherries, stoned
20 ml (½ fl oz/1 tablespoon) 'Guignolet'
   (or cherry liqueur)

LITTLE DUCK PIES
500 ml (17 fl oz/2 cups) (or more) duck
   or veal stock
250 g (9 oz) good-quality puff pastry
60 g (2¼ oz) duck livers (about 2), diced
1 tablespoon thick cream
2 teaspoons chopped flat leaf (Italian) parsley
1 egg wash (1 egg beaten with 1½ tablespoons
   of milk)

Cuissot de chevreuil, sauce poivrade, gâteau de céleri-rave

ROAST VENISON WITH PEPPER SAUCE AND CELERIAC GATEAU

SERVES 4

VENISON IS ONE RED MEAT THAT MUST BE EATEN VERY RARE.

1 tablespoon coarsely ground black peppercorns

sea salt

1 kg (2 lb 4 oz) fillet of venison, trimmed (reserve trimmings)

1 teaspoon redcurrant jelly

1 teaspoon dijon mustard

250 g (9 fl oz) jar good-quality preserved redcurrants

POIVRADE SAUCE

2 teaspoons olive or grapeseed oil

100 g (3½ oz) diced pancetta (or prosciutto) along with venison trimmings (see above)

1 onion, diced

1 carrot, diced

2 French shallots, diced

1 teaspoon roughly crushed black peppercorns

2 tablespoons red wine vinegar

1 teaspoon tomato paste (concentrated purée)

500 ml (17 fl oz/2 cups) good strong red wine

1 garlic clove, chopped

300 ml (10½ fl oz) veal or chicken stock

1 small bouquet garni

CELERIAC GATEAU

butter, to grease

280 g (10 oz) celeriac, peeled and cubed

2 small eggs

120 ml (4 fl oz) cream

freshly grated nutmeg, to taste

TO MAKE THE PEPPER SAUCE: Heat the oil in a heavy-based saucepan over medium heat. Brown the pancetta and venison trimmings until they stick to the bottom and turn brown. Add the onion, carrot, shallots and cook until caramelised. Add the peppercorns and vinegar, and reduce. Stir in the tomato paste, wine, garlic, stock and bouquet garni. Stir well, cooking very slowly over a low heat for 1 hour, skimming often. When it is reduced by about half, strain through a very fine sieve, apply pressure to extract the juices from the vegetables and meats, then discard the solids. Bring the sauce to the boil again, skim the fat from the top, check seasoning and set aside. Combine peppercorns and sea salt and roll the venison in it. Sit at room temperature for at least 30 minutes, while you make the gateau.

TO MAKE THE CELERIAC GATEAU: Preheat the oven to 180°C (350°F/Gas 4). Butter 100 ml (3½ fl oz) capacity ramekins. Line the base of the ramekins with greased baking paper. Place in a deep roasting pan and set aside.

Steam the celeriac for 10–15 minutes or until very soft. Drain well, then purée in a food processor until smooth; mix in the eggs one at a time and the cream. Season with the nutmeg and salt and pepper. Process again and divide the mixture between the ramekins. Pour enough hot water into the roasting pan to come halfway up the sides of the ramekins. Cook for about 20 minutes or until set in the middle. Leave in hot water, covered, until time to serve.

Increase the oven temperature to 225°C (425°F/Gas 7). Preheat the roasting pan in oven. Place venison in roasting pan and roast for 8–10 minutes, depending on the thickness of the meat. It must remain rare. Rest in another oven at 80°C (165°F/Gas ¼) for 8 minutes.

To serve, heat the sauce, then whisk in redcurrant jelly and dijon mustard. Unmould celeriac gateaux onto warm plates, scatter with redcurrants. Slice the venison and divide between plates. Spoon some sauce onto each plate and serve the remainder separately.

Pigeonneau, crème de petits pois et oignons nouveaux

ROAST YOUNG PIGEON, FRESH PEA PURÉE AND CONFIT BABY ONIONS

SERVES 4

A RECIPE FOR EARLY SPRING WHEN THE NEW YOUNG PEAS ARE SWEET AND TENDER, AS ARE THE PIGEONS.

4 farm pigeons (about 500 g/1 lb 2 oz each)

4 large thyme sprigs

2 small garlic cloves

8 thin pancetta slices

grapeseed oil, to drizzle

30 ml (1 fl oz) port

250 ml (9 fl oz/1 cup) chicken stock

PEA-PURÉE AND ONIONS

350 g (12 oz/2¼ cups) shelled fresh green peas,

350 ml (12 fl oz) (or more) chicken stock

80 ml (2½ fl oz/⅓ cup) cream

20 baby round spring onions

20 g (¾ oz) butter

1 tablespoon grapeseed oil

TO MAKE THE PEA PURÉE AND ONIONS: Steam the peas for 8–10 minutes, depending on the size, they should be soft, but still green. Plunge immediately into cold water, then strain. Purée in a food processor, as finely as possible, adding a tablespoon of the chicken stock to ease the process, if necessary. Push through a fine sieve with the back of a ladle or a wooden spoon into a small saucepan, season, stir in cream and set aside.

Peel the onions, leaving a 2 cm (¾ inch) green 'tail'. In a saucepan over medium heat cook the onions slowly in the butter and oil for 5–10 minutes, adding a pinch of salt and sugar. When lightly browned, half cover with the stock and cook, covered, for 15–20 minutes or until soft but not falling apart. Set aside in the saucepan and keep warm.

Preheat the oven to 220°C (425°F/Gas 7). Season the pigeons inside and out with salt and pepper, place a sprig of thyme and half a clove of garlic, crushed, inside each bird. Place pancetta over the breast of the birds and secure with string. Place in a flameproof roasting pan, drizzle with some grapeseed oil and bake for 12–15 minutes for rare, depending how rare you like them, you may like to cook them longer. When cooked to your liking, remove the garlic and thyme from the insides and place into the roasting pan, remove the pigeons from the roasting pan to another warm dish, keep covered, in a warm area or low oven. Discard the fat from the roasting pan, deglaze with the port and add the chicken stock, reduce by half, then strain into a small saucepan ready to heat.

To serve, cut the strings from the pigeons, crisp the pancetta, cut the pigeons in half or into 4 pieces. Heat the pea purée over low heat, stirring. Heat the sauce and heat the onions. Spoon the pea purée onto a warm serving platter. Place the pigeons on purée. Place the onions around the platter and place the pancetta on top of pigeons.

Noisettes d'agneau, barquette à l'ail

LOIN OF LAMB WITH A LITTLE GARLIC TART AND LAMB JUS

SERVES 4

LAMB AND GARLIC IS A MARRIAGE MADE IN FOOD HEAVEN, AND THIS TARTLET OF ROASTED GARLIC PURÉE SERVED WITH ROAST LAMB MAKES FOR A VERY SPECIAL DISH. YOU'LL NEED TO START THIS RECIPE 24 HOURS IN ADVANCE.

GARLIC TARTLETS

175–200 g (6–7 oz) pâte brisée (short crust pastry)
    (see recipe page 328)
1 whole large head garlic
1–2 tablespoons tomato concassé, strained
1–2 tablespoons cream

2 loins of lamb, boned out, flaps left on
    (about 875 g/1 lb 15 oz each)
4 thyme sprigs, leaves picked
2 rosemary sprigs, leaves picked
olive oil, for drizzling
2 tablespoons tomato concassé (see recipe page 230)

LAMB JUS

1 tablespoon olive oil
1 kg (2 lb 4 oz) loin bones, or other lamb bones,
    chopped roughly, and lamb off-cuts
2 carrots, sliced
3 garlic cloves, skin on, crushed
1 celery stalk, sliced
5 parsley sprigs

TO MAKE THE GARLIC TARTLETS: Preheat oven to 220ºC (425ºF/Gas 7). Roast the garlic for 20 minutes or until soft.

Meanwhile, roll out pastry to 3 mm (1/8 inch) thick and line five 8 cm (31/4 inch) diameter tartlet tins. Line with aluminium foil and fill with dry beans or pastry weights. Place on a tray and refrigerate.

Using a food processor, blend the roasted, peeled garlic with the tomato sauce until very smooth, add some cream and season with salt and pepper. It should be pale pink and the consistency of a thin purée. Transfer to a saucepan and set aside.

Reduce oven temperature to 200ºC (400ºF/Gas 6). Bake the tartlet cases for 10 minutes or until pale golden. Reduce temperature to 180ºC (350ºF/Gas 4). Remove foil and weights and cook for another 3 minutes. Set aside on tray.

Increase oven temperature to 220ºC (425ºF/Gas 7). Remove any extra fat from the loins of lamb, being careful not to pierce the flaps, chop herbs together and sprinkle all over the loin and inside the flaps and season with salt and pepper. Roll the flaps to enclose the meat and secure with string at 2 cm (3/4 inch) intervals. Place in a roasting pan and drizzle with a small amount of oil. Roast for 10–15 minutes for medium rare. Rest, covered, in a warm area for 8–10 minutes.

Reduce oven to 160ºC (315ºF/Gas 2–3). Reheat pastry cases for 4 minutes. Add the tomato concassé to 250 ml (9 fl oz/1 cup) of the jus, season with salt and pepper and simmer for 3 minutes. Reheat the garlic mix over very low heat.

Cut each loin into 4 noisettes. On each plate, place a warm tartlet filled with garlic purée, 2 lamb noisettes and moisten with warmed sauce.

TO MAKE THE LAMB JUS: In a heavy-based saucepan, heat oil over medium heat and sauté the bones and vegetables until golden. Pour out the fat and discard. Cover with water, cook until all the liquid has evaporated, cover again with water to the level of the contents, reduce heat to low and cook very slowly for 2 hours. Strain, pressing out all the vegetable juices and reduce by half. Jus may be frozen.

deep-fried *beignets* of dates stuffed with pistachios and *crème patissière* and served with honey ice cream.

One day an ex-art teacher from Orange came to us at Cleopatra and introduced himself as 'the Beaver', whose job it was to forage for hard-to-find ingredients such as brook trout, chestnuts, walnuts, berries, figs, and baby lamb. The Beaver also sourced fresh white asparagus, which, up until then, we'd only ever found sold in a can in Australia. The Beaver also found fig leaves for me. I discovered that by braising peeled chestnuts under the fig leaves they were infused with a wonderful flavour. Thanks to the Beaver, I also made walnut liqueur and *vin de noix*, which, according to very old Périgourdine recipes, had to be macerated in glass jars for forty days in the sun with a quarter turn every day. I found such biblical instructions to be very appealing. There wasn't much sun in the misty mountains so we had to leave them in our brightest patch at the end of the tennis court. Of course, we'd then forget about them. Ten days later, Trish would say: 'Guess what is still at the end of the tennis court?' Even after ten days and with no turning the *vin de noix* were still good and I would use it in a sauce for guinea fowl served with chestnut purée; the combination was delicious.

Every time a new dish appeared on the menu, I'd be like an actor with stage fright; worrying about how my interpretation would be received. I attribute these first-night jitters to the fact that I didn't have any professional training ...

Often the Beaver would turn up with things that he couldn't recognise, especially mushrooms, and I'd have to say, 'Um no. That's very poisonous!' He eventually bought a big ute and he would squirrel away his stash of ingredients under potato bags, scared I would try and procure them for my own purposes. I knew his secret stores were destined for Sydney restaurants, but I was always so nosy and just had to have a peep ...

In September 1993 Marcelline the wood-fired Godin stove had to go. We sold it and bought a brand-new gas stove, a stainless-steel kitchen table and a salamander grill. We also converted the garage into a coolroom and office. For years, the wonderful old French pâtisserie table had been the centrepiece in our country kitchen. Trish would never tell me what it cost and when I grumbled about it being impractical and difficult to clean she would just shrug it off and say, 'but it is really beautiful'. Trish finally agreed to take her lovely old table home when one of the male cooks broke the ancient marble slab at one end; the incident happened during a bone-crushing display of machismo while he was making praline. Finally I could have my purpose-built stainless-steel centre table; although it was far more practical, it was much less beautiful.

Our new stove meant we had more oven space, which meant I could dare to try Michel Bras' *le biscuit de chocolat coulant*. After weeks of trial and error with the mixes, temperature and *centre du noyau de gianduja*, I finally achieved success! All the time spent tweaking the dish was obviously worth it; with its warm, gooey chocolate centre it proved to be one of our most popular desserts. The dish was also very practical during a hectic service because all the hard work was done in advance. Once an order came in, all you had to do was bake it in the oven for just eighteen minutes, and *voilà*. I also made a sensational sheep's milk yoghurt ice cream with poached cherries and a *tuile*; and a fig and pistachio parfait with a strawberry sauce.

As we progressed through the 1990s I made dishes such as: *les petits farcis du vieux Nice* (which featured a baby eggplant, baby squash and roma tomato, all stuffed with different ingredients); as well as a summery *feuilleté de brandade* (very thin slices of deep-fried zucchini, layered with a warm purée of salt cod with olive oil and milk and a fresh tomato *concassé*). A kangaroo fillet with a *poivrade* sauce was also a speciality of the house. I treated the kangaroo like venison, but served it with a sweet potato garnish. I also invented an oyster and spinach recipe that I was especially proud of; it consisted of wilted English spinach with warm poached oysters and fresh mushrooms stuffed with pork and crabmeat, dried *cèpes*, sherry, truffle juice and *nuoc mam* and a tablespoon of vermouth and butter sauce. This was one of my very few ventures into fusion, but after years of experience, you do acquire a good sense of *recoupement*, of cross-referencing flavours and knowing what will work well together. Sometimes this meant breaking with tradition. But every time I used coriander in *navarin d'agneau*, I knew Grandmère Rachel would be rolling in her grave.

———————

ALTHOUGH I WAS VERY SELF-ASSURED IN THE KITCHEN, I never considered myself to be an inventive or creative chef. I was an artisan, always poring over the pages of French regional cookbooks or those by famous chefs and then arranging the dishes to suit my own taste and level of ability; I also had to consider whether the staff and equipment would be up to the task. My guiding principle was always to presume that if I liked a dish, other people would too and not the other way around. If you started cooking a certain way because you assumed the customers preferred it that way you would end up being a master of mediocrity. It was great having our own space in our own kitchen in our own home where I could experiment and try new things. Trish would taste the dish and we would discuss how it could be improved and presented before putting it on the menu. Every time a new dish appeared on the menu I'd be like an actor with stage fright; worrying about how my interpretation would be received. I attribute these first-night jitters to the fact that I didn't have any professional training and was perhaps venturing into territory that might be considered beyond my station. To help alleviate my nerves, Trish would return to the kitchen to show me the plates wiped clean. (She was far too kind to ever show me the ones that weren't and if someone left, say, a beautiful piece of juicy pink lamb, she would hide it so I wouldn't be upset.) Also bolstering my confidence was the fact that the box where we emptied the plate scraps was always surprisingly empty.

The greatest compliments I've ever received as a chef have been when keen home cooks have come into the kitchen at the end of service with a big smile to say: 'Oh Dany, did you put such-and-such in that dish? I think so.' That is what has always given me the greatest thrill of all: to know that I can communicate with everyday people through their palate and that they really appreciate it. It's during those moments that all the hard work seemed suddenly worth it; such compliments meant a lot to me.

My favourite customers have never been the high-profile chefs or celebrities. In fact, my perfect customers were those who arrived with a sense of anticipation and a sense of occasion. These were the customers that were open to suggestion who possessed a healthy appetite and took great pleasure in all that we took pride in offering. The greatest compliment was for them to make a booking for 'next time' before they'd even left the restaurant. There were also those who called at the start of the year to make a series of bookings throughout the coming year so they'd have 'lots to look forward to'.

If I knew that certain customers had stayed with us at the same time the previous year I'd revamp the menu entirely. But there were also those who wanted to see their favourites on the menu; one family who always came for a week in winter insisted on being served *cassoulet* for at least three of their meals. Knowing they had been looking forward to these meals for up to a year sometimes added extra pressure. What on earth were they expecting? But I had no choice; I simply had to come up with the goods, disappointing them was not an option.

In the end, what wore us down at Cleopatra was the staff. We'd invest all this time training the waiters and kitchen staff only to see them go off and leave us and we'd have to start all over again. It was relentless. One of the worst staffers we had was a certain chef whom I will call 'Bruce'. Bruce could cook. He was passionate, had a great palate and was very capable. But whenever the pressure was on, instead of putting his head down and upping his game like the rest of us, he'd flip his lid. The first time Bruce lost the plot in the kitchen was on Easter Sunday. We had been exceptionally busy Thursday, Friday and Saturday, and there were over fifty people booked for both lunch and dinner. But when I arrived to start work at 10.30 am Bruce was nowhere to be seen. As time ticked on, the housekeeper told me Bruce had come in early that morning, had eaten breakfast and then declared he was off to collect some mushrooms. *Mushrooms?* In short, Bruce had done a runner. I had to do his job as well as my own for lunch and dinner that day, with everyone pitching in the best they could. The atmosphere in the kitchen was silent and grim. Bruce's wife felt so bad that she came to apologise and ended up washing up for us, too, as our kitchenhand had also left us in the lurch. What a day!

To add insult to injury, almost everyone over the course of the Easter weekend paid in cash, rather than using their credit cards. Trish locked the money in a box, which was then stored in a locked filing cabinet in the locked office. Someone broke through the window, jimmied the filing cabinet open and took the lot. And it *was* a lot, too.

A few years down the track we again needed a chef and word came back to us through the network that Bruce wanted his job back. I threw a fit and said no. Leaving us as he had was unforgivable; there is no greater crime for a chef to abandon the kitchen during service. But Trish and Monique argued that everyone should have a second chance and that he really was a good chef and we needed him. Bruce came back to us with tears in his eyes, begging to be reinstated. I was so exhausted from not having enough help that I said 'okay'. Things were fine for a couple of months, but then we had a big event scheduled and Bruce did a no-show. He knew not to show his face at Cleopatra again.

A few days later I asked an apprentice to go to the coolroom and bring back the gruyère, which we kept in a wooden cheese box. I knew that there should have been a huge quarter of a round, wrapped in muslin. 'It's not there,' said the young apprentice.

'What do you mean, it's not there?' I grumbled, tired of having to deal with finding things for him twenty times a day. 'Of course it's there. Go and look again.' He returned minus the cheese again and so I went in to have a look and found he was right. It was gone. Then I looked to see where the fillet of beef should have been, but there was no fillet of beef. I kept looking around and thought, 'Uh-oh'. A ham was missing; the gravlax was gone and a bucket full of roasted bones, which were ready to make demi-glaçe had also disappeared. What kind of demented burglar would steal roasted bones? But then we worked it out: if you were to add up the missing ingredients, you could have made an entrée, a main course (with sauce), cheese and dessert! We had to laugh, but we also had to ring up the police to report the theft. Of course, neither they nor the insurance company were interested because the coolroom didn't have a lock. We had to put bars on the window and a padlock on the coolroom and in so doing moved another step away from having a 'beautiful life, creating beautiful food in beautiful surroundings'.

Yes, our dream now had a few downsides. But there were lots of positives, too, especially with regards to some of the people we met. There was the lovely Kerry Anne, a waitress extraordinaire and real professional who would proudly announce that she had ended up with eighteen walk-ins on a Tuesday night – when just she and the chef were on – and that 'everyone had gone home happy'. We also had Chui Lee Luk, the then twenty-nine-year-old lawyer who suddenly decided she wanted to be a chef. Chui had already worked for several restaurants in Sydney, when she came to me, saying: 'Dany, I want to work with you. I just really need to learn.' Chui was a fast learner. When I taught her how to make pastry she took it very seriously; she was very refined and dedicated and soon highly skilled. Before too long, Chui was in charge of doing all the entrées on the new gas stove and, as soon as she'd finished those, she'd swap to doing desserts. She was exceptionally talented.

We also had a group of macho men in the kitchen who were led by an arrogant and dispassionate male chef, who was also French. These men were all professional and highly trained, but they were cocky and competitive, too, and, because of their adversarial approach, the atmosphere in the kitchen changed. Staff dinners, which were once lovingly prepared, were now thrown together at the last minute. Complicating matters even further were the tangled love affairs between the chefs and waitresses. Staff would arrive for work exhausted, hungover and snarling at each other. Adding to the levels of aggression was the fact the housekeepers suddenly decided to hate each other. It became a struggle to maintain the convivial atmosphere we had always had at Cleopatra. The

Aumonière de crêpe aux pommes

SAUTÉED APPLES WRAPPED IN A CRÊPE WITH SPICED RED-WINE SAUCE

SERVES 4

THIS RECIPE WAS INSPIRED BY *LA CUISINE DE BRETAGNE* BY FLORENCE ARZEL, AND TYING THE PANCAKES UP TO LOOK LIKE LITTLE PURSES MAKES A LOVELY DESSERT 'GIFT'.

TO MAKE THE CRÊPE BATTER: Mix together the flours, sugar and salt in a bowl, gradually stir in the combined eggs, add the milk and melted butter to make a smooth batter. Cover and rest the batter at room temperature for at least 1 hour.

TO MAKE THE CANDIED ORANGE STRINGS: Using a vegetable peeler, cutting around the circumference of the orange, cut about six-eight 15–20 cm (6–8 inch) lengths of zest, without pith, then with a sharp knife cut these into thin 'strings'. Blanch in boiling water, drain and refresh. Bring the sugar and 250 ml (9 fl oz/ 1 cup) of water to the boil and cook until a syrup. Add the 'strings' and cook gently until transparent, remove from heat and cool. Store in a jar in the refrigerator.

TO MAKE THE SPICED RED WINE AND APPLES: In a saucepan, combine the wine, sugar, orange strings, spices and 100 ml (3½ fl oz) water, stir over medium heat until the sugar dissolves. Bring to the boil and cook for 10–15 minutes or until reduced by half. Strain and set aside. Peel and cut the apples into 1 cm (½ inch) cubes; then sauté in a frying pan over medium heat very quickly in the butter with some extra sugar. until golden Add apples to the spiced wine, and macerate for 1 hour. Strain and set the apples and the spiced wine aside separately.

Batter should be the consistency of thickened cream, if not, thin with a little water. Heat a little grapeseed oil in a 23 cm (9 inch) frying or pancake pan, spoon two tablespoons of batter at a time rotating to coat pan evenly and cook for 1–2 minutes on each side, until golden. When all the crêpes are cooked, place 2 tablespoons of the spiced apple in the centre of each crêpe, gather up the edges of the crepe into the shape of a little purse, and tie in place with an orange string. Preheat the oven to 200°C (400°F/Gas 6). Heat the spiced wine sauce. Whisk the cream to soft peaks and refrigerate until needed. Heat the 'purses' on a baking tray in the oven for 5–7 minutes or until heated through. Serve in shallow soup bowls, surrounded with hot spiced wine sauce and whipped cream.

200 ml (7 fl oz) cream, for whipping

CRÊPE BATTER
100 g (3½ oz/⅔ cup) plain (all-purpose) flour
25 g (1 oz) rye flour
30 g (1 oz) caster (superfine) sugar
3 eggs
300 ml (10½ fl oz) milk
1 tablespoon unsalted butter, melted
grapeseed oil, to cook the pancakes

CANDIED ORANGE STRINGS
1–2 large oranges
250 g (9 oz) sugar

SPICED RED WINE AND APPLES
330 ml (11¼ fl oz/1⅓ cups) strong red wine
60 g (2¼ oz) caster (superfine) sugar, plus a little extra for cooking the apples
1 clove
1 juniper berry
½ vanilla bean, split, seeds scraped
1 cinnamon stick
7 coriander seeds
4 apples (granny smith or braeburn)
20 g (¾ oz) unsalted butter

Gratin de brugnons et framboises

NECTARINE AND RASPBERRY GRATIN

SERVES 4

THIS IS A DESSERT FOR THE END OF SUMMER, WHEN THE NECTARINES AND BLACKBERRIES ARE AT THEIR BEST. EARLIER IN THE SEASON, USE STRAWBERRIES AND RASPBERRIES — WHATEVER IS PLENTIFUL AND IN SEASON. IT IS EASY TO MAKE BUT LOOKS VERY SPECIAL WHEN BROWNED UNDER THE GRILL JUST BEFORE SERVING.

Mix the egg yolks, cream, orange juice and honey together and cook in a saucepan over low heat, stirring constantly with a wooden spoon (in the same way as for a crème anglaise), being careful not to let it boil. When it thickens and coats the back of a spoon remove from the heat and strain into a bowl. Set aside and allow to cool. It can be kept in the refrigerator until ready to use.

Preheat the grill (broiler) to high. Before serving, cut the nectarines into wedges and arrange in 4 shallow soup plates, place under the grill to warm. Meanwhile whisk the extra whipping cream, and fold into the egg yolk mixture. Sprinkle the raspberries over the nectarines and pour over the cream mixture. Sprinkle with icing sugar, place under the grill and cook until light golden brown. Place each bowl on a folded napkin placed on a plate to make them easier to serve, be careful, as the edges of the bowls will be hot.

4 egg yolks

60 ml (2 fl oz/¼ cup) cream

60 ml (2 fl oz/¼ cup) fresh orange juice

1 tablespoon honey

4 ripe nectarines

60 ml (2 fl oz/¼ cup) cream, extra, for whipping

200 g (7 oz) raspberries or whatever berries
    are available (such as strawberries, blackberries etc)

icing (confectioners') sugar, for dusting

Tarte feuilletée aux figues, glace aux coings

PUFF PASTRY FRESH FIG TARTLET WITH QUINCE ICE CREAM

SERVES 4

DECEPTIVELY SIMPLE, THESE FIG TARTLETS ARE SERVED HOT AND CRUNCHY FROM THE OVEN WITH FRAGRANT AND COOLING QUINCE ICE CREAM.

TO MAKE THE QUINCE ICE CREAM: In a saucepan, stir in the sugar and 800 ml (28 fl oz) water over medium heat until the sugar is all dissolved. Bring to the boil. Add the quince and simmer for 1–2 hours or until mid-pink and very soft. Strain and reduce the cooking liquid to a thick, pink syrup, approximately by two-thirds. Cool. In a food processor, finely purée the quince, then if there are any hard bits left, push the purée through a sieve. Add one-third of the reduced syrup, or to taste, you may not need it all as you don't want it to be too sweet. Whisk the cream lightly and fold into the quince purée. Freeze in an ice-cream machine (sorbetière) according to the manufacturer's directions.

TO MAKE THE FRESH FIG TARTLETS: Roll puff pastry about 3 mm (⅛ inch) thick and use it to line four 10 or 12 cm (4 or 4½ inch) loose-based tartlet tins without touching the edges of the pastry (and squashing the layers together). Prick the bottoms all over with a fork and place the tartlets on a baking tray and refrigerate.

Preheat the oven to 220ºC (425ºF/Gas 7). Stand the figs on their bases and with a sharp knife, finely slice them. Arrange slices of fig overlapping in lined tartlet tins and sprinkle with caster sugar. Bake for 12–15 minutes or until the pastry is puffed up and golden. Glaze the fruit with warmed quince jelly. Scoop some quince ice cream into little china dishes (to keep the ice cream cold) and place next to a hot fig tartlet on each plate.

QUINCE ICE CREAM
400 g (14 oz) sugar
3 large quinces, peeled, cored and quartered
200 ml (7 fl oz) cream, for whipping

FRESH FIG TARTLETS
250 g (9 oz) good-quality prepared puff pastry
8–10 small fresh purple figs
caster (superfine) sugar, for sprinkling
2 tablespoons quince jelly

Pina colada vacherin

MERINGUE WITH COCONUT, PASSIONFRUIT AND RUM ICE CREAM

SERVES 12

THIS IS A GREAT RECIPE FOR ENTERTAINING AND CAN BE MADE AHEAD OF TIME. THE MERINGUES WILL KEEP IN AN AIRTIGHT CONTAINER AND THE ICE CREAM WILL KEEP IN THE FREEZER. IT IS EASY TO MAKE IF YOU HAVE AN ICE-CREAM MAKER AND A JUICER.

MERINGUE
5 egg whites (or 150 g (5 1/2 oz) egg whites)
250 g (9 oz/2 cups) caster (superfine) sugar
250 g (9 oz/2 cups) icing (confectioners') sugar,
    plus extra to sprinkle

ICE CREAM
1 pineapple, ripe and sweet, plus extra for serving
5 small oranges, peeled, plus extra for serving
350 g (12 oz) passionfruit pulp with seeds (about
    13 juicy passionfruit)
200 ml (7 fl oz) tinned coconut cream
175–225 ml (5 1/2–7 3/4 fl oz) sugar syrup
    (boil together 500 g (1 lb 2oz) sugar and 500 ml
    (17 fl oz/2 cups) water); keep remainder in fridge
    for future use
50 ml (1 3/4 fl oz) dark rum, or to taste
figs, for serving (optional)

CHANTILLY CREAM
300 ml (10 1/2 fl oz) cream
1 large tablespoon thick cream
1 teaspoon caster sugar
2–3 drops vanilla extract

TO MAKE THE MERINGUES: Preheat the oven to 100°C (200°F/Gas 1/2). Lightly grease a baking tray and line with baking paper. Using an electric mixer beat the egg whites until very stiff. Combine the sugars and gradually pour onto the whites while still beating for about 8–10 minutes or until stiff and glossy. Put the mixture into a piping bag with an 8 mm (3/8 inch) plain nozzle and pipe 9 cm (3 1/2 inch) circles onto the prepared tray, giving the mixture the shape of a small nest. Sprinkle with a little icing sugar and bake for 1 hour. Turn off oven and cool meringues completely in the oven. Keep in an airtight container nestled in crumpled baking paper if not being used the same day.

TO MAKE THE ICE CREAM: Cut the pineapple and orange into segments to fit easily through the hole of the juicer. Put the pineapple, oranges and passionfruit pulp through the juicer. Strain, then stir in the coconut cream, sugar syrup and rum, to taste.

Freeze in an ice-cream machine according to the manufacturer's directions.

TO MAKE THE CHANTILLY CREAM: Combine all the ingredients in a bowl and whisk until stiff peaks form. On each plate, put half a teaspoon of cream and place a meringue shell on top to stop it sliding. Fill the cavity of the meringue with the chantilly cream and place a scoop of ice cream on top. Decorate with slices of fresh fig, peeled pineapple wedges and/or orange segments.

TOP: DANY AND CHUI IN THE CLEOPATRA KITCHEN

BOTTOM: JENNY KEE WITH TRISH, DANY AND MONIQUE

boys gave Chui, who was very sensitive, such a hard time that Trish would sometimes find her near to tears in the coolroom and say: 'Chui, you must not cry. When you cry, they've won. How many times do you think I'd love to burst into tears in the kitchen? You can't! You must be strong.'

Chui did learn to be strong and today runs Claude's in Woollahra, a restaurant awarded three hats in the *Sydney Morning Herald Good Food Guide*. It's an achievement that not one of those macho boys can match.

We became so busy around this time that Barney would come to Blackheath to work weekends. Barney could handle the machismo and it was great to have him on our side; he has a cool, quiet ability to get along with everyone and he could handle the aggressive French chef with sarcasm. 'Are you sure this is something that Dany would send out?' he'd say, and shame him into doing better. He was a godsend; we could leave Barney there on his own on Sunday nights – when we were completely exhausted – knowing Cleopatra was in good hands. He and Kerry Anne made a great front-of-house team; they did not want anyone else to help them. They'd say: 'Nah, go home, we can handle it.'

In September 1998 I received the *Sydney Morning Herald's* Award for Professional Excellence. Terry Durack wrote: 'If French cuisine is the model for modern Australian cooking, then Chouet, the winner of the 1998 Award for Professional Excellence, has been its midwife … since 1984, when the pair opened Cleopatra, the Three Sisters have had some serious competition as a tourist attraction in the Blue Mountains.'

It was lovely to receive this recognition. But we were tired. We always wanted to go on a high, and all the stress was grinding us down and I didn't want it to show in my cooking. The reason why there are so few female chefs in restaurants is because it is so demanding – both physically and mentally. You really have to be tough, and neither Trish nor I are naturally that way, so it was a constant effort to manage other people and make them get along and do their work. I also wanted to return to France before I was too old to enjoy it; I wanted to buy a house and go to markets and learn to cook *foie gras* and do all the things I had never learned when I was young.

Trish was keen to move to France, too; it had always been her dream and she no longer had family ties to hold her back. Trish's mum, Nanna Jane, had sadly passed away in 1998 and her boys were all grown up and had their own lives.

We very quietly put Cleopatra on the market, which was the start of a very awkward time for us. Rumours leaked through the restaurant network, and Kerry Anne and people we really cared about would come up and say: 'What's going on? I've just heard Cleopatra is for sale!' and we'd have to say 'Oh no, we're just testing the market.' Although we eventually told Kerry Anne the truth, we made her promise not to tell anyone. When an estate agent in Leura brought over a buyer to inspect the property Trish had gone to great lengths to look fresh and relaxed. In fact, she looked so content that the prospective buyer commented: 'The reason why I'm interested in your property is because you're the only owner who doesn't look tired and exhausted; you look as if you enjoy the work.' Trish just smiled.

Of course, Trish and the estate agent banned me from having anything to do with the prospective purchaser as I was far 'too fond of the truth'. He thought running a guesthouse and restaurant would be a relaxing way to spend his retirement and we both worried he had absolutely no experience and no idea. We reassured ourselves we were not selling the business – we had been advised by all the agents that it was too famous, too personal – we were only selling the real estate and therefore he would be getting a very beautiful house.

One night when we were close to finalising the deal, the phone rang. It was an old chef friend of ours, Damien, ringing for a chat. Trish told him what was going on – that we were on the verge of selling and the buyer had bargained us right down. Trish and Damien chatted a bit and then said goodbye. About fifteen minutes later, the phone rang again and it was Damien. 'At that price, I want to buy it,' he said. The sale went through on 31 December 1999.

COMING HOME

A good daughter of the Périgord

DANY AT HOME IN THE GARDEN, PÉRIGORD, FRANCE, 2009

I HAD TRULY FORGOTTEN HOW LOVELY MY COUNTRY COULD BE IN THE SPRING.
OVER THE PREVIOUS THIRTY YEARS MY TRIPS TO PÉRIGORD HAD ALWAYS BEEN
DURING SUMMER OR IN DEEPEST WINTER. SUCH VISITS WERE ALWAYS BUSY
AND FLEETING AND USUALLY REVOLVED AROUND VISITING MAMAN AND PAPA
IN VÉLINES. SO IT WAS VERY DIFFERENT IN MARCH 2000, WHEN TRISH AND
I ARRIVED FOR A SIX-MONTH STINT TO SEARCH FOR A PROPERTY IN FRANCE
AND FINALLY HAD THE LEISURE TIME TO DRINK IT ALL IN.

WE WERE BOTH STRUCK BY THE BEAUTY OF THE
countryside: the incredible green lushness of the rolling meadows and budding oak
forests; the immaculate order of well-tended vineyards; and fruit trees laden with
blossoms and humming with bees. Colour was everywhere: adding a burst of brightness
to the landscape were the yellow forsythia flowers; deep-red japonicas; and cascades of
purple wisteria hanging heavy and fragrant against sun-soaked limestone. We travelled
down narrow roads bordered with lipstick-red poppies to explore towns and villages
and tiny hamlets and to visit churches and châteaux. Trish was truly in heaven; every
house she saw was more beautiful than the last and she pointed out a new *maison de rêves*
(dream house) at every turn.

My Grandpère Armand had always told me there was no need to travel outside
France because we lived in the most beautiful country in the world. His words made me
realise that I had to leave France in order to return and fully appreciate my homeland.

Rural South-West France was a far more prosperous place in the twenty-first century
than during my childhood. This was reflected in the dizzying array of activities that
people now had the time, money and inclination to enjoy. The entertainment options
were many and varied and reached far beyond the age-old weekly markets, fairs and
Saint's Day fêtes. Our arrival in spring coincided with an explosion of *brocantes* (flea
markets), *vide-greniers* ('attic emptiers') and jazz or classical music concerts held in
lustrous, old churches. Every day there was something going on in one village or another
and Trish and I tried our best to zip about to all of them, especially if food was involved.
We saw a poster for the *Fête des Fraises* (strawberry festival) at Vergt and dutifully set off
to visit the village regarded as the strawberry capital of the Dordogne. What we found
was a scene straight out of a Jacques Tati comedy film: the hosting confraternity of mostly

middle-aged men with paunches were wandering about with nonchalance wearing red leggings and red shirts with glittery capes and green hats shaped like leaves. Really, you haven't lived until you've seen grown men dressed up as strawberries!

Local women wearing fetching red bonnets also joined in the fun doling out free aperitifs of Monbazillac wine with strawberries. Périgord strawberries are renowned for their quality and the announcement of awards crackled through the loudspeakers all day. A special guest from the local truffle appreciation society (dressed in black velvet) was introduced and a small group dressed as *cèpes* were resplendent in swirling cream velvet capes with brown collars and floppy velvet caps. The *cèpes* looked very hot and flushed and were very happy to quaff several glasses of the strawberry aperitif. Included in the day's itinerary were interminable speeches made by members of the strawberry *confrérie* who should never have been allowed to get hold of a microphone, let alone wear tights. After the communal lunch, which fed about 600 people and featured strawberries in every course, the accordions started squawking and the strawberries, mushrooms and truffles tangoed in the square. A giant strawberry tart, some three metres (ten feet) in diameter, was then wheeled out before being sliced, segmented and distributed. As well as buying a mound of bright-red strawberries, we purchased dozens of plants for Maman's potager. Ahhh! It was good to be home again!

During our six months off, Trish and I had set ourselves two goals: buy our dream house in France and treat ourselves to a month's holiday in Spain. One of the things we most looked forward to was the opportunity to travel to places without first sitting on a plane for twenty-four hours! Périgord may not be everyone's idea of the centre of Europe, but the Mediterranean is only a four-hour drive away; the Atlantic only three; and London, Morocco, Amsterdam or Rome just a couple of hours away by air.

The first thing we did when we arrived to stay with Maman was to buy a car. At age eighty-seven, Maman was still a force to be reckoned with. Although she was still very fit and determined to get her own way, Maman had conceded that she needed a bit of help around her big old house: a man now helped in the garden; and Dede, a sweet *femme de ménage*, kept her company when she came to clean and fuss over the geraniums in the front of the house. There were no longer any chickens or ducks in the outbuildings, nor rabbits in the lovely old cages under the horse-chestnut tree. Another noticeable change was that the big vegetable garden that Papa had been so proud of had now shrunk to a couple of rows, a few raspberry bushes and herbs.

During all my years spent living in Australia, Maman had never given up trying to lure me back to France; she was suitably thrilled to have finally got her way. She was also fond of mentioning the devoted daughters she knew of who kindly went to live with their ageing mothers to care for them in their old age.

Trish and I had such a wonderful time rediscovering how to live without the restaurant and guesthouse dominating our every day. We immersed ourselves in French life and let it seep into our pores. We spent days wandering around the labyrinthine lanes of Sarlat and the medieval quarter of Périgueux without worrying about squeezing in another Michelin-starred restaurant or researching the latest food trends. We were off duty and enjoying life in the slow lane. We loved not having to think about how we could adjust this dish, replicate that flower arrangement or redecorate a guest bedroom.

We were gluttons for the nearby *marchés*: ingredients that had been so hard and expensive to source in Australia were suddenly at our fingertips. Our first stop was always the cheese truck, which sold a phenomenal range of French *fromages*. Also worthy of exploration were the many stalls piled high with everything from garlands of garlic to green and white asparagus and glistening red strawberries. It was also impossible to bypass the butcher who very quickly understood that Madame Chouet was to receive only the 'best of the best'. The fishmonger in Castillon was our last port of call; he always had the most exciting display of ultra-fresh fish, brought in from the Atlantic each day.

We told Maman we were happy to take over the task of shopping and cooking. But the problem was we had completely forgotten how to buy food for just three people and so ordered kilos of everything; we would return triumphantly from our visit to the market with our car groaning under the weight of all our goodies. On one such excursion, Trish was enthused to the point of folly when she purchased a live chicken. Neither Trish nor I had ever slaughtered a bird before so Maman blithely told Dede to kill it and pluck it and prepare it. She also suggested that in future we resist the urge to return with livestock.

I FOUND IT BOTH ENDEARING AND SURPRISING TO SEE how little things had changed in Vélines and how deeply 'local' and engrained the culinary heritage was. One morning I stood in a queue outside the *cremerie* truck in the huge Sainte-Foy-la-Grande *marché*, waiting to be served. When it was my turn to order I asked for some delicious salted butter, which was sliced off the giant pat and wrapped in waxed paper. To add to this, I also requested 500 millilitres of cream. The nuggetty, peasant woman at my side pulled at my sleeve. 'What are you doing? You're from around here, aren't you, Madame?' she asked, eyeing me suspiciously. 'You certainly have the right accent. So what are you doing buying cream? What do you do with cream? We don't use cream. Not here!' And she was right: nobody in my family ever used cream except in desserts, and then only rarely. Adding cream to sauces or pasta or vegetables was a foreign idea and I began to feel like a bit of a traitor. I had to explain to the woman that I was a chef and that I had adopted many strange, foreign habits while living overseas for many years. She was not at all impressed and assured me that cream was not only bad for my health but totally unnecessary. As a good 'daughter of the Périgord' she suggested I mend my ways.

In the meantime, Maman was doing everything she could to sabotage our house-hunting efforts. She would smile at us beatifically and announce: 'My, my, my. Aren't we happy here … just the three of us, all together … aren't we happy?' And we'd chirp back: 'Yes, aren't we happy?' We were far too polite to tell Maman the truth: that we couldn't wait to find our dream house and get started on the renovations.

Foie gras de canard frais aux pommes

PAN-FRIED FRESH DUCK FOIE GRAS, WITH APPLES AND MONBAZILLAC

SERVES 4

DESPITE LIVING IN THE MIDDLE OF *FOIE GRAS* COUNTRY, AND BEING ABLE TO BUY IT ALL YEAR ROUND, WE DON'T EAT IT EVERY DAY – IT REMAINS A FESTIVE ENTRÉE OR HORS D'OEUVRE FOR A SPECIAL OCCASION. AN ENGLISH FRIEND OF OURS ATE IT FOR LUNCH EVERY DAY FOR THE FIRST MONTH SHE LIVED HERE, THINKING THAT WAS NORMAL, ALONG WITH CROISSANTS FOR BREAKFAST, AND LOTS OF BAGUETTES AND WINE WITH EVERYTHING UNTIL HER JEANS WOULD NO LONGER ZIP UP. HER FRENCH NEIGHBOURS HAD TO EXPLAIN THAT ONE MUST BE *RAISONNABLE* ABOUT THESE THINGS. IF YOU LIVE IN A COUNTRY WHERE *FOIE GRAS* IS UNAVAILABLE, YOU WILL JUST HAVE TO DREAM ABOUT THIS DISH. REALLY THERE IS NO SUBSTITUTE FOR FRESH *FOIE GRAS*.

3 apples (braeburn or other cooking apples)

20 g (¾ oz) butter

1 tablespoon grapeseed oil

caster (superfine) sugar, for sprinkling

500 g (1 lb 2 oz) fresh duck foie gras

½ teaspoon sea salt

¼ teaspoon white pepper

¼ teaspoon four spice (quatres espices)

40 g (1½ oz) potato flour (potato starch)

2 tablespoons cider vinegar

125 ml (4 fl oz/½ cup) Monbazillac (sweet white wine – serve the rest of the bottle to accompany the dish)

100 ml (3½ fl oz) duck demi-glaçe or reduced chicken stock

1 tablespoon lemon juice

Preheat oven to 80ºC (165ºF/Gas ¼).

Peel, core and cut the apples into eighths. Sauté the apple in the butter and oil in a non-stick frying pan over medium heat for 5–10 minutes until golden on both sides. Sprinkle them with a little sugar and salt during the cooking. Transfer to a tray and place in the warm oven. Clean the frying pan for re-use.

With a sharp knife dipped in hot water, slice the foie gras evenly into 1 cm (½ inch) thick slices, and lay them on a chopping board.

Mix together the sea salt, white pepper and four spice, and season the slices on both sides with this mixture, turning them over carefully, as they are fragile. Dust them all over with the potato flour on both sides.

Heat the non-stick frying pan until it is hot, but not burning. Without any fat in the pan, sauté the *foie gras* slices in batches for no more than 1 minute on each side. Remove them immediately to a tray lined with paper towel and keep warm in the oven.

Discard the fat which has come from the *foie gras*, and return the pan to the heat. Deglaze with the cider vinegar for 3–5 minutes until the liquid has totally evaporated, then add the Monbazillac wine and reduce almost completely. Stir in the duck demi-glaçe, bring to the boil, add the lemon juice and heat only for 10 seconds. Leave the pan covered on a warm corner of the stove. Arrange 6 slices of apple on each of the warm plates, divide the *foie gras* between the plates and spoon over the sauce. Serve immediately. Chilled Monbazillac is excellent to drink with this dish.

Soupe à la citrouille

PUMPKIN SOUP

SERVES 8–10

THIS RECIPE WAS INSPIRED BY LA MAZILLE. I MAKE IT IN AUTUMN AND WINTER USING THE PUMPKINS FROM OUR
GARDEN, WHICH ARE FUN AND EASY TO GROW. I TELEPHONE TATIE DENISE TO CHECK WHEN IT IS TIME TO PICK
THEM, AND STORE THEM IN THE DARK ON A COLD TILED FLOOR IN THE GRANGE, WHERE THEY KEEP HAPPILY
FOR MONTHS, PROVIDING SOUP AND VEGETABLES THROUGH THE WINTER.

250 g (9 oz) podded fresh borlotti beans
   (about 625 g in pod) or
   150 g dried beans, soaked overnight
2–3 tablespoons duck fat
2 onions, sliced
2 leeks, thinly sliced
1 kg (2 lb 4 oz) 'Potimarron' squash
   (or butternut pumpkin), diced
2 carrots, diced
1 turnip, trimmed and cubed
1 celery heart, sliced
2 garlic cloves, chopped
2.5 cm (1 inch) fresh ginger, chopped

If using dried beans, drain them and place in a saucepan of cold water and bring
to the boil. Cook for 1 hour or until tender, then drain.

In a large heavy based saucepan, sauté in a tablespoon of the duck fat the
beans, onions and leeks together, keeping them white. Add 2½ litres (88 fl oz)
of boiling water.

At the same time in a separate large frying pan sauté the pumpkin, carrot and
turnip in the remaining duck fat until they caramelise slightly. Add this to the
bean mixture, as well as the celery, garlic and ginger. Season with salt and freshly
ground black pepper and add more water if it is too thick. Let this boil gently
for 30 minutes or more until the pumpkin, carrots and beans are tender. Once
cooled, put the soup through a mouli, or blend with a hand-held blender.

Reheat and serve in a soupière (soup terrine) in the middle of the table
so friends and family can readily access seconds if they desire. This soup can be
kept in an airtight container in the refrigerator for a couple of days.

Courgettes rapées, sautées

STIR-FRIED ZUCCHINI WITH GARLIC AND PARSLEY

SERVES 4

A VERY EASY AND QUICK RECIPE FOR THE SUMMER WHEN THERE IS AN ABUNDANCE OF ZUCCHINI. IN OUR GARDEN THEY SEEM TO APPEAR OVERNIGHT, AND WE EVEN HAVE A PACT WITH OUR FRIENDS, 'PLEASE, DON'T BRING ME ANY ZUCCHINI FROM YOUR GARDEN!' IT IS SO DIFFICULT TO KEEP UP WITH PRODUCTION.

Wash and trim the zucchini, keeping the skins on. Coarsely grate the zucchini by hand or in a food processor, using the disc with the largest holes. Place in a colander above a tray or a larger bowl and arrange the grated zucchini in layers, alternating with the salt. Place a plate and a heavy weight on top, to extract the liquid from the zucchini and leave to drain for about 1 hour.

Press out as much liquid as possible by hand, then wring the zucchini in a clean tea towel or dry with paper towel, so it is as dry as possible.

In a very hot wok, or a large frying pan, place the olive oil and butter, add the garlic and sauté very quickly, do not let the garlic go brown, add the zucchini all at once and stir fry constantly for about 5 minutes. Keep it firm and a little 'al dente'. Remove from the heat and season with freshly ground black pepper, add the parsley and serve as an accompaniment for veal, pork, lamb or chicken.

4 large green zucchini (courgettes)
2 teaspoons fine salt
2¼ tablespoons olive oil
3 teaspoons unsalted butter
2 garlic cloves, crushed
½ bunch flat-leaf (Italian) parsley, chopped

Périgord is chock-full of lovely houses filled with character. But back in 2000, it was a seller's market. We felt like children in a sweet shop: although bewildered by the choices, we couldn't find anything we liked in our price range. Even arranging an inspection was difficult. In France, real estate agents don't have exclusive rights to sell a property. So though you may see several likely looking houses in an estate agent's window, they'll never tell you where they are, for fear that you'll find the house, knock on the door and negotiate a private sale, thus depriving them of their commission.

For some reason, proximity was everything: according to most agents, being close to a *pharmacie* and *boulangerie* far outweighed any aesthetic considerations. It was always pills and bread before beams and dovecotes. To even get a look inside a house you had to book a block of time in the morning or afternoon, a week or two in advance. It was then you were likely to discover that the inspection was a complete waste of time as the agent had neglected to inform you the house was near a highway or had high tension wires slicing through the front garden.

At this time, mobile phones were still a relatively new phenomenon in rural France and although I would leave the agents my number, they would still invariably phone Maman's landline. When Maman answered the phone, she would take a message and then promptly 'forget' to pass it on. As a result, we were constantly missing appointments. If we actually succeeded in making a date to look at some properties, Maman would then stop us at the door: 'But *mais non*! You can't go. You have to take me to the doctor in Ste-Foy at three o'clock!' She may have been as fit as a fiddle, but Maman made countless appointments with doctors, heart specialists, dentists, bureaucrats and lawyers so she could ambush us at the last minute.

To make ourselves more contactable, we bought a laptop computer and fax machine. Maman regarded both technological aids as being works of the devil – mainly because she didn't know what we were doing with them. Maman had to know everything, so the minute we stepped out of the house, she'd sneak into the bedroom and fiddle with the computer trying to figure it out. One of the few English words Maman recognised was 'she'. If her ears picked up a 'she'-type sound she was convinced that we were talking about her – even if that word was 'sheet', or 'shop' or 'shelf'.

We found it impossible to relax in Maman's house. There was nowhere comfortable to sit and even if Trish did manage to curl up in the stiff, upright Louis XVI canapé in the salon, Maman would open the door a minute later and say: '*Ça va*, Treeesh? *Ça va?*' Trish would say '*Oui, merci*'. Maman just wouldn't accept that Trish and I liked to have a bit of peace and quiet to go off and read a book. She would turn to me and say: '*Elle fait la tête!*' I would have to explain that, no, Trish wasn't sulking and that once in a while, we both liked to escape the incessant background chatter and enjoy a bit of time to ourselves. This was difficult for Maman to fathom; members of my family never sat down to read a book. For them, reading meant sitting at the table with the newspaper and a cup of coffee. If Trish and I dared to sneak into the salon together to read at the same time, Maman would follow us in with her daily copy of the *Sud-Ouest*. 'This is such a *bonne idée*! Aren't we all happy here, reading together?' We'd have one glorious minute of silence before

Maman would start reading news stories aloud, especially the obituaries: 'Oh, she was the cousin of so-and-so.' 'Oh my, I knew his niece!' And, of course, the refrain was always the same: 'Oh, Madame X was so very fortunate. She lived with her daughter who looked after her dear mother until the end! She won't have any regrets now her mother has gone.'

In keeping with French tradition, Maman wanted her main meal at lunch. Trish and I are not early risers and we had long become accustomed to eating a simple meal in the middle of the day. But Maman was also a creature of habit: she simply had to have her soup, entrée, main course, fruit and cheese on the table the second the bells rang out that it was *midi*. In order to please Maman, we had to make a few adjustments to the order of our day. Even though we didn't want to eat our main meal at noon, we joined Maman at the table just to be polite. If she had prepared the meal herself, she would pile up our plates with extra food and make little hurt noises if we didn't eat it all. 'Why aren't you eating that? Don't you like it?' Of course we liked it, but we preferred eating our main meal in the evening; our waistbands soon became very tight.

EVEN COOKING DINNER BECAME A STRUGGLE, TRISH used to laugh to see Maman and I fighting over a frying pan. 'Now sit down, Maman,' I'd say sweetly. 'Let us look after you. Get comfy in your chair and watch *Questions pour un Champion* (her favourite television show) while we cook.' But Maman was not used to being looked after and she'd soon be back in the kitchen, sniffing around. 'I'm not helpless, Dany! I can do something. And besides, you don't do it like that.' If I left something simmering on the stove and went upstairs to change for dinner I'd warn Maman not to touch a thing. The second I was out of sight she'd sneak into the kitchen and turn the burners up. When I returned to the kitchen, I would find Maman had ruined the dinner again. She wanted things done her way; if I was cooking green vegetables she would insist on boiling them until they were grey. Such incidents provided Trish with the perfect cue to disappear down the road to the *boulangerie* to buy a baguette. 'Oh, *c'est pas possible! Tu as tout changé ça! Tu as tout demoli! C'est foutu!* No one in my restaurant kitchen brigade would have ever dared to interfere like that. But my own mother in her own kitchen was another story. It drove me crazy.

Even when the weather was gorgeous and we were desperate to eat out in the cool, green garden, Maman wanted to sit inside at the table. All she had to do was walk down the steps and sit there to be served like a queen. But she didn't want to; she just wasn't used to it. And nor were we used to sitting at the table with an eighty-seven-year-old, who, midway through the meal, would suddenly jam the cork back in the wine bottle and declare: 'Well, that's that! We've all had enough wine!'

Maman was convinced she had to keep an eye on Trish and would follow her around to make sure everything was done 'the French way'. She would lecture her at the washing line about how she had hung out the clothes and even accuse her of 'wasting' pegs. It was sometimes *trés difficile* to stay calm in Maman's presence.

Even though she was driving us crazy, Trish and I tried to be tolerant. We knew Maman wasn't getting any younger so we tried to find our dream home as close as possible to Vélines. All the estate agents in the area knew what we wanted: an old house with character, with up to four bedrooms and enough space to fit a swimming pool. On paper, our criteria seemed simple enough. But the agents continued to dither about, showing us properties that didn't even remotely fit our brief. We were taken to see an assortment of ghastly houses that were a total affront to the senses; many were covered in layers of concrete and hideous tiles and featured ugly, modern windows that had often replaced lovely old ones. One enterprising DIY fanatic had even installed a giant circular spa bath on a pedestal and covered it with streaky purple tiles. The spa bath was positioned smack-bang in the middle of the living area. Not surprisingly, there weren't too many takers for that house.

Although we did find a few old stone houses that oozed charm and character, few of them featured sitting rooms. In rural France it had long been the tradition that one either sat at the table or went to bed. At 'Chez Maman' the salon was kept clean and shut, with only upright Louis XVI chairs arranged around a table. It was very uninviting. What we wanted and sorely missed was a spacious room to fill with plump, comfortable sofas. In ninety-nine per cent of the farmhouses we went to visit, sitting rooms simply did not exist. However, what was stock-standard in most of these properties was an enormous *chais* full of winemaking equipment. One owner tried to convince us that it would be a simple task to transform such a space into a sitting room. 'How on earth could we remove those massive concrete vats?' I asked. 'Oh, *très facile*, Madame. You can demolish them in an afternoon,' he said. When we asked if he could do it for us, he said he was unfortunately too busy to do so.

In May 2000, Trish and I decided to travel to Spain. To our horror Maman announced she wanted to come, too; I had to work very hard to convince her to stay home. She would have hated it. I told her we intended to live like the Spaniards and eat lunch at two o'clock in the afternoon and dinner just before midnight – long after she usually went to bed. That little titbit tipped the scales; she decided to stay home.

On the morning of our departure we were up and about at eight o'clock to find Maman in the kitchen; she had been up for hours cooking lamprey à la Bordelaise! In my family, this dish was considered to be a treasured delicacy – something to serve on special occasions. Maman was proud of her recipe and knew it was pretty irresistible, especially if you loved lamprey (an eel-like marine animal) as I do. There she was busily cooking away, sautéing the onions, leeks and ham, saucepans everywhere. The aroma engulfed us. 'Maman! What are you doing cooking lamprey at this hour of the morning?' I asked. 'You knew we were leaving this morning!'

'Well if you want any you'll have to stay!' she retorted, convinced that one whiff of the delicious and very distinctive aroma emanating from the kitchen would enchant us into cancelling our holiday. 'If you go you will miss out and, well, who knows? Maybe I will never cook it again!' My mother: the lamprey temptress! We went anyway and had a great month down in Andalucía.

Galettes de courgettes à la Grecque

DANA'S KOLOKYTHOKEFTEDES

THIS MAKES ABOUT 24; SERVES 8 AS A STARTER

THIS IS MY TAKE ON OUR FRIEND DANA'S DELICIOUS GREEK RECIPE.

Boil the whole potatoes until half cooked, cool, then coarsely grate them and set aside. Coarsely grate the zucchini and the onions and lightly salt them, mix together with the potatoes and leave in a colander in the sink to drain, with a heavy weight on top, for about ½ hour. Then take handfuls of the mixture and squeeze out as much water as you can (or until you can't stand it any more) – this is very important to the process.

Mix in the eggs, cheese and mint. Season with freshly ground black pepper and salt to taste. Form the mixture into little patties, if they aren't holding together, add a little cornflour until they do. Heat the olive oil in a large frying pan, coat the patties in a little flour and fry for 5–10 minutes until golden, then drain on paper towel. Serve hot or at room temperature.

500 g (1 lb 2 oz) potatoes that are good for mashing
   (such as desiree or Dutch cream), peeled
1 kg (2 lb 4 oz) zucchini (courgettes)
1 kg (2 lb 4 oz) onions
3 eggs, lightly beaten
130 g (4¾ oz/1 cup) grated cheese (any hard
   yellow cheese with a bit of bite works)
1 large bunch fresh mint, finely chopped
   (or dried if need be)
1 teaspoon salt
1–2 teaspoons cornflour (cornstarch), if needed
olive oil, for frying
flour, for coating

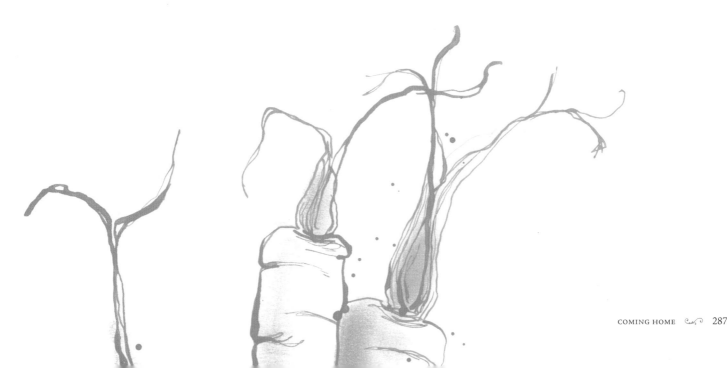

Gougère aux petits légumes

CROWN OF CHEESE CHOUX PASTRY, WITH BABY SPRING VEGETABLES AND HERB BUTTER

SERVES 4-6

I COOKED THIS ENTRÉE AT OUR BLACKHEATH RESTAURANT, CLEOPATRA, IN AUSTRALIA FOR MANY SPRINGS AND EARLY SUMMERS. NOW BACK IN FRANCE, I SERVE IT IN SPRING FOR LUNCH IN THE GARDEN. THERE ARE NEVER ANY LEFTOVERS AND EVERYONE ASKS FOR THIS RECIPE.

HERB BUTTER
100 g (3½ oz) unsalted butter
1 teaspoon finely shredded basil
1 teaspoon sliced chives
½ teaspoon chopped tarragon
½ teaspoon chopped chervil

GOUGÈRE PASTRY
75 g (2¾ oz/½ cup) plain (all-purpose) flour,
  plus extra for dusting
75 ml (2½ fl oz) milk
75 ml (2½ fl oz) water
55 g (2 oz) unsalted butter, diced
2 eggs
55 g (2 oz) Gruyère cheese, finely diced
freshly grated nutmeg, to taste
1 pinch cayenne pepper
1 teaspoon dijon mustard

BABY VEGETABLES
A selection from the following, about 650 g
  (1 lb 7 oz) in total when cleaned: asparagus tips
  (green asparagus), tiny squash or baby zucchini
  (courgettes), broccoli florets, spring onions, snow
  peas (mangetout), fresh baby peas, broad (fava)
  beans (double peeled, and very small), baby corn

TO MAKE THE HERB BUTTER: Soften the butter to a paste, add all the herbs at once, season with salt and freshly ground black pepper, mix well and set aside.

TO MAKE THE GOUGÈRE PASTRY: Preheat the oven to 210ºC (415ºF/Gas 6–7). Grease a heavy baking tray with butter, place a 24 cm (9½ inch) round cake tin on the tray and dust around the edge with a little extra flour, to mark a ring on the tray. Remove the tin.

Place the milk, water and butter in a heavy-based saucepan over medium heat and bring just to the boil. Immediately remove the saucepan from the heat, add the flour all at once and beat energetically with a wooden spoon until the dough forms a ball. Put the saucepan back over a very low heat and keep rolling the dough around for 1–2 minutes to dry it. Transfer to the mixing bowl of an electric mixer, add the eggs, Gruyère cheese, spices and mustard and season with very little salt (because of the cheese and the mustard) and pepper. Beat well to combine.

Spoon the dough inside the circle drawn on the baking tray in the shape of a thick ring. Bake for 15 minutes, then reduce the temperature to 200ºC (400ºF/Gas 6) for a another 15 minutes. Check at this point, if the pastry is not golden and smelling wonderful, reduce the temperature to 180ºC (350ºF/Gas 4) and cook for another 5–8 minutes until very firm. Remove from the oven, slide onto a wire rack, and when it is cool enough to handle, slice in half horizontally.

Place the herb butter in a warm mixing bowl. Steam each vegetable separately and cook to your liking. Add to the butter and stir to combine. Arrange them in the base of the gougère, replace the lid and serve.

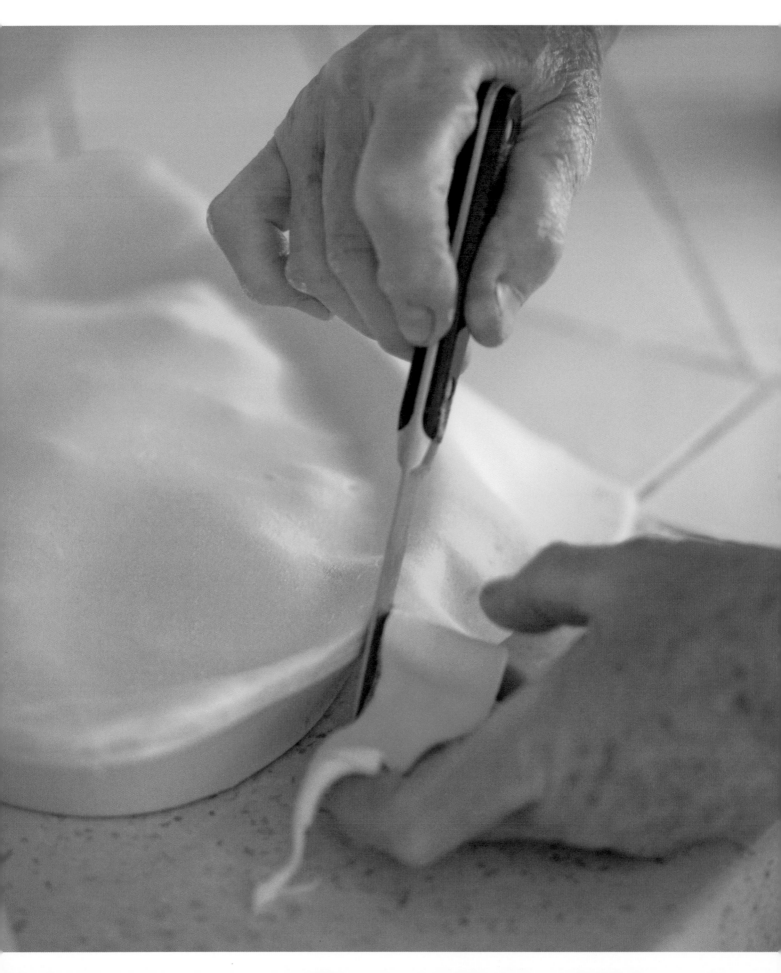

Tourte de pommes de terre Berrichonne

HOT POTATO PIE FROM THE BERRY

SERVES 8

THIS RECIPE WAS INSPIRED BY THE BERRY REGION IN THE CENTRE OF FRANCE, WHERE POTATO PIE OR GALETTE IS A TRADITIONAL DISH, TYPICAL IN ITS RUSTICITY. IT IS VERY HEARTY AND CAN BE EATEN AS A MAIN COURSE WITH A GREEN SALAD.

*500 g (1 lb 2 oz) pâte brisée (short crust pastry)
(see recipe page 328)*
2 onions, finely sliced
125 g (4½ oz) unsalted butter
120 g (4¼ oz) prosciutto, finely diced (optional)
1.2 kg (2 lb 12 oz) desiree or bintje potatoes
100 g (3½ oz) Gruyère cheese, grated
2 tablespoons chopped flat-leaf (Italian) parsley
1 egg yolk mixed with 1 tablespoon milk
400 ml (14 fl oz) cream
¼ cup finely snipped chives

Roll out two thirds of the pastry and line the bottom and sides of a 24 x 30 cm (9½ x 12 inch), 4.5–5 cm (1¾–2 inch) deep terracotta, ceramic or cast-iron dish. Roll out the remaining pastry and cut a lid the size of the dish, then place both pastries in the refrigerator.

Cook the onions very slowly in a frying pan with 1 tablespoon of the butter over a low heat, keeping them white. Set aside to cool. (If you are using the prosciutto, mix it with the cooled onions. In this case use a little less salt in the seasoning below to allow for the saltiness of the prosciutto.)

Preheat the oven to 180°C (350°F/Gas 4). Peel the potatoes and slice them very thinly (using a food processor). Melt the remaining butter in a small saucepan.

Place half the potatoes, onions, cheese and parsley in alternate layers in the prepared pie dish and season with salt and freshly ground pepper, then drizzle over half of the melted butter. Repeat with the remaining ingredients. Place the pastry lid gently on the top and stick the edges of the pastry together using a fork. Cut a hole in the centre and make a little aluminium foil 'chimney' for the steam to escape. (Roll the foil around the handle of a wooden spoon to form the chimney.) Score the pastry with a very sharp knife to make a pattern. Brush the egg-wash over the top of the pastry lid. Bake for about 1 hour. Prick with a skewer to check the cooking of the potatoes. Cover the pie with a sheet of aluminium foil if the pastry is getting too dark and the potatoes need more time to cook. Meanwhile, boil the cream in a saucepan to thicken slightly (reduce to about 300 ml/10½ fl oz), season with salt and pepper and add the chives at the end. To serve, cut the pie into serving pieces in the dish and lift out with a spatula. Serve the cream sauce separately.

When we returned to France in June, Trish and I continued our house-hunting with a renewed sense of urgency. In France, the paperwork associated with a house sale contract takes about three months to process. We were running out of time; we had return flights back to Australia in October and it was imperative that we sell our house in Blackheath before returning to our French farmhouse.

A week after returning from Spain we were walking through the charming township of Lalinde after exploring the bustling Thursday *marché* when Trish – in passing – picked up a brochure from a real estate agent's office. While casually flicking through the leaflet Trish spotted a postage-stamp-sized picture of a property that looked quite promising. Trish thought: 'Hmmm. I must tell Dany about that.' She then tucked it away and forgot about it until a week later when she found it languishing in the bottom of her handbag: 'Oh look, Dany! This one looks cute, doesn't it?'

The agent engaged to sell the property was situated in the centre of Bergerac. When I called him I found the house was still on the market and asked if we could arrange an inspection. He said: 'Well, the house is located near Issigeac and it just so happens that I'm going to be very close to there this afternoon. I could arrange to meet you on the road and take you over.' Now, this was a first – to be able to see a house straightaway!

It was the most perfect house we'd seen within our price range and – as luck would have it – even came complete with a sitting room and large fireplace. The rambling property comprised a pretty stone farmhouse, a couple of stone barns and enough space for a swimming pool. It was far from any main roads and offered a very pretty view of the verdant fields and neighbouring homesteads. Adding to its appeal was a little stone building that housed an ancient bread oven and a well. Although the property was full of character and charm, it also needed a lot of attention: there were walls to knock down and bathrooms to re-do and it needed painting and plastering, too. Trish and I had both 'been there and done that' on the renovation front and agreed it all seemed very achievable.

One thing the property did have that was slightly off-putting was a *chemin rural* – a narrow public lane running between the house and the barns. But even this problem didn't seem insurmountable to us! At the end of the lane it was a dead end and there was only one neighbouring farmer who lived down the lane. We were convinced it would actually be rather nice to have him going to and fro on his tractor, tipping his beret and wishing us 'bonjour'. Trish and I revisited the property a few days later and made a formal offer. The estate agent rang back that very night and said the owner had agreed to our bid price.

After signing our *sous-seing* (agreement to purchase), paying the deposit and waiting for the seven-day cooling-off period to pass, Trish and I took Maman to see the farmhouse. She examined every little detail, but was uncharacteristically quiet. As we drove down the big hill towards Bergerac on the way back to Vélines, Maman broke her silence. 'Sell it,' she said. I looked at her in astonishment. 'What do you mean "sell it" Maman? We just bought it! Why should we sell it?' 'Because of the *chemin rural*.' We thought she was mad. But what was worse was when we later found out that we should have taken her advice!

In the meantime, Trish and I had a lot of fun dashing about, back and forth to *brocantes* to buy bits of furniture. I was also pleased to rediscover the old table and rush-bottom chairs from my Paris days, which Maman had been storing for me all these years. Trish also busied herself with painting some old bits of furniture from the *grenier* (attic) with her favourite shade of distressed grey. Maman thought we were mad.

The first friend to visit our new farmhouse was Sandy! He showed up the day after we moved in and even had to take the manufacturer's plastic off his bed before we could make it for him. It was always great to have Sandy around: the day after he arrived he was, as per usual, all gung-ho: 'Come on, girls, off we go to Bricomarché to buy the stuff you need for the garden!' We bought secateurs, a wheelbarrow, an electric chainsaw and hoses and shovels and before we knew it, there he was, bare-chested, out in the garden, sorting us out. Dire pruning has always been his forte.

When Trish and I had more or less settled in, we held a housewarming party (a *pendre la crémaillère*, which literally means 'the hanging of the chimney hook'). Many of my extended family members were on the guest list and it was great to see them all after so many years. We also invited all our new neighbours, including an Englishwoman named Sally, with whom we are still great friends. Sally had moved into another house in the hamlet and we often had curry nights together and shared a lot of laughs.

The farmer, his wife and son at the end of the *chemin rural* raised *cochons* (pigs) and we secretly called his place the '*cochonnerie*', which is a play on words: in French a *cochonnerie* is a filthy joke or an obscenity. In the other direction was a farm owned by a man who bred cattle and grew mixed crops. Our house, we learned, had belonged to the cattle farmer and he had lived there with his wife and four children. When they divorced, the wife kept the house. He thought he would live next to his barn in a rather splendid-looking *pigeonnier* of 1762, but – *quel surprise* – this living arrangement didn't work out and she was forced to sell.

I THINK THE CATTLE FARMER THOUGHT WE WERE ALL slightly mad. Both Sally and Trish engaged him in conversations in their version of French, which – at times – he found incomprehensible. It led to many misunderstandings. One evening the cattle farmer dropped in on Sally unexpectedly and, in an act of generosity, she invited him to stay for supper. The farmer – who was a man of few words – graciously accepted Sally's invitation, which then sent her into a bit of a fluster as she tried to keep the somewhat stilted conversation flowing.

'*Oh, vous devez avoir beaucoup des femmes!*' she started with, meaning to say he must be hungry (*vous devez avoir trés faim*)? Instead, she had asked him if he had had many women! Realising her error, she became even more flustered and so burnt the sausages. Sally then initiated another conversation about the fact that his daughter had just given birth, and how proud he must be, what lovely grandchildren he had and so on. Unfortunately, a question about the son-in-law was also lost in translation.

'Are you sure he is the father?' Sally asked. It was only when the farmer replied, 'I certainly hope so' that Sally realised what she must have said.

Trish was also way out of her depth with the farmer when she launched into a conversation about baby calves. Trish didn't have a clue about anything remotely rural, but somehow found herself engaged in a discussion about how many of the farmer's cows seemed to be pregnant. 'Are cow pregnancies like wine, with good years and bad years?' Trish asked. The farmer looked at her as if she was seriously mad. '*Insemination artificielle*,' was the deadpan reply. After this I usually did my best to be present during such interchanges, so as to avoid any more misunderstandings.

Although Trish and I did quite a lot of the restorative work on the farmhouse, there were some jobs that were way beyond us. One of our two stone barns had a huge rotten beam over the entrance, which was supported, somewhat precariously, by a collection of sticks. The real estate agent put us in contact with a tradesman named Christophe, who turned out to be a real treasure. Christophe told us he only worked for people he found '*sympa*'. Christophe would arrive at 9 am and enjoy a cup of coffee and a chat. He would chat, and chat, and chat, and we felt lucky if that chat lasted less than an hour. Once Christophe actually got around to working, he was fast and efficient and turned his hand to everything from wiring to masonry, to plumbing and hanging curtains. Christophe liked to feel needed. One day he took us to meet a stonemason he knew; the three of us bounced along in Christophe's bashed-up van all the way into the lonely forest behind Saint-Avit, where the stonemason and his ancient father owned a quarry. After a lengthy conversation, during which we compared photos from his battered album with images from Trish's stylist folder of fireplace shots, we finally made a decision. We ordered a fireplace, which would be ready the following year.

Although the farmhouse was starting to look fabulous, there was one mysterious corner of the dining room/sitting room that needed a complete overhaul. It was comprised of lumps of stone and bits of concrete and seemed completely incongruous with the rest of the house. When Christophe finally found the time to get in there with a chisel and hammer he unearthed a beautiful *evier* (old-fashioned stone sink) carved from stone and set in a niche in the thick, stone walls. It seemed everything was going swimmingly; before returning to Australia, Trish and I received word from the local *maire* that the plans for our swimming pool had been approved.

Back in Blackheath we sold our house, sent a container of furniture back to France and held an auction for everything we no longer wanted. We were surprised when crowds of people came to the auction and bought everything that was for sale. While in the process of packing up our lives in Australia we also made a nice discovery: our old friend Mary Moody, of ABC-TV's *Gardening Australia* fame, had bought a village house in the Lot, in a place called Frayssinet-le-Gélat. 'What? Frayssinet the frozen?' Neither of us had ever heard of the village, named after a stream called Le Gélat, but the wonderful news was that it was only about half an hour's drive from our new house. We promised to keep in touch with Mary – which we have done – catching up with her whenever she is in France.

When we returned to France in March 2001 we also learned of some other old Sydney friends who spend six months of every year in the nearby Lot valley. Ken Hom, the Chinese-American chef, TV presenter and author, also owned a house in the Lot and it was through Ken that we met his two American friends, Morgan and Bill, who had bought a house to restore not too far from us. These were exciting times: we had a new house; a new project; and an ever-widening circle of friends.

It was about two months after our arrival back in France that work finally began on our swimming pool. As anyone who has installed a pool in France will tell you, this sort of undertaking will always turn into somewhat of a soap opera. For us, the drama was delivered in the form of the neighbouring pig farmer at the end of the *chemin rural* who, it turned out, was not the jovial, rosy-cheeked, beret-wearing French peasant we'd hoped for. On the very day we moved in, the pig farmer marched over to the house, and abruptly asked: 'What are you doing here?' Startled by his rudeness, I replied, 'I'm from here. I was born near here and I've come back to live here. I am not an *étranger*.'

———

THE PIG FARMER, AS IT TURNED OUT, HAD A LONG-HELD reputation for being rather difficult. He was in his seventies, and the nearby locals had lost count of the number of lawsuits he had initiated over the years. He was apparently scandalised by the fact that two women who were living together had moved into his beloved hamlet.

The fact that the farmer was reminded of our presence every day he passed by on the *chemin rural* meant he could never quite manage to put us to the back of his mind. He just couldn't seem to 'live and let live' – an attitude I had taken for granted after living in Australia for so long. In fact, our neighbouring pig farmer was so unfriendly that he made the plodding, conniving locals in *Jean de Florette* look like the good guys.

There were other factors, too, that conspired to turn him against us. I may have been from Périgord, but, as the estate agents said, we had 'wiped the plate' (*on a essuyé l'assiette*) – meaning we had changed things irrevocably; we were the first people to move into that part of the hamlet who weren't farmers, and our old neighbour believed in his heart that was wrong.

He told other people that we had arrived like 'conquerors' from the other side of the world. How ridiculous! Trish and I had worked very hard all our lives – we certainly hadn't been plucking gold from the gutter, as he seemed to think.

Everyone in the hamlet knew we were putting in a pool and – right from the start – there were ominous signs that it might run into trouble. Our neighbouring cow farmer was the first to warn us there was an old water mains pipe cutting through the field. And even the pig farmer – in his inimitable manner – instructed us not to dig behind the barn. Concerned, I visited my contact at the water board who double-checked the plans and said: 'Yes, the pipe does cross the field, but it's far from you and will not pose a problem.'

Pissaladière

ONION, OLIVE AND TOMATO TART

SERVES 6—8

THIS TART IS MADE IN NICE USING BREAD DOUGH AS A BASE, BUT I USE MY OWN SHORT CRUST PASTRY. IT COULD BE SERVED AS AN ENTRÉE OR AS A CASUAL LUNCH WITH A GREEN SALAD ALL THROUGH SPRING AND SUMMER. WE LIKE TO SERVE IT AS AN ENTRÉE WHEN ENTERTAINING, USING TOMATOES AND BASIL FROM THE GARDEN AND ACCOMPANIED WITH THE LOCAL ROSÉ. THERE ARE NEVER ANY LEFTOVERS.

Place olive oil in a heavy-based saucepan with the onion and sauté over high heat for 5–7 minutes, stirring often until the onion shrinks down. Add the garlic and thyme, turn the heat to low, cover and braise for 30–45 minutes until they are very soft and make a compote – keep watching, they should just melt and stay pale, not catch or brown. Season with salt and freshly ground black pepper. When the onion is cooked, strain in a colander above a large bowl (this fabulous juice can be used in soups, or as a base for stews etc) and set aside until cool.

Meanwhile, roll out the pastry until 3 mm (1/8 inch) thick and use to line a loose-based 28 x 18 cm (11 1/4 x 7 inch) rectangular or 32 cm (12 1/2 inch) round tin and refrigerate for at least 20 minutes or until pastry is firm.

Preheat the oven to 200°C (400°F/Gas 6). Slice the tomatoes into 3 mm (1/8 inch) thick rounds. Spread the cold onions evenly over the pastry, arrange the tomato slices in a pattern, then make a criss-cross pattern with the anchovies. Dot the black olives around and drizzle with olive oil. Sprinkle with chopped basil if desired. Bake for 25–30 minutes, do a first check after 20 minutes, turn it around so that it cooks evenly, cook for another 10–15 minutes or until the pastry is a lovely golden colour. When it is ready to serve, the delicious smell will invade the house. It is good served warm.

2 tablespoons olive oil, plus extra for drizzling

6 large onions, very thinly sliced (about 1.25 kg/ 2 lb 12 oz)

6 garlic cloves, crushed

4–5 thyme sprigs, leaves picked

300 g (10 1/2 oz) pâte brisée (shortcrust pastry) (see recipe page 328)

6 very ripe tomatoes (preferably straight from the garden)

15–20 large anchovies in oil, sliced in half lengthways

120 g (4 1/2 oz) black olives, stoned

1 bunch fresh basil

Lapin aux pruneaux, mique de maïs

FARM RABBIT WITH PRUNES, COOKED IN RED WINE WITH TRADITIONAL MAIZE DUMPLINGS

SERVES 4—6

OUR LOCAL BUTCHER GETS HIS RABBITS FROM A LOCAL *MAMIE* (GRANDMOTHER) WHO HAND-FEEDS THEM. THESE RABBITS HAVE A WONDERFUL FLAVOUR AND PERFUME, AND WHEN COOKED IN FULL-BODIED LOCAL RED WINE, WITH LOCAL PRUNES D'AGEN, AND SERVED WITH MAIZE DUMPLINGS, THERE IS NO DISH MORE EMBLEMATIC OF THIS BEAUTIFUL RURAL AREA. IT IS A DISH THAT REQUIRES LOVING PREPARATION AND LONG, SLOW COOKING. YOU'LL NEED TO START THIS RECIPE 24 HOURS IN ADVANCE.

TO MARINATE THE RABBIT: Cut the rabbit into serving-size pieces, keeping necks, flaps etc to make the rabbit stock. Place the rabbit pieces into a large bowl and add all the remaining ingredients. Cover and refrigerate overnight, turning occasionally.

TO PREPARE THE PRUNES: Preheat the oven to 100°C (200°F/Gas ½). Place the prunes in an ovenproof dish and cover with wine and port. Cook for 30 minutes to swell the prunes. Cool, cover and set aside overnight.

TO MAKE THE DUMPLINGS: Place all the ingredients except the parsley in an electric mixer with a dough hook attachment, and mix until the dough forms a ball, adding a few drops of water if the mixture is too dry. Place the dough in an oiled bowl and cover with greased plastic wrap and allow to rise in a warm place until doubled in size. Punch down the dough and mix in the parsley. Shape the dough into walnut-sized balls and refrigerate covered with plastic wrap until you are ready to cook them.

TO COOK THE RABBIT: Remove the rabbit from the marinade and dry the pieces with paper towel. Pour the marinade into a large pot and cook over low heat for about 1 hour, or until reduced by half.

In another large heavy-based saucepan heat 2 teaspoons of the olive oil or duck fat over medium heat and sauté the pancetta and onions. At the same time, in a large frying pan over medium heat, brown the rabbit pieces in the remaining olive oil or duck fat. Season to taste with salt and ground pepper. When the onions are golden, add the browned rabbit to the pot and sprinkle with the plain

1 medium-size farm rabbit
1 bottle (750 ml/26 fl oz/3 cups) full-bodied
   red wine
2 onions, thinly sliced
2 carrots, thinly sliced
6 parsley sprigs
¼ bunch fresh thyme
1 bay leaf
4 juniper berries
2 teaspoons black peppercorns
45 ml (1½ fl oz) olive oil
45 ml (1½ fl oz) cognac
   (or brandy)

THE PRUNES
20 prunes
250 ml (9 fl oz/1 cup) red wine
30 ml (1 fl oz) port

flour. Toss the mixture over low heat for about 5 minutes to cook the flour. Strain the reduced marinade and discard the solids, pour the marinade liquid over the rabbit and add enough stock to cover. Cook over a very low heat for 30–40 minutes.

TO FINISH THE DUMPLINGS: Poach the dumplings in boiling salted water for 8 minutes until they rise to the surface and are cooked through. Lift out with a strainer, and drain on paper towel and set aside in a warm place.

Remove the rabbit pieces from the saucepan and set aside in a warm place. Push the sauce through a sieve, pressing to get as much flavour from the vegetables as possible. Discard the solids. Simmer the sauce until it is thick, then add 2–3 tablespoons of prune liquid, then whisk in the grated chocolate and warm very gently for about 5–10 minutes. Meanwhile, warm the prunes in a saucepan with a little of their juice.

To serve, place the rabbit pieces in the centre of a serving platter, arrange the prunes and pour some sauce over the rabbit. Serve the dumplings to the side and the rest of the sauce in a sauceboat.

THE DUMPLINGS

100 g (3½ oz/⅔ cup) plain (all-purpose) flour

50 g (1¾ oz/⅓ cup) maize (meal) flour

5 g (⅛ oz) dried yeast dissolved in 2 teaspoons tepid water

½ teaspoon salt

2 eggs

25 g (1 oz) duck fat (or pork fat)

1 tablespoon chopped parsley

TO COOK THE RABBIT

1½ tablespoons olive oil (or duck fat)

150 g (5½ oz) pancetta, finely diced

2 onions, thinly sliced

2–3 tablespoons plain (all-purpose) flour

500 ml (17 fl oz/2 cups) rabbit or chicken stock

1½ teaspoons finely grated dark chocolate

It was an exceptionally hot day when the *terrassiers* and diggers arrived on site. A pool seemed like a brilliant idea and we couldn't wait for it to be finished! Within a few hours, the digger had opened up a great big hole in the earth. Then, at exactly two minutes to noon, the machine hit the mains, sending an enormous plume of water into the air and causing instant chaos. I raced to the phone to call the water board and begged them to send someone straightaway; it was urgent. Even the threat of nuclear war might not be enough to keep the French from eating their lunch. *'Non, Madame, c'est impossible*! But we will send someone over after lunch, at about one-thirty this afternoon!'

During the intervening time, the pig farmer went berserk, marching over to our house red-faced with rage. The water was cut off to his house and piggery and it was probable his pigs would die in the heat. 'But it's not my fault!' I pleaded with the pig farmer. 'I went to the water board and they stamped the plans and said it was all right!'

'But I warned you it wasn't!' he yelled. What could we do? There I was running from the gushing fountain to the telephone, trying to calm things down while the whole hamlet gathered to watch. The pig farmer stood on our property, shouting and insulting not only us but also the *terrassiers*, who were a rough bunch all too ready for a punch-up. As if that weren't enough, the son of the pig farmer started screeching back and forth in his truck shouting coarse invective at us. This provoked the digger driver, a large, fit muscular man, to jump out of the cabin, ready to punch the son in order to defend our honour. Everyone was shouting at everyone else; it was total mayhem.

The water people reconnected the water pipe by three o'clock in the afternoon. Luckily, the pigs survived. By the end of the day, when the neighbours, water board, pig farmers and *terrassiers* had finally left us in peace we were hot and filthy and desperate to have a nice cool shower.

I turned on the tap only to find that in fixing the main water pipe, the workers had mistakenly bypassed our house and left us with no water!

It was now too late to call the water board so we grabbed plastic buckets and went to the cow farmer to beg for some water. He begrudgingly agreed and then stood there watching us struggle to bring water from his well. Not once did he offer to lift a finger, help draw water or even carry a bucket. All in all, the day was a low point in the annals of French chivalry. After a lot of stressful telephone calls and endless meetings, the pool was finally built. We had the surrounding area landscaped and it looked beautiful.

The arrival of winter brought with it another unexpected challenge on the home front. When we bought the house we had never thought to enquire if the central heating was functional and, of course, the previous owner had not brought up the subject. So, of course, when it came time to crank up the central heating, we found that the hot water was going everywhere except into our radiators. We then had to ask permission from the mayor to dig up the *chemin rural* and it all became very complicated, time-consuming and expensive.

Maman, who could have said 'I told you so', and would have taken great pleasure in doing so, had sadly started to lose the plot. She was forgetting to cook and eat and was behaving erratically. As well as burning her cheque book she had taken to writing nonsensical letters to the bank and it very quickly became apparent she could no longer take care of herself. We found a *maison de retraite* for her in a lovely old house north of Bergerac. When we visited her she was always sweet, yet vague and distant, off in the la-la land of senile dementia and miles away from her feisty control-freak former self. Although Maman had become very absent-minded she still had a beautiful voice and, with little prompting, would sing for the nurses and other patients and recall every single verse of any song she knew. In 2003, we had to sell the house in Vélines to pay for Maman's fees at the nursing home. It was the end of an era.

Cleaning out Maman's house to make way for the new owners was a mammoth task. Monique came from Australia to help Trish and I and the three of us became hysterical on more than one occasion; although it was depressing and a lot of hard work, we decided it was better to laugh than cry. Trish was adept at keeping our spirits up. Just when she thought she had finished emptying a chest of drawers or a cupboard, she would

One balmy night in summer we entertained thirty-five people at an elaborate sit-down dinner in the open grange ... The wine flowed and the music drifted over the fields.

open a drawer to find it full of religious artefacts: holy cards, crucifixes, religious pictures, rosary beads. She would shriek: 'Oh *non*! More *bondieuserie*!'(Good Lord things). Our religious upbringing precluded us from throwing away our boxes of *bondieuserie* so we donated them to nuns in a nearby convent.

Life carried on. There was a lovely Sunday market in Issigeac, the nearest village, and another to visit in Bergerac, which was not too far away. While waiting for our container of furniture to arrive from Australia we had fun making do: besides the table and chairs from my time in Paris, we had a cupboard that Maman had given us and some wine boxes that Trish made into bedside tables. We hadn't bought any furniture for years, so it was fun looking for pieces in the *brocantes*. The garden also needed sprucing up. Many people advised Trish to pull out all the old mangy-looking roses and start from scratch; she didn't. She cut them back and nurtured them until they reached their full potential. The resulting two-metre-tall hedge was so beautiful people would drive by just to admire it.

Our house soon began to feel like a home. As well as hosting a lot of old friends who made the pilgrimage from Australia, our local social circle continued to widen, providing us with many opportunities to host some wonderful dinner parties.

One balmy night in summer we entertained thirty-five people at an elaborate sit-down dinner in the open *grange*. We lit hundreds of candles and placed buckets of fresh-cut wildflowers around the barn; it looked beautiful. The cow farmer donned a new shirt for the occasion and the locals were mightily impressed with everything from the elegant menu to the eclectic mix of guests from around the world.

For the hors d'oeuvres we had: chick pea purée with cucumber; an aubergine compote and cream of fresh goat's cheese with chillies. The entrée was *pissaladière* hot from the oven and for main course there was a huge pot of veal ribs and shanks cooked *osso buco*-style and served with grated lime and couscous. The sublime array of desserts included: *crème au trois parfums*; *tarte au chocolat*; *financiers*; apricot sorbet; and fresh strawberries with cream. The wine flowed and the music drifted over the fields.

It was great to have my cousin Véronique on the guest list. Véronique, who was the grand-daughter of dear Tatie Antoinette, had married an architect named Philippe and been to visit us twice in Australia. Philippe, a man of impeccable taste, owned a stunning, beautifully handcrafted wooden yacht that had been built in Hong Kong in the 1950s. The yacht was moored in La Rochelle and Trish and I often joined the couple on weekends to go sailing along the coast.

Although Trish and I were living a rich and rewarding existence, the pig farmer continued to dominate our days. Following the fiasco surrounding the swimming pool, everything that involved him became *un problème*. Every time he drove past our property he would blast the horn on his tractor; he claimed the roses blocked his view and he couldn't see oncoming traffic. This was despite the fact he lived at the end of the *chemin rural*, which was a no-through road. He also drove huge semi-trailers and cistern trucks full of pig food down the lane, and decided that our beautiful bed of irises edging our property was also *un problème*. He claimed they were in the public right of way and had to be removed. Trish tidied up the bed of bulbs but the pig farmer still went out of his way to drive over them. When we complained, the clump of irises was suddenly elevated from being merely *un problème* to *quelle horreur*! He raged at us but we refused to give in so he took us to court for planting a garden on a public property.

This would have probably been the sensible time to cave in to the farmer's demands. Instead, we both agreed it was now a matter of principle: we had been pushed one step too far and so dug in our heels. We told the pig farmer: 'You can take us to court but we aren't digging up the irises!' We thought the case would be over with very quickly. Instead it dragged on for months and inspired many longwinded debates over *bornage* involving surveyors and *géomêtres* whose task involved determining the boundaries between the two properties. They measured every inch of our garden to see if the slightest centimetre protruded on the *chemin rural*, which was public property.

One freezing cold morning we woke to find a bunch of people in our garden, busy trying to define the limits between the two neighbouring properties. The group comprised; ten members of the village council; the *géomêtre* and his two assistants; our cow farmer neighbour, and the pig farmer, his wife and son. Barney, who was living in London at the time, had come down to the Dordogne for a visit. He was absolutely aghast at the stressful situation we were in, as was our friend Michel, who arrived to give us moral support.

Despite the fact we won the first court case, the pig farmer lodged appeal after appeal which made it horribly stressful for us; every day there were endless legal affairs or meetings with the *avocat* and all the attendant paperwork. Even though we went on to win the final court case, we still felt defeated. This was not what we had come to France for. Although we loved our house, we would never be able to relax or feel comfortable as long as the pig farmer lived next door. We began looking for another house. As well as our ongoing feud with the pig farmer, the other reason that motivated us to move was the fact the kitchen and house just weren't big enough. We had been retired for a few years now and both Trish and I had begun to feel the urge to try something new; something involving food. Trish was always talking wistfully of finding a *maison des rêves* and although she found many properties full of promise, it took a while before we did in fact find our dream home.

One house Trish was really taken with was an ancient *gendarmerie* once owned by Louis XIV; it had seven spectacular stone fireplaces and a kitchen Trish adored. She said it was straight off a movie set. I wholeheartedly agreed – but the movie I had in mind was one about wretched, starving, medieval peasants. The walls were black and smoke-stained, the plaster was cracked and the DIY renovations were disastrous! Trish took the point that it would probably take an army of cats to kill all the rodents that had infested the house. Trish was also seduced by the charm of a vast manor that she felt had huge potential. Unfortunately we just couldn't afford to fund what would be a radical revamp: it needed a new roof, floors and staircase and more than twenty sets of new shutters.

The house was located in a lovely little hamlet overlooking a spectacular vista of rolling hills and dense forest.

Trish and I were right in the midst of our house-hunting frenzy when Sandy made his annual pilgrimage to France. I had to stay very focused when Sandy and Trish both got madly excited about the prospect of us owning an ancient hospital. The property had been used by the Knights of Malta in the twelfth century as a hospice for returning pilgrims suffering from the Plague. Sure, it had an enclosed monastic courtyard garden (or the vestiges of one) and lots of pretty windows, too. And, yes, there were many rooms 'en enfilade' and the cross of the Knights of Malta was carved in stone over the entrance. But as well as all the delightful detail, there were quite a few drawbacks too, including: a tree growing through the ruined kitchen; a rear wall that was ready to collapse; and a roof that needed to be replaced. Add to this the fact there was no heating, no bathrooms, and eleven hectares of untended, overgrown garden. In short, Trish's dream house was my worst nightmare. Even if we could have afforded the renovations, I just could not picture the two of us rattling around in the space. Suffice to say there were tears before bedtime.

After a few frustrating months of scouting the area in search of our Shangri-la, Trish and I finally found what we felt was the perfect property. The house was located in a lovely little hamlet overlooking a spectacular vista of rolling hills and dense forest. It had a country kitchen that was large enough to host cooking demonstrations for up to eight people and an enclosed *potager* right outside the kitchen door.

The home also featured a good-sized sitting room with an enormous fireplace; a dining room that could seat about thirty guests; a paved terrace area and swimming pool;

Gâteau de noix

WALNUT GÂTEAU — THE ULTIMATE WALNUT CAKE

SERVES 8-10

EVERYONE HAS THEIR FAVOURITE WALNUT CAKE RECIPE. THIS RECIPE WAS GIVEN TO US BY OUR FRIEND MONIQUE PÉBEYRE. IT IS AN EXAMPLE OF THE OLD WAY OF MEASURING CAKES BEFORE KITCHENS HAD ELECTRONIC SCALES OR ELECTRIC MIXERS. LIKE ALL REALLY GOOD THINGS IT IS INCREDIBLY SIMPLE, AND USES THE LOCAL PRODUCE — THERE ARE WALNUT TREES EVERYWHERE AND WALNUTS ARE SOLD IN ALL THE *MARCHÉS*. THE OLD RECIPE BEGINS WITH 'COLLECT A LARGE BASKET OF WALNUTS, SORT AND SHELL THEM'.

220 g (7¾ oz/2¼ cup) walnuts
100 g (3½ oz) butter
30 g (1 oz) plain (all-purpose) flour
caster (superfine) sugar, measure in a measuring jug
   up to the 400 ml (14 fl oz) mark
6 egg whites
icing (confectioners') sugar, to serve

Preheat the oven to 200ºC (400ºF/Gas 6). Grease a 24 cm (9½ inch) loose-based tart tin with butter, and cut a circle of baking paper for the base of the tin, even if it is non-stick, because this cake will stick!

Grind the walnuts in a food processor, not too finely and take care not to over-process or it will form a paste.

Melt the butter slowly and set aside.

Mix the walnuts, flour and sugar in a bowl. Mix in the egg whites, using a wooden spoon. Lastly add the melted butter, mix well and pour into the tin. Bake for 20–25 minutes. It should be quite brown and will go crunchy at the edges.

Remove to a wire rack and turn out after 5 minutes, peel off the baking paper while it is still warm.

To serve, sprinkle with icing sugar. If you like, you can serve this cake with whipped cream or ice cream and red berries in summer, or with chocolate sauce in winter. If there are any leftovers, this cake keeps well for a few days.

Confiture de quatre fruits rouges

MY VERSION OF TATIE ANTOINETTE'S FOUR-BERRY JAM

MAKES ABOUT 16 'BONNE MAMAN' JARS, 325 ML (11 FL OZ) EACH

ON ONE OF MY TRIPS TO FRANCE IN THE LATE EIGHTIES I VISITED MY TATIE ANTOINETTE IN LA RÉOLE, A PRETTY TOWN ON THE EDGE OF THE GARONNE RIVER. AFTER AN ELEGANT LUNCH, SHE DICTATED TO ME THE RECIPE FOR HER FAMOUS FOUR-BERRY JAM, A GREAT COMPLIMENT AS SHE DID NOT GIVE THIS RECIPE TO JUST ANYBODY. THERE ARE JUST A FEW WEEKS IN THE YEAR WHEN IT IS POSSIBLE TO MAKE THIS TRULY DELUXE JAM: WHEN THE CHERRY SEASON IS JUST FINISHING AND THE RASPBERRIES ARE COMING IN, THE STRAWBERRIES ARE AT THEIR PEAK AND THE REDCURRANTS ARE JUST BEGINNING. YOU'LL NEED TO START THIS RECIPE 24 HOURS IN ADVANCE.

1.6 kg (3 lb 8 oz) strawberries and 950 g (2 lb 2 oz) sugar

1.3 kg (3 lb) raspberries (checked) and 1 kg (2 lb 4 oz) sugar

2 kg (4 lb 8 oz) cherries (not stoned) and 1 kg (2 lb 4 oz) sugar

1.5 kg (3 lb 5 oz) redcurrants (not cleaned) and sugar as required

The day before, place the strawberries and their sugar in a large bowl. Mix the raspberries with their sugar in a separate bowl, then add to the strawberries. Cover and refrigerate overnight.

ON THE DAY: Drain the strawberries and raspberries in a colander above a large bowl, let them drip for 20–30 minutes, shaking the colander from time to time.

Stem, then poach the cherries with 200 ml (7 fl oz) water in a large saucepan for 15–20 minutes. Cool, then strain the cherries, keeping their juice. Remove the stones, then mix the cherries with their sugar in a saucepan stir over medium heat until the sugar dissolves. Cook over a high heat for 20–30 minutes. Remove from the heat and set aside.

When the strawberry/raspberry mixture is drained, cook the syrup in a very large pot for about 10 minutes, or if you have a sugar thermometer, to 112°C (233°F). Add the berries and cook on high heat until 'thread' stage (106°C/223°F on a sugar themometer). Keep skimming the foam which rises to the top. Remove from the heat when ready.

Meanwhile, remove the stems from the redcurrants, place in another pot, add the reserved cherry juice and cook until tender. Pass this through a food mill or a very fine mouli. Measure the amount of juice, add the sugar (800 g/1 lb 12 oz sugar per litre of juice) and put this back in the pot and cook on a low heat for 5–10 minutes until it forms wrinkled skin on the surface when a small amount is cooled on a chilled saucer and you push your finger through it. This can happen very quickly. Stop cooking instantly, or the jam might not gel. Pour the redcurrant jelly into the strawberry/raspberry saucepan, and add the cherries. Ladle jam into clean jars while still hot, seal tightly and turn jars upside down and cool overnight.

Tarte aux noix et chocolat

CARAMELISED WALNUT TART
WITH CHOCOLATE ICING

SERVES 8-10

AFTER MUCH EXPERIMENTATION, THIS IS MY VERSION OF THE *TARTE AUX NOIX*: IN THE PÉRIGORD EVERY
PATISSERIE HAS A SPECIAL VERSION, WITH A CLOSELY GUARDED SECRET RECIPE. THEY ARE SOLD IN THE *MARCHÉS*,
SOMETIMES AS INDIVIDUAL-SIZED TARTS, AND THE QUALITY CAN VARY FROM THE ORDINARY TO THE SUBLIME.
THIS IS A RICH TART, SO CUT IT INTO SMALL SLICES AND THERE WILL BE PLENTY FOR SECONDS.

Preheat the oven to 200°C (400°F/Gas 6). Roll out the pastry until 3 mm (¹/8 inch) thick and use to line a 27 cm (10¾ inch) greased loose-based tart tin, trim and refrigerate until firm. Line the pastry with foil, and dry beans or pastry weights. Bake blind for 10 minutes. Remove from the oven and remove the aluminium foil and weights. Let the pastry case cool in its tin on a wire rack.

TO MAKE THE WALNUT MIXTURE: Bring the cream to the boil in a saucepan. Meanwhile, place the sugar in a separate stainless-steel or copper pan with 60 ml (2 fl oz/¹/4 cup) water and stir over medium heat until sugar dissolves. Bring to the boil and cook, without stirring, until it is blond, just turning golden. Take it off the heat and add the boiling cream, stirring all the time (take care as it will splutter and could burn). Mix well, add the ground walnuts. While still hot, before it sets, pour this onto the pastry shell and spread evenly. Bake for about 10 minutes, the pastry edge should be golden and the walnut mixture bubbling like a fudge mixture. Remove and let it cool down completely on a wire rack.

TO MAKE THE CHOCOLATE ICING: In a saucepan bring the cream to the boil, remove from the heat and stir in the chocolate. Keep stirring from time to time with a wooden spoon until completely amalgamated, then add the liquid glucose (this will make the icing shiny and velvety smooth). Cool the mixture a little before it is poured carefully over the tart to give a perfectly smooth and shiny surface. Before it sets decorate with walnut halves around the edge. When the icing has set completely, unmould the tart onto a serving plate.

350 g (12 oz) pâte sucrée (sweet shortcrust pastry)
(see recipe page 329)
walnut halves, for decorating

WALNUT MIXTURE
500 ml (17 fl oz/2 cups) cream
250 g (9 oz) caster (superfine) sugar
350 g (12 oz) walnuts, ground in the food processor
to a 'crumb'

CHOCOLATE ICING
160 ml (5¼ fl oz) cream
160 g (5¾ oz) best-quality dark chocolate, grated
1 tablespoon liquid glucose (optional)

a barn with a pair of guest rooms and a hectare of beautiful gardens surrounded by the long sweep of fields and forest. An actor had purchased the house in 1987 and done all the major renovation work that it required. As well as giving the house a new roof, he had exposed its ancient stone walls and oak beams and, in so doing, faithfully restored it to its former glory. The nearest towns for shopping were Villeréal and Monpazier, two medieval towns (known as bastides) dating back to the time of the Hundred Years' War (a prolonged conflict lasting from 1337 between the English and the French). The focal points of both villages were arcaded squares, where weekly *marchés* have been held for more than 750 years. We bought the house in 2005 and have had no regrets ever since! We both adore it.

In spite of all the troubles we'd had with the pig farmer, we didn't feel guilty about selling our old house on the condition that the new owners weren't two women, which would surely continue to fuel the feud. All the finicky problems had been sorted; the dispute over the *bornage* had been resolved; the barn had a new roof; and the central heating was back to full working order.

Once again, as was often the case when I was at the crossroads in my life, Sandy came to the rescue. The real estate agents didn't seem to be very proactive about selling our property so Barney designed a website to promote the sale of the property and we placed a tiny advertisement in the *Times*, in London. Sandy emailed the address of the website to a friend of his in the UK who replied straightaway and said it looked 'fabulous'. Sandy's friend flew to France the following weekend and fell in love with the property. On the very day the new owners moved in, the pig farmer and his wife arrived at their doorstep with a jar of *foie gras*. Maybe they had learned their lesson, after all.

After years of icing cakes I was a natural at plastering and quite proficient at painting, too, and Trish and I immediately set about sprucing up our new place. Because the core of the house dates back to the thirteenth century, some of the interior stone walls are more than a metre thick. The biggest, dirtiest job by far was definitely adding an upstairs doorway. From the day Trish and I moved into our new home, we knew we had managed to get it right. Both the house and the hamlet are so extraordinarily beautiful that there isn't a day that goes by where we don't stop, take a deep breath and truly appreciate our environs. In stark contrast to the pig farmer, our new neighbour is very sweet. And the mayor? Well, he had our driveway resurfaced as a welcoming gift.

Even when things go wrong, the residents of the tiny little commune pull together to help each other out. The South-West of France was recently buffeted by the worst storms to hit the region for a decade. When a nearby tree went down in the winds it took electric cables with it, cutting off our power. The next morning, we had barely opened our eyes before we found the mayor at our door, chainsaw at the ready: he had come to survey the damage and to ensure we were all right. The mayor also offered us his personal computer to check our emails, loaned us a generator and sent a team of electrical workers to our house to get us back on the grid.

The mayor was proud when Barney asked him to officiate at his wedding and in his speech said how wonderful it was that people came from all around the world to his village. However, Barney and Jane were quite taken aback when they received their *Livret de Famille* (a booklet issued by the French government). Included is the government-recommended *marché à suivre* for the wedding itself: three weeks before, you should visit the beautician to plan your make-up and hair for *Jour J* (D Day); you should undergo your first of three facials on the nineteenth day, and so on.

Although Trish and I had bought our new house because it was well-equipped for entertaining, Barney and Jane's wedding reception really put the house through its paces. They wanted a dreamy French country wedding 'like in a film' with *foie gras*, oysters and prawns to start, followed by duck brochettes with a little *gâteaux* of potato and *cèpes* and salad, a buffet of desserts and the *de rigueur pièce montée*. It was tremendous fun to be arranging a big party again, and in the process we made lots of useful, local contacts. We learned where to source the best of everything – from the Champagne and wine and fresh-cut flowers to the DJs and caterers and local B&Bs where some of the wedding guests would stay. Many of these contacts have come in handy often in our now well-established business as event organisers.

In 2008 we organised a huge fiftieth birthday party for owners of a nearby château. We were slightly taken aback to learn our neighbours were 007 fanatics and wanted a James Bond theme. Fortunately, they supplied their own gold Bond-style 1933 Rolls Royce – which would have been quite difficult to find in South-West France. We did,

We were slightly taken aback to learn our neighbours were 007 fanatics and wanted a James Bond theme. Fortunately, they supplied their own gold Goldfinger-style 1933 Rolls Royce – which would have been quite difficult to find in South-West France.

however, manage to organise everything else – from the food and wine to the casino, chandeliers, hair and make-up, Bond girls and so on. It was, they said, the 'party of the decade'.

Our everyday life is somewhat less flashy. Trish and I still love to cook and our addiction to the local *marchés* is as incurable as ever. Every Saturday morning you can find us there. In summer, we usually make our way down to the *marché* in Villeneuve-sur-Lot, where the stalls are arranged around the fountain in the pretty, arcaded square. The vibrant colours and heady fragrances of the fresh-picked apricots, strawberries and peaches are almost overwhelming.

The nearby village of Villeréal is also exceptionally pretty and hosts a thriving Saturday-morning *marché* all year round. It is amazing what one can buy in a village of just 1300 souls: there are five hairdressers, two pharmacies, a large *supermarché*, and a few brilliant bakers selling crispy warm baguettes. Our preferred butcher is also located in Villeréal. I love his poultry – ducklings, chickens, pigeons, guinea fowl and quail –

Terrine de canard

DUCK AND PORK TERRINE WITH COGNAC

MAKES 15–17 500 ML (17 FL OZ/2 CUP) JARS

LIKE A LOT OF PEOPLE WHO LIVE IN THE COUNTRY IN THE SOUTH-WEST, WE TAKE THE TIME TO MAKE AND PRESERVE TERRINES FOR THE NEXT YEAR. IT IS A LARGE-SCALE PRODUCTION AND TAKES A COUPLE OF DAYS, BUT THE RESULTS ARE WORTH IT. THE JARS ARE KEPT IN A DARK, COOL CUPBOARD IN THE GRANGE WHERE THEIR FLAVOURS DEVELOP – THE PÂTÉ TASTES BETTER AFTER AT LEAST SIX MONTHS, AND KEEPS IMPROVING FOR A FEW YEARS. MAKING PRESERVES LIKE THIS IS NOT JUST A PASTIME FOR APRON-CLAD GRANNIES: MEN AND WOMEN, YOUNG AND OLD ALIKE ALL GET BUSY. THE LOCAL SUPERMARKET GETS OUT SPECIAL SHELVING FULL OF COLANDERS, BULK SALT AND PEPPER, CHEESECLOTH, GIANT WOODEN SPOONS, THERMOMETERS, PACKS OF JARS AND RUBBER CAPSULES AND GIANT JAR BOILERS. EVERYONE SEEMS TO BE AN EXPERT AND WE HAVE GREAT FUN DOING THE PRESERVING WITH FRIENDS. THERE IS LOTS OF MEASURING AND MIXING, DISCUSSION AND LAUGHTER, THEN WHEN WE HAVE FINISHED, WE SHARE OUT THE JARS. THIS IS MY 'SECRET' RECIPE. YOU'LL NEED TO START THIS RECIPE 24 HOURS IN ADVANCE.

EQUIPMENT

One 'bouilleur à bocaux' or preserving boiler,
   (a giant metal pot to fill with jars and water with
   a thermometer)
15–17 500 ml (17 fl oz/2 cup) preserving jars
   and rubber seals (capsules)
1 food grinder attachment for your electric mixer
scales that measure grams

2 kg (4 lb 8 oz) boneless and skinless pork belly
2 kg (4 lb 8 oz) duck leg meat, skinless
120 g (4¼ oz) fine salt
24 g (1 oz) ground black pepper
400 ml (14 fl oz) strong red wine
200 ml (7 fl oz) cognac
200 g (7 oz) French shallots, finely sliced
duck fat, for sautéeing
2 kg (4 lb 8 oz) duck livers, cleaned
400 g (14 oz) ham
4 large garlic cloves, crushed
1 handful stale bread, for cleaning
6 eggs

THE DAY BEFORE: Cut pork and duck meats into large cubes or strips. Mince together through the large hole of a food grinder, twice. Place in a large bowl and add the salt, pepper, red wine and cognac. Wash your hands well and then mix (using your hands) thoroughly for a long time, until all the liquid is well incorporated. Cover well with plastic wrap and leave in the refrigerator overnight.

ON THE DAY: Remove the large bowl of meats from the refrigerator. Sauté the shallots in a little duck fat gently over medium–low heat for 3–4 minutes. Allow to cool. Mince the livers and ham together with the shallots, through the large hole of the mincer twice. Add crushed garlic.

Put a handful of stale bread through the grinder to remove any meat bits stuck inside. Add the ham/liver mixture to the pork/duck mixture, then add the eggs, mixed spices and thyme.

Now, pull up your sleeves and mix for a long time with your hands until the mixture becomes a bit elastic and sticky. It is ready to be cooked.

Make sure the jars are sterilised, line them up on the table, get a bowl of tepid water near you. Fill each jar up to the level mark on the side with the meat mixture, pressing it in with the back of your hand so there are no air bubbles in the mixture, dipping your hand into the tepid water often so that the meat doesn't stick to your hand. Before you seal the jars, make sure the top edge of the glass is perfectly clean. Place the seal on the jars and then the screw caps. Place the jars in the boiler, fill with tepid water to come 7 cm (2¾ inch) above the top of the jar. Put the thermometer in place and put the lid on. Bring to the boil, then cook at 100°C (200°F) for 3 hours. Keep an eye on the water level, it should constantly be 7 cm above the top jars, add more boiling water when necessary. After 3 hours turn off the heat and let the jars cool down in the water. Ideally, you should do this overnight.

Remove the jars one by one from the cool water, and wipe dry, drain out any water trapped between the seal and the screw top lid. Write and stick the labels on the jars (don't forget the date), they are ready to store away in a cool, dry place.

MIXED SPICES: Mix the spices together well and keep them in an airtight jar.

1 teaspoon mixed spices (see below)
1 small handful thyme flowers
  (or fresh thyme leaves), chopped

MIXED SPICES
10 g (3 teaspoons) freshly grated nutmeg
5 g (3 teaspoons) ground cloves
5 g (2½ teaspoons) ground cinnamon
10 g (3 teaspoons) ground white pepper
5 g (2 teaspoons) ground fennel seeds
3 g (2 teaspoons) star anis, ground
10 g (1 tablespoon) ground mace
5 g (3 teaspoons) ground coriander

Lamproie de Madeleine

MAMAN'S BORDELAISE LAMPREY

WHEN I WAS GROWING UP, WHENEVER WE HAD A SPECIAL OCCASION, MY MOTHER USED TO SAY, '*ON VA OUVRIR DE LA LAMPROIE*' (WE WILL OPEN SOME LAMPREY JARS). IN SPRING WHEN THE LAMPREY COME UP THE DORDOGNE RIVER TO LAY THEIR EGGS, AND THE LEEKS IN THE MARCHÉ ARE HUGE, IT IS TIME TO *FAIRE LA LAMPROIE*. IT IS ALWAYS AN HONOUR TO HAVE IT SERVED TO YOU AND EVERYONE IN MY FAMILY KEEPS THEIR OWN SECRET RECIPE. MY MOTHER'S RECIPE SAYS YOU CAN COOK LARGE EELS THE SAME WAY, BUT WITHOUT THE BLOOD LIAISON AT THE END. THIS DISH DESERVES YOUR BEST RED WINE.

EQUIPMENT

One 'bouilleur à bocaux' or preserve boiler, (a giant metal pot to fill with jars and water with a thermometer)

Sterilising jars: 2 x 1.5 litre (52 fl oz/6 cup) capacity jars, 4 x 1 litre (35 fl oz/4 cup) capacity jars and 4 x 750 ml (26 fl oz/3 cup) capacity jars

10 kg (22 lb) whole lampreys (7–8 individuals), scraped cleaned and bled (drain the blood into a container, add a little red wine and refrigerate)

olive oil

200 ml (7 fl oz) cognac

20–25 very large leeks, 3 cm (1¼ inch) diameter, white part only

500 g (1 lb 2 oz) Bayonne ham or prosciutto, finely minced

14 onions, thinly sliced

2½ tablespoons plain (all-purpose) flour

7 x 750 ml (26 fl oz/3 cups) bottles or 5.25 litre (185 fl oz) good red wine

1 very large bouquet garni (3 bay leaves, 1 bunch fresh thyme, 1 bunch parsley)

6 large garlic cloves, crushed

1½ teaspoons freshly grated nutmeg

Cut off and discard the head and the tail end of each lamprey. Cut them into 6 cm (2½ inch) chunks and season with salt (not too much salt, because of the ham) and pepper. In a large frying pan over medium heat, and working in batches, lightly brown the pieces of lamprey in olive oil for 3–5 minutes, then flambé each batch in cognac and set aside.

Cut leeks into 6 cm (2½ inch) cylinders, you should have the same number of leek pieces as lamprey pieces. In a large frying pan over medium–low heat, fry the leeks in olive oil for 7–10 minutes, keeping them pale. Season and set aside.

In a very large heavy-based saucepan gently brown the minced ham, then add the onion; let this cook slowly for quite a while, stirring often. Sprinkle the flour over the onions and ham, and cook gently, stirring, for about 5–7 minutes.

Meanwhile, pour the wine into a large saucepan, bring to the boil and flambé until there are no more flames. Pour wine over the onion mixture a little at a time, stirring all the time. Add the bouquet garni, garlic and nutmeg. Simmer for 20–30 minutes, then add leeks and cook for 10 minutes. Add the lamprey and cook for 15–20 minutes. Check the lamprey by inserting a wooden skewer, the lamprey should stay firm and not fall apart. Remove the saucepan from the heat and with a skimmer strain out the pieces of lamprey and leek onto separate trays.

Return saucepan to a low heat. Add some of the hot sauce to the blood and wine container, dilute well and pour back into the saucepan. Stir until the sauce thickens but do not let it boil. Distribute equal pieces of lamprey and leeks into the jars, ladle in the sauce up to the filling level, clean the jar tops thoroughly, seal them and place in the preserving boiler, add tepid water to come 7 cm (2¾ inch) above the top of the jars. Bring to the boil and cook at 100ºC (200ºF) for 1 hour 15 minutes. Let the jars cool in the water. When cool, dry, label and store in a cool, dark place. Wait at least 6 months before eating. Serve with toasted bread.

Confit de Canard

DUCK CONFIT

SERVES 12

IF THESE CONFIT DUCK LEGS ARE TO BE USED FOR A CASSOULET, THEY MUST BE STARTED AT LEAST THREE DAYS BEFORE. THEY TASTE BETTER AFTER A FEW WEEKS AND MAY BE PRESERVED IN THE REFRIGERATOR FOR UP TO TWO MONTHS AS LONG AS THEY ARE COMPLETELY BURIED IN DUCK FAT AND NO AIR BUBBLES REMAIN. THEY CAN ALSO BE VACUUM-PACKED. IF THEY ARE PRESERVED IN STERILISED JARS THEY WILL LAST FOR A FEW YEARS. THE RECIPE IS FOR TWELVE LEGS, IT IS NOT WORTH MAKING FOR LESS. YOU CAN DOUBLE OR TREBLE THE RECIPE FOR THE FULL FRENCH FARMHOUSE EFFECT: PLENTY OF CONFIT ON HAND FOR ANY UNEXPECTED VISITORS. YOU'LL NEED TO START THIS RECIPE 24 HOURS IN ADVANCE.

---

12 large duck legs

1 bunch thyme, leaves picked and chopped

1 sprig rosemary, leaves picked and chopped

2 fresh bay leaves, crushed and chopped

3 garlic cloves

4–5 tablespoons salt

2 tablespoons freshly ground black pepper

2 teaspoons freshly grated nutmeg

2 kg (4 lb 8 oz) rendered duck fat (or goose fat)

Clean the duck legs, but leave all the fat on them. Combine the thyme, rosemary, bay leaf and garlic in a large bowl, add the duck legs, salt, freshly ground black pepper and nutmeg. Mix to coat the duck legs. Cover and leave in the refrigerator for 24 hours.

The next day, melt the duck fat in a large saucepan or casserole dish over a very low heat. Meanwhile, remove the legs one by one and thoroughly wipe off salt and spices with paper towel. When the fat is just warm, but not boiling, plunge the legs carefully into the saucepan. Cook very slowly, barely simmering, for 1½ –2 hours or more. The confit is cooked when the duck legs are easily pierced with a wooden skewer. Using tongs remove the duck legs from the pot, arrange in a ceramic or earthenware dish and set aside. When the fat is lukewarm, strain it through a fine sieve over the meat. The meat must be well covered with the fat. Make sure not to pour in the meat juices at the bottom, keep them separately, they can be used with restraint in stews, with potatoes etc. but will be very salty. When it has cooled, cover the dish and refrigerate.

To preserve for longer, cook the meat for only 1½ hours which will keep the legs a little firmer. When cool enough to handle, put 2 to 3 legs in each sterilised jar, then pour strained duck fat half way up each jar. Seal and place them in a 'bouilleur à bocaux' (preserving boiler). Add lukewarm water to cover with 7 cm water above the top of the jars. Bring to the boil and sterilise at 100ºC (200ºF) for 1½ hours. Cool jars in the water (this can take overnight). When cool, label and store in a cool, dry, dark place. The flavour improves with age.

sourced from his collection of reputable suppliers who, with great pride, breed and feed their animals with only the very best.

Trish and I feel rather smug when we watch TV chefs extolling the virtues of organic food; it seems so irrelevant to us here as we know that almost everything we buy was produced nearby with tender, loving care. It's all extremely seasonal, too. One day the market is chock-a-block with asparagus, the next day it's: 'Sorry, Madame. *C'est fini*. You'll have to wait until next year.' It keeps you on your toes. Every year I make Tatie Antoinette's four-berry jam, but it's essential to know just when all the raspberries, strawberries and redcurrants are at their best. I then spend a couple of days driving around the various markets buying the very best berries. For me, that's half the fun.

───────────

IN THE PAST FEW YEARS A LOT OF *MARCHÉ NOCTURNES* or *marché gourmands* have also sprouted up over summer. There is one held every Monday evening in Villereal and another every Wednesday night in nearby Salles. The colourful local stallholders all sell different dishes made from ingredients produced on their own farms. As well as the sumptuous displays of bread and summer fruits, you can buy barbecued duck breasts, sausages, pork chops, snails and steak grilled to order. There are also specialty products such as home-made goat's cheeses, walnut cakes, fruit tarts and wine. There is no better way to spend a summer evening than gathering at a long table with a group of friends and feasting under a sky pin-pricked with stars. Everyone brings a basket with their own place settings and you get to choose exactly what you feel like eating – all for only a handful of euros. Children, especially, love being able to choose and buy their own food and then tear around the village while the accordion band plays on. I recall one night when I saw a table of six very serious small children seated together around a table sharing a big bowl of snails cooked in tomato and garlic. They were picking the snails out of their shells with toothpicks and making appreciative noises.

The *brocantes* are always an adventure. The season for secondhand markets extends from Easter time to November. And you never know what you're going to find – there's everything from heirloom-inspired handbags and Art Deco mirrors to chic vintage fashions and antique lace bridal gowns. As well as unearthing treasures such as silvery cutlery and gorgeous linen, there's the usual household rubble – old jam jars, used phone cards and calendars as well as broken plastic toys and rusty garden chairs and tables.

At Cleopatra we aimed to create a cosy haven that was far from the rat race, but in rural France the pace of life is really much slower. Although we initially resisted having our main meal at *midi*, we have finally acquiesced; everything stops from *midi* until about three o'clock so it seems churlish not to join in this national pastime. Now, when we go to the *brocantes*, we always allow time for a lazy, three-hour lunch!

Flowers also feature on France's festival calendar. There's a lovely yearly celebration in May that takes place by the romantic ruins of the Abbaye-Nouvelle, a Cistercian abbey founded in 1242, when you can pick up everything you need for the garden. As well as flowers, there are many plants you would never have found in the rural France of my childhood, including hot chilli plants, lemongrass and even Japanese eggplants. In line with our new rural lifestyle, we are now more likely to be found lingering in the tractor shop looking longingly at a lawnmower rather than leafing through a fashion mag,

Another one of my new obsessions is growing tomatoes. The *coeur de boeuf* variety are really 'essential tomatoes' and in August we spend days bottling the excess fruit, making enough to last a full year. I also love to grow pumpkins and in winter there's nothing like a hearty soup made from home-grown pumpkins and beans. Although I adore courgettes, I always plant too many of them and am always calling on friends to inspire me with new ways to cook them. I like to stir-fry them in a wok with garlic; our neighbour Bill

One of our lovely winter traditions is to get together to make a year's worth of pâtés and terrines.

does a tasty courgette soup; and our Greek friend Dana makes courgette fritters with the impossible-to-say name *kolokithokeftedes*.

You know it's summer in France not just because of the heat; it's also Tour de France time, when cycling enthusiasts clad in pink-and-lime-green latex start swarming all over the roads. Similarly, the blaze of orange-red and scarlet leaves on the trees and vines are not the only indicator that autumn has arrived. The other clue comes from the clumps of camouflaged men with rifles slung over their shoulders standing about in the fields and forests waiting for a wild boar or deer to happen by. And winter in France is heralded not only by the frosty mornings and amazing light in the sky but because the *Intermarché* in Villeréal wheels out a set of special shelves that sell all the equipment you need to make your *confits de canard* – oversized spoons, jars, labels and pots. Though time-consuming, this annual ritual of making *confits de canard* is both fun and rewarding and involves everything from making the marinades to the cooking, canning and label-writing process. If you don't raise your own ducks (and we are not tempted), the *marché au gras* – which literally means the 'fat market' – will oblige, selling huge lobes of foie gras, as well as whole ducks and stripped, fatty carcasses called *demoiselles*. I never cooked with these ingredients in Australia because they were very hard to find and up until this point I'd never cooked with them in France because they were considered *produits de luxe*. That said, my mother, Tatie Denise and Tatie Antoinette all had their own special foie gras recipes.

Our new friend Bill also loves to cook, and when he and his partner Morgan (who just happens to love washing up) are in France, the four of us often gather to talk about food, visit each other and cook up a storm. One of our lovely winter traditions is to get together to make a year's worth of pâtés and terrines. This is another two-day job which requires a lot of organisation, extensive shopping lists and lots of chopping, mincing, weighing and measuring. The end result is always worth it: home-made pâtés and terrines are definitely superior. But cooking is thirsty work and the chilled refreshing rosè flows like water, often resulting in a certain level of confusion with regards to the labelling. Did one red dot of nail varnish on the base of the jar mean with or without foie gras in the middle? What did three dots mean? How many dots for the duck? Another time-honoured family tradition I love is stocking Barney and Jane's car with jars of terrine when they visit us – exactly the way Maman used to do for me.

Every winter I now receive a phone call from the head of the *comité des fêtes* in the village, wondering if I'll help make the crêpes on 2 February for *Chandeleur* (Candelmas) and the traditional pancake ball in the Salle de Fêtes. The *mairie* provides all the necessary ingredients in commercial-sized quantities; we go through nine kilograms of flour, dozens and dozens of farm eggs and fresh cow's milk, which arrives direct from the farm in a large metal can. To prepare the pancakes, Trish and I spend a lovely afternoon with the village ladies in the 'kitchen' in the basement of the *mairie*. Though it's a convivial atmosphere, there is also an element of competition about the whole operation: one of the women is proud of being able to cook four pancakes at a time, so she appropriates the kitchen's only four-burner stove; the rest of us have to be content with little two-burner gas camping stoves. After a pile of pancakes have been cooked they are then sprinkled with sugar, rolled and kept ready to be heated and served during the ball along with lots of cold, sparkling cider.

The last weekend of August is when the patron saint's day fête is held in our village. The festivities kick off on the Friday night with a bingo game that gives punters the chance to win a *demi cochon* (half a pig), some fat ducks or a leg of venison. This is followed by a *bal musette* dance on Saturday night and a Sunday morning *randonnée* (ramble around the fields and village) before a church service. This is followed by a five-course lunch enjoyed under the trees where you must bring your own plate and cutlery.

Every November, the local village hosts yet another ball, this time dedicated to chestnuts. We womenfolk spend hours slitting the hard shells of the chestnut before handing them over to the menfolk who roast them over roaring fires built in giant, tumbling drums. When we arrived to our first chestnut festival we were startled to see our neighbouring farm folk line-dancing to live country music: the ladies all wore glittery garments and had beautifully coiffed red-tinted hair while the men were decked out in smart, checked shirts. Trish and I had no idea how to line-dance so watched in awe from the sidelines as the couples earnestly concentrated on each and every move. All this action in a village with a population of ninety-seven! Who needs the bright city lights?

Although Maman was no longer able to participate in these annual events, she remained remarkably fit and was treated with dignity and respect by the lovely nurses at the *maison de retraite*. We went to visit her often and I always left feeling melancholy – she just wasn't the mother I had known and loved and fought with for all those years. When I called her on the telephone she usually just listened and didn't speak; it was very unlike her! Maman was slowly shutting down. Sandy, who adored my mother and thought she was a great character, came to visit in 2007 and we took him to see her. She sang one of her old songs for him and it was quite poignant; we all had tears in our eyes. Although she had become very fragile, Maman was still up and around and walking every day. Her brother Jeannot came down from Paris to stay with us and visit her for a few days and it was not long after that we got the call: on 30 December 2008 Maman died peacefully in her sleep. When we went to the *maison de retraite*, the nurses were crying; after six years they had come to know and love her, too. Maman was ninety-five and I was totally unprepared for the wave of sadness and loneliness that engulfed me after a lifetime of loving and arguing with her.

Monique and James flew over from Australia for the funeral and I was so glad to have them. There were endless arrangements to make and an enormous pile of paperwork. Amid the sadness, Monique and I couldn't help laughing when we found that Maman had left us a little notebook entitled *Au Sujet de Mes Obsèques*, featuring precise instructions penned with ink in her immaculate handwriting. The notebook contained details of: who we were to notify of her demise and who we were NOT to notify; who was to be invited to the funeral and who was NOT to be invited; exactly which newspapers should run her obituary; what kind of wood she wanted for her coffin and what colour material it should be lined with. She wanted a proper funeral mass in Vélines and wanted to be buried next to her parents in Port Sainte-Foy. We did our best to respect Maman's wishes, which included convincing her favourite priest to come out of retirement and preside over the ceremony. On the day of the funeral there were huge snowfalls, making it extremely difficult for people to get to the church. Although we decided to go ahead with the ceremony, the weather was so cold and inclement that the roads had turned treacherous and we were forced to cancel the wake. 'This is just so Madeleine,' cousin Véronique remarked with a smile. 'Snow and ice … and difficult to the bitter end!'

It was around this time that Véronique and Philippe sold their glamorous boat at La Rochelle and bought a vineyard on a hill near Saint-Emilion. With great enthusiasm we offered to help – not by picking the grapes but by cooking lunch and dinner for their thirteen friends who had come from all over France to help out. The *vendageurs* and *vendageuses* would be rewarded with fantastic food and wine in exchange for their free labour and it was up to us to prepare the perfect feasts.

In France, there's never any doubt as to when it's time to eat lunch as all around the country there's a chorus of ringing church bells and screaming sirens, announcing that it's *midi* and time to stop work. Right on cue, our red-cheeked, tired and hungry grape-pickers tramped in from the cold, grey day to take their seats around the long table near the fire. After hours of preparation, we felt the pressure of expectation and scrambled to set down the food, which included: huge steaming bowls of tagine or hearty *petit salé aux lentilles*; chicken with *vérjus*; or – a popular favourite – *tourte aux pommes de terres* hot from the oven. This rich, diet-destroying pie is filled with potatoes, butter and cream layered into a home-made pastry, accompanied by a gorgeous green salad and red wine.

Véronique also loves doing things the traditional way. Even though she could do what most *vignerons* do these days – hire gypsies to do the *vendange* and then not have to

Le sandwich aux truffes

TRUFFLE SANDWICHES

SERVES 8–10

THE GREATEST LUXE IN LIFE IS SURELY BABÉ PÉBEYRE'S RECIPE FOR TRUFFLE SANDWICHES. UP UNTIL I'D TASTED THIS TREAT I HAD THOUGHT MY DREAM DISH WAS THE TRUFFLE AND FOIE GRAS WRAPPED IN PUFF PASTRY THAT I SWOONED OVER AT L'AMBROISIE IN PARIS MANY YEARS AGO. BUT BILL MADE TRUFFLE SANDWICHES TO SERVE AS HORS D'OEUVRES ON NEW YEAR'S EVE AND THE AROMA PERMEATED THE HOUSE. THE SECRET IS TO HAVE LOTS OF TRUFFLES, SALT AND TOP-QUALITY BUTTER.

1 really good country bread loaf, thinly sliced
200 g (7 oz) unsalted butter
2 fresh truffles
sea salt flakes

First you cut the crusts off the bread. Next, you butter one side of each slice generously and then sandwich the thinly sliced truffles between the bread slices, stacking them as you go. Sprinkle with the sea salt flakes. After pressing down the top layer of bread, cut the bread into elegant little sandwiches. Wrap the sandwiches very tightly in plastic wrap and refrigerate overnight so the flavours are infused.

Just before serving, preheat the oven to 200°C (400°F/Gas 6). Unwrap the sandwiches and place them on a tray in oven and cook for about 7–8 minutes. When the bread is golden and sizzling hot, the perfume will be almost overpowering. Of course, the sandwiches must be served hot from the oven and accompanied with frosty flutes of Champagne.

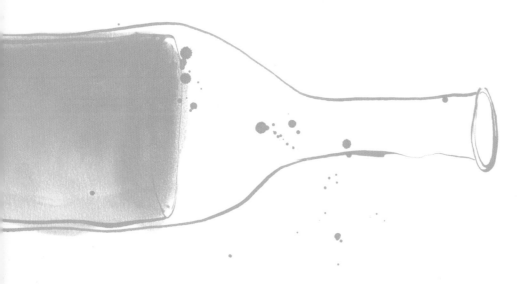

Pâte brisée

SHORTCRUST PASTRY

MAKES ABOUT 1 KILOGRAM

---

375 g (13 oz) unsalted butter, diced

500 g (1 lb 2 oz) plain (all-purpose) flour

15 g (½ oz) fine salt

15 g (½ oz) caster (superfine) sugar

2 eggs

2 tablespoons cold water

METHOD 1 (BY HAND): Leave the butter at room temperature for about one hour. In a large bowl combine the flour, salt, sugar, butter and eggs, then using the tips of your fingers rub butter and eggs through dry ingredients until it looks like coarse sand. If necessary add the of cold water to help bring it together, gather the pastry into a ball, kneading gently once or twice. Work quickly, never work it too long. Flatten into a disc and wrap in a cloth or plastic and refrigerate for at least 1 hour, or if possible overnight – as the pastry will be easier to roll.

METHOD 2 (USING A FOOD PROCESSOR): Place all the ingredients except for the egg and water into the bowl of a food processor. Pulse for 15 seconds, until the mixture looks like coarse sand.

Then add the egg and pulse, just a few seconds until it forms a ball, if necessary add the cold water to help bring it together. When it forms a ball, tip out onto the bench, kneading it gently once or twice. Work quickly, never work it too long. Flatten into a disc and wrap in a cloth or plastic and refrigerate for at least 1 hour or if possible overnight – as the pastry will be easier to roll.

You can also freeze the pastry – after the initial one hour resting period, cut the pastry into three blocks of approximately 320 g (11¼ oz) for future use.

Pâte sucrée

SWEET SHORTCRUST PASTRY

MAKES ABOUT 1 KILOGRAM

METHOD 1 (BY HAND): In a large bowl combine all dry ingredients, make a well in the centre and add the eggs, vanilla and the softened butter in little pieces. Using your fingertips and working quickly mix and rub in the butter until you can form a large ball. If the mix is too dry, add a few drops of milk, gather the pastry into a ball, kneading gently once or twice. Work quickly, never work it too long. Flatten into a disc and wrap in a cloth or plastic and refrigerate for at least 1 hour or if possible overnight – as the pastry will be easier to roll.

METHOD 2 (USING A FOOD PROCESSOR): Place all the ingredients except for the eggs into the bowl of a food processor. Pulse for 15 seconds, until the mixture looks like coarse sand.

Then add the egg and pulse, just a few seconds until it forms a ball, if necessary add 1–2 drops of milk to help bring it together. When it forms a ball, tip out onto the bench, knead gently once or twice. Work quickly, never work it too long. Flatten into a disc and wrap in a cloth or plastic and refrigerate for at least 1 hour, or if possible overnight – as the pastry will be easier to roll.

Pastry may be frozen for future use.

500 g (1 lb 2 oz) plain (all-purpose) flour
125 g (4½ oz) ground almonds
80 g (2¾ oz) caster (superfine) sugar
10 g (¼ oz) salt
2 eggs
¼ teaspoon natural vanilla extract
350 g (12 oz) softened butter
few drops of milk, if necessary

Les tomates du jardin

PRESERVED TOMATOES FROM THE GARDEN

THERE IS A MOMENT IN MID-SUMMER WHEN THE TOMATO PLANTS PRODUCE KILOS AND KILOS OF THE MOST MAGNIFICENT TOMATOES. WE CANNOT KEEP UP WITH THE SUPPLY BY EATING THEM AS THEY RIPEN, SO WE PRESERVE THEM. OPENING A JAR OF THIS SAUCE IN THE MIDDLE OF WINTER IS SUCH A MIRACLE. THIS OPERATION TAKES A FEW DAYS AND USES EVERY BOWL AND BIG POT IN THE KITCHEN. AT THE END, THERE IS A MOUNTAIN OF WASHING UP AND USUALLY A GLASS OR TWO OF COLD ROSÉ. IT'S HOT, HARD WORK BUT IT IS SO REWARDING.

THE TOMATOES: The tomatoes are picked as they ripen on the vine, and are left on the cool tiled kitchen bench to accumulate for a few days until there are enough. 'Enough' is probably at least 20 kilos (44 pounds), being such strangely shaped tomatoes, they vary in weight, my proudest specimen weighed nearly a kilo! You need a huge heavy based stainless steel pot, and at least four or five large stainless steel or china mixing bowls. Sharp knives, strainers, aprons and a continuous supply of boiling water should be on standby.

Firstly, one cuts the stem end from the tomatoes, then cut out any damaged bits, and make a criss-cross in the bottom of the tomato skin with a very sharp knife. Put these tomatoes into a large bowl and then pour over boiling water to cover. They only have to stay in the hot water for about three minutes. Keep the production line going: check, cut, make cross, pour boiling water, etc. When the first bowl is ready remove the tomatoes one at a time and with a sharp knife peel off the thick skin, cut into quarters and squeeze out any seeds (the joy of the 'coeur de boeuf' is that they have very few seeds). Keep the skin and seeds in a big bowl, put the flesh into another bowl. Keep going like this, the bowls of flesh will mount up, and when the bowl of seeds and skins is full, tip it into a strainer set over yet another bowl to catch the juice. Eventually you will end up with many bowls of chopped flesh, bowls of juice, and piles of skin debris for the compost. Peel and chop the garlic cloves, about half a head of garlic per big bowl (3 kg/6 lb 12 oz) of tomato flesh.

TO MAKE THE SAUCE: In the bottom of the heavy-based saucepan (which will hold about 3 bowls of tomato flesh), pour enough good olive oil to cover the base to a depth of about 2 cm (¾ inch). When it is hot throw in the garlic and stir with a wooden spoon, it should cook but on no account go brown, it must stay white, but cook over a gentle flame for a few minutes. Then tip in enough tomatoes to come three-quarters of the way up the sides of the pot, turn up the heat and stir well, adding a good handful of chopped fresh thyme from the garden, a handful of rock salt and about 3 tablespoons of freshly ground pepper. Keep stirring until it begins to boil, then lower the heat and keep cooking, stirring often, for about half and hour – maybe 45 minutes depending how juicy the tomatoes are. When it has reduced by one-third, keep an eye on it and stir often, this is when it could catch and burn and be spoilt. At this stage, strain in the juices collected from the seeding process and stir in and let reduce. The whole cooking process should take about one hour, not longer, as you don't want to lose the taste of the tomatoes.

While the tomatoes are cooking, clean up the kitchen (there will be tomato everywhere) and put the preserving jars through the dishwasher, without soap, on a high temperature, to sterilise them. Then drain them upside down on a clean cloth.

When the tomatoes are cooked, throw in a few handfuls of clean and plucked basil leaves, but do not chop or tear them, leave whole. Stir into the hot and bubbling sauce and leave to cool a little.

When cooled enough to handle, ladle the tomato sauce into the preserving jars up to the filling level marked, and with a clean cloth and a bowl of clean very hot water wipe the top edges of the jars. Then place the capsules (rubber seals) on the top, and wipe again and screw the tops on the jars. This can be a joint, or indeed a group effort, and at this stage put the boiler on the stovetop, and stack the jars into the boiler, fitting them carefully with old clean rags to wedge them in. We also find that some suitably sized rocks (washed clean) from the garden are very handy for wedging purposes. Now fill the boiler with tepid water (never try to fill it on the ground and then lift it onto the stove – it weighs a ton) up to at least 7 cm (2¾ inch), above the top layer of jars. Bring to the boil, insert thermometer and boil for 30 minutes at 100ºC (200ºF). Then turn off and leave to completely cool down in the water – this can take hours, even overnight.

When cold, remove the jars, unscrew the lids, wipe with a dry cloth, and re-screw the lids on. Write labels with the date, and store in a cool, dry, dark place. The preserve can be used immediately, or will keep for well over a year.

spend a fortune feeding her workers, the fact that the volunteers are all her friends means she goes the extra mile in thanking them for their efforts. But the very fact the *vendageurs* and *vendageuses* are all close friends means she can't then say: 'Right, lunch is finished; off you go back to work!' Because of this, the lunches tend to go on rather longer than perhaps they should. When the well-fed workers roll back to the fields, it's then time for us to start making dinner. After four or five days of this routine we leave the vineyard feeling exhausted, yet satisfied. It's always such good fun.

SOME FOOD CRITICS IN FRANCE WORRY THAT ALL THE recipes we learned from our mothers and grandmothers are in danger of disappearing. My young cousin Véronique should give them hope. Véronique inherited her grandmother Antoinette's recipe notebook and guards it with her life; she also passes the supreme test of culinary obsession by cooking lamprey *à la bordelaise* every year. Because both recipes descended from the same grandmère, my cousin's version is very close to mine. This dish is also a real labour of love: it's made every April when the lampreys are caught in nets in the Dordogne River, where they have swum from the Atlantic to spawn. Cooking the lampreys involves endless pots and pans and blood and wine and mess and jars; I have very clear memories of Maman plunging the lamprey into boiling water before then scraping and hanging them. She'd then slit their tails so the blood dripped into a dish that contained red wine, which prevented it from coagulating. This precious blend of wine and blood is added to the sauce at the end. Nowadays, of course, we ask the fishmonger to do this.

If it's not too cold, I always suggest leaving the windows open when cooking this dish because the heavy lamprey, wine and leek smell clings to your skin and seems to seep into the walls of the house. It's also not something to eat immediately after cooking and is best after spending at least six months in a jar. Lamprey is not something you approach lightly and nor is it something you would ever waste on anyone who didn't absolutely love it. Whenever Uncle Jeannot comes, I open a jar especially for him. It's also on hand whenever Monique visits Trish and I – we three then become members of a secret society, sharing a lovely lamprey night together.

Now that we are well and truly settled in France, we have once again set up a business, which we've called Périgorgeous. As well as arranging parties, we offer five-day tours for people interested in going on a gourmet tour of the region. Because we are now firmly ensconced in the local community we are given behind-the-scenes access to vineyards, restaurants and markets that have refused to change with the times. Top of our list is always the old-fashioned duck farm run by a very sweet family near the Château de Biron. On Wednesdays during summer the family hold a little *marché*, selling such delicacies as duck, walnut oil pressed fresh on the spot, honey and little inexpensive *assiettes* of duck to eat at a table under the trees. The family hosts an informative class for us, and afterwards we all eat a big duck lunch with the family in their dining room.

On the menu is: duck pâté, duck *foie gras* and duck ham (served with Monbazillac sweet wine) followed by a confit of duck with potatoes and wild mushrooms cooked in duck fat. To finish we are treated to cheese and salad and fruit tart, all served with local wines!

In late summer we also cook a lunch or two for Mary Moody's tour groups, which is always great fun; there are usually a couple of old Cleopatra customers among them and it's always great to catch up on industry gossip from the other side of the world.

In winter we tend towards truffle tours. Both Périgord and the Lot produce a large percentage of France's annual haul of melanosporums. We take visitors on tours of the Cahors' truffle 'factory' owned by the local Pébeyre family and go on truffle hunts with a pig and dog, organise truffle-themed dinners and go to the truffle market in Lalbenque.

It was the lovely Pébeyre family that made our Christmas 2008 so very special. The festive season started off extremely quiet and low-key. With Barney and Jane staying in London and Stephen enjoying a Sydney summer, we planned a quiet couple of days with our close friends Bill and Morgan. It was to be just the four of us – all cooking and eating together. And it didn't seem like anyone had much to celebrate. The headlines were all about: bank bailouts; plunging stock markets; bankruptcies; plummeting exchange rates; and massive job losses. With pension funds and trust funds hit hard and bank stocks disappearing into thin air, the bad news kept pouring in.

We were feeling completely depressed when Morgan and Bill arrived to stay, bearing a huge bag of truffles. It was a Christmas present from the ever-generous and completely lovely Pébeyre family. We couldn't stop laughing at the complete absurdity of it all. Here we were facing a very uncertain future yet eating like Louis XVI!

For Christmas I made foie gras with truffles and pigeon with a truffle stuffing; Boxing Day brunch was a huge bowl of scrambled eggs made black with truffles. We were snowed in, but we had a roaring fire, and drank Champagne as we watched the deer outside in the field, uncertainly exploring the snow. The day after Boxing Day there were still so many truffles left over that we made a truffle risotto … it actually reached the point where we were giggling about our predicament, saying: 'Oh no, not truffles again!' Of course we were also very conscious that we may all be living on beans next year; *l'année prochaine, on mangera des haricots.*

The greatest luxe in life is surely Babé Pébeyre's recipe for truffle sandwiches. Up until I'd tasted this treat I had thought my dream dish was the truffle and foie gras wrapped in puff pastry that I swooned over at L'Ambroisie in Paris many years ago. But Bill made truffle sandwiches to serve as an hors d'oeuvre on New Year's Eve and the aroma pervaded the house. The secret is you need to have lots of truffles, and they need salt and top-quality butter.

Yes, there are certainly many positives about living so far from sophisticated cities, here in *la France profonde.*

In this index the initials DC refer to Dany Chouet. Page numbers in italics indicate recipes. Bold page numbers indicate photographs.

Published in 2010 by Murdoch Books Pty Limited

Murdoch Books Australia
Pier 8/9
23 Hickson Road
Millers Point NSW 2000
Phone: +61 (0) 2 8220 2000
Fax: +61 (0) 2 8220 2558
www.murdochbooks.com.au

Murdoch Books UK Limited
Erico House, 6th Floor
93–99 Upper Richmond Road
Putney, London SW15 2TG
Phone: +44 (0) 20 8785 5995
Fax: +44 (0) 20 8785 5985
www.murdochbooks.co.uk

Publishing Director: Kay Scarlett
Publisher: Jane Lawson
Photographer: Alan Benson
Stylist: Trish Hobbs
Designers: Sarah Odgers and Emilia Toia
Illustrator: Tracy Loughlin
Project editor: Livia Caiazzo
Editor: Carla Grossetti
Food editor: Adelaide Harris
Production: Alexandra Gonzalez

National Library of Australia Cataloguing-in-Publication Data
Author: Chouet, Dany.
Title: So French : A lifetime in the provincial kitchen / Dany Chouet.
ISBN: 9781741964943 (hbk.)
Notes: Includes index.
Subjects: Chouet, Dany.
                 Cookery, French.
                 Cooks--France--Biography.
Dewey Number: 641.50944
A catalogue record for this book is available from the British Library.

PRINTED IN CHINA

IMPORTANT: Those who might be at risk from the effects of salmonella poisoning (the elderly, pregnant women, young children and those suffering from immune deficiency diseases) should consult their doctor with any concerns about eating raw eggs.
OVEN GUIDE: You may find cooking times vary depending on the oven you are using. For fan-forced ovens, as a general rule, set the oven temperature to 20°C (35°F) lower than indicated in the recipe.

Expedition· N· CHOUET· Bd d

Fran

Destin

miss CHOUE

H, Cleopatra

2785- Blac

australia